CULTURE**SHOCK!**

A Survival Guide to Customs and Etiquette

ECUADOR

Nicholas Crowder

Marshall Cavendish
Editions

This edition published in 2006 by:
Marshall Cavendish Corporation
99 White Plains Road
Tarrytown, NY 10591-9001
www.marshallcavendish.us

Other Marshall Cavendish Offices:
Marshall Cavendish International (Asia) Private Limited. 1 New Industrial
Road, Singapore 536196 ▪ Marshall Cavendish Ltd. 119 Wardour Street, London
W1F 0UW, UK ▪ Marshall Cavendish International (Thailand) Co Ltd. 253 Asoke,
12th Flr, Sukhumvit 21 Road, Klongtoey Nua, Wattana, Bangkok 10110,
Thailand ▪ Marshall Cavendish (Malaysia) Sdn Bhd, Times Subang, Lot 46,
Subang Hi-Tech Industrial Park, Batu Tiga, 40000 Shah Alam, Selangor Darul
Ehsan, Malaysia

Marshall Cavendish is a trademark of Times Publishing Limited

ISBN 10: 0-7614-2495-4
ISBN 13: 978-0-7614-2495-6

Please contact the publisher for the Library of Congress catalog number

Printed in Singapore by Times Graphics Pte Ltd

Photo Credits:
All photos from the author. ▪ Cover photo: Photolibrary.com

All illustrations by TRIGG

ABOUT THE SERIES

Culture shock is a state of disorientation that can come over anyone who has been thrust into unknown surroundings, away from one's comfort zone. *CultureShock!* is a series of trusted and reputed guides which has, for decades, been helping expatriates and long-term visitors to cushion the impact of culture shock whenever they move to a new country.

Written by people who have lived in the country and experienced culture shock themselves, the authors share all the information necessary for anyone to cope with these feelings of disorientation more effectively. The guides are written in a style that is easy to read and covers a range of topics that will arm readers with enough advice, hints and tips to make their lives as normal as possible again.

Each book is structured in the same manner. It begins with the first impressions that visitors will have of that city or country. To understand a culture, one must first understand the people—where they came from, who they are, the values and traditions they live by, as well as their customs and etiquette. This is covered in the first half of the book.

Then on with the practical aspects—how to settle in with the greatest of ease. Authors walk readers through topics such as how to find accommodation, get the utilities and telecommunications up and running, enrol the children in school and keep in the pink of health. But that's not all. Once the essentials are out of the way, venture out and try the food, enjoy more of the culture and travel to other areas. Then be immersed in the language of the country before discovering more about the business side of things.

To round off, snippets of basic information are offered before readers are 'tested' on customs and etiquette of the country. Useful words and phrases, a comprehensive resource guide and list of books for further research are also included for easy reference.

CONTENTS

INTRODUCTION

When I was a young man, my father always encouraged me, in a light-hearted manner, to take a banana boat down to South America. He probably did not realise that the thought stayed in my subconscious and determined my future.

In my early twenties, when working in a department store, I met a wealthy Ecuadorian by chance. He was visiting the United States and had lost his passport. With my Spanish 101, I did my best to help him and he explained to me that he was a banana farmer and was in Arizona studying water resources to help combat some of the droughts in Ecuador. A stout muscular man with a genial smile, he had a very attractive wife with bronze skin and brown eyes, who looked as if she were descended from an Indian princess.

Later, I had a Spanish professor from the Sierra (mountain area) region of Ecuador who did not look or speak like my newfound acquaintance from the coastal plains of Ecuador in the city of Guayaquil. My professor was slight in build and had a distinct accent, sounding very different from the man from Guayaquil. I was intrigued with the differences in these two men and it was an early introduction to the wide range of differences in people within a very small geographical area.

It was on a jet that I finally made my first trip to Ecuador in the early 1980s, not on a banana boat. Ecuador captured my soul. In this small country, I found a dose of all that was good and bad in life. Within its borders, it is a country steeped in the human spirit and every human experience. If James A Michener had lived long enough, he would probably have discovered the tiny jewel of Ecuador and found more than enough material to write a number of epic novels.

If you are lucky enough to have the opportunity to move to or visit Ecuador, you are in for an adventure. Despite its small size, it is not a homogeneous country. It possesses many divisions socially, culturally and geographically. A constant factor about Ecuador is that it always seems to be in transition. Whether it is suffering from natural catastrophes or expanding substantially due to oil exports, it is always changing.

Superficially, however, much of the country does not appear to have changed from the time the Spanish conquered it. On the surface, it appears similar to other Latin American countries.

Ecuador, however, has a unique way of conducting life. One of the most profound statements I have ever read regarding Ecuador can be found in Walker Lowry's rare masterpiece *Tumult at Dusk: Being an Account of Ecuador*. During his visit to Ecuador, he and his companions became aware of a murder at a ranch named Ila. They were concerned, as many North Americans would have been, and thought something had to be done. But a colonel offered this advice: "That is right Señores. Whatever you do you will only make things worse. Forgive me for saying it but you do not understand this country. You do not understand its people. You think that because we have houses, cars and clothes like yours, because we talk of democracy and freedom, because we read your books, borrow your money, buy your goods, we are like you.

"But we are not. We look like you, sometimes we talk like you, but we do not think like you. The difference, Señores, is not great but it is important. If you do not see it, the things you do in this country will be wrong. You will only make trouble. Your motives will be good but you will always be misunderstood. You will try to make friends and find only enemies. You will be disappointed. You will condemn this country. Or you will make fun of it. You will go home and say this country is ridiculous, that everything is hopeless.

"But who are you to say, you who have never understood us? Señores, try to understand. Look at this country with open eyes believing only what you see. Look at our people. Look at our history. Look at our land. Do this, Señores. Do not worry about Ila. Ila is not your affair. Adiós, Señores."

What about you, my dear visitor friend? Do you wish to understand Ecuador? Do you wish to look at this country with open eyes? If you do, it is for you that this book has been prepared. It will guide you through the maze of cultural differences and help you understand its people, history and land and help you believe what you see.

ACKNOWLEDGEMENTS

When I began my experiences in Ecuador, over 20 years ago, I never expected that I would have the good fortune to meet so many individuals who would provide me with such valuable insight into this small and immensely complicated country. Numerous people have helped me in the writing of *Culture Shock! Ecuador* and I regret that I only have the space to thank some of them here.

Phone numbers, addresses and so on seem to be in a constant state of flux here. I have tried my best to ensure this material is as accurate as possible and I take full responsibility for all the facts in this book.

I wish to offer my special thanks and deepest appreciation to the following people: Marc Becker, Mercedes Crowder, Jenny Estrada Ruiz, Michelle O Fried, Amalia V Garzón, Dr Angel Gustavo Guevara, Angela Hamilton, Rodolfo Perez Pimentel, Milly Rivadeneira, Professor John Schechter, Luz Maria De la Torre and Tim Virnig.

*I would like to dedicate this book to
my Ecuadorian wife and our children.
I feel the same way as a good friend of mine,
who also married an Ecuadorian—
"Isn't it wonderful how the two cultures blend to produce
wonderful children who understand different points of views!"*

*This book is also dedicated to my mother and father
who made it possible for me to attend the
American Graduate School of International Management for
Advanced Studies. That opportunity exposed me to numerous
cultures and it was there that my passion for travel and to
understand people from distant lands was honed.*

MAP OF ECUADOR

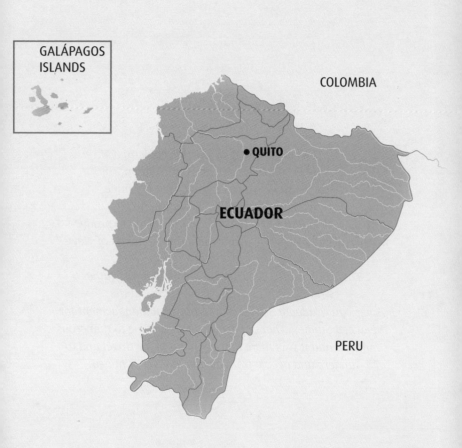

GALÁPAGOS
ISLANDS

COLOMBIA

● QUITO

ECUADOR

PERU

FIRST IMPRESSIONS

CHAPTER 1

'The geography of Ecuador has always dominated the
humans who have come to make their homes on her soil.'
—Albert B Franklin, *Ecuador: Portrait of a People*

First impressions are important to all of us during our lives. Our parents and teachers always tell us 'make a good first impression'. Countries are that way too, in that our first impressions often shape our feelings about a certain place as to whether we like it or not. While I have travelled to numerous countries throughout the world, Ecuador has been the place that has captured my wanderlust and love of other cultures the most.

I learned that there are few places in this world where, in such a small geographical area, you can find such a diverse geography and a melting pot of different cultures as in Ecuador.

I was in my bedroom at age 12, sitting at my desk in Phoenix during a winter rainstorm in January. I had received a large, leather-encased, GE transistor shortwave radio for Christmas with instructions on listening to country broadcasts. My father helped me string a large antennae across the roof and I was so excited that voices and music would soon arrive from all parts of the globe to my small house. I turned on my radio and clicked the band selector to shortwave and all types of sounds and signals began sputtering from the speaker. I slowly began to turn the dial and I heard Spanish and the announcer say "Santiago Chile". Then, I moved my fingers across the dial and sweet guitar music came to my ears and I was captivated. The announcer then came on and said "HCJB, Voice of the Andes from Quito Ecuador". I was mesmerised by the music and began to imagine this station perched high in the Andes, sitting in the middle of the world.

Again, I was exposed to Ecuador by having a professor in graduate school who came from the Sierra and by helping an Ecuadorian one day find his passport in Phoenix, as mentioned in the introduction. Quite honestly, my interest in Ecuador really catapulted when I saw the wife of the man who had lost his passport. Bronzed and shapely, her beauty was inspiring and I would later learn she would be what many men in Ecuador referred to as one who possesses *full equipo* or a woman who is beautiful with all the feminine attributes. At that point, I decided I would go to Ecuador someday. Maybe for fame, maybe for fortune but most definitely in search of a beautiful woman of my own.

Finally the time arrived. I took a job with an export company out of Chicago and they hired me to build up their Latin American sales. My first trip took me through Central America and on to Colombia. Finally, on my itinerary was the chance to visit Quito, the city which I had thought about since age 12. Taking an overbooked, late night flight to Quito would be a turning point in my life. Landing hard on the tarmac, the altitude made me gasp for breath and the cool of the night made my bones ache.

I arrived at the old Hotel Quito, which at that time was still one of the most elegant places to stay in Ecuador. The hotel sat perched on a ridge overlooking a valley, lights twinkling away in the distance.

A Memorable Experience

I went to the restaurant on top of the hotel. It was enclosed with glass to provide views of Quito. I felt as if I was in an old Alfred Hitchcock film as the fog surrounded the restaurant in a very short period of time. It was quite eerie as a music trio played haunting melodies while I ate my shrimp cocktail and steak. I looked out over Quito and thought of the history of the place, the love, the violence, the art and the music.

Quito was magical and spoke to my soul. That first week in Quito was amazing as I tried to learn the business practices and walked the cobblestone streets wondering about all the tales the old walls from the 1500s could tell if only they could speak.

During my first stay, I was successful at making several large sales. One of the advantages of being young and travelling for a company is the amount of time you have to entertain yourself at night and at weekends. I walked a great deal throughout old Quito and along Avenida Amazonas and took in the smells of the food being cooked and felt the music being played. As you will learn, music is deep in the soul of Ecuadorians. I felt reborn. However, I was a little surprised that I did not see many women in Quito who appeared similar to the goddess that I had seen in Phoenix. Don't get me wrong. The women in Quito are alluring with their dark eyes and features. I made a comment to a cab driver on my last night in Quito as to why the women here weren't more 'cinnamon' coloured? He asked if I was going to Guayaquil and I told him I would be going the next day. He said, "Patience *amigo*—you will see".

The next day, I made the thirty-minute flight from 2,743 m (9,000 ft) in the Andes, soaring down the avenue of volcanoes, amazed at the landscape and how quickly it changed. My God, the humidity stepping off the plane and the smell of insecticide in the airport was overbearing. And, at first sight, I noticed how significantly different the people in Guayaquil looked. Short, squared, bronzed and proud. The place oozed sensuality. A more open and easy going nature than the highlands, and, of course, I had to speak of the women. Shapely and cinnamon in colour, they possessed a feminine mystique of romance and passion. Had I gone to heaven? Hell yes. In fact, I met my future wife on my first day in Guayaquil. For some reason, I knew this was where I belonged despite the elements that would not make it a destination popular with many travellers at that time. Everything was here—this was my destiny. And as I would find out later, Guayaquil is a tough place to make a life, despite all of its attributes.

Years have passed now and while I don't live in Guayaquil at the present, it still impresses me, and each time I return, my impressions are invigorated for the way Ecuadorians live and survive despite social injustice, corruption, environmental elements and economic downfalls. Don't let the negatives discourage you—Ecuadorians are an unusual breed and live in a magical country. It is very unique and if you open your eyes and see, you will be changed permanently for the better. Your heart will be touched, and you no doubt will want to return. And be sure to open your ears and move to the Ecuadorian rhythm of life.

THE LAND AND ITS HISTORY

CHAPTER 2

'Ecuador is a sombre land.'
—Walker Lowry, writer of the classic
Tumult at Dusk: Being an Account of Ecuador

IN YOUR QUEST TO UNDERSTAND ECUADOR, you will find that it is one of the most unique geographical places on Earth. It is a very small country with lots of geography. Imagine being near glaciers, hours later tramping in the rainforest, then a few hours later boating through the mangroves on the Pacific coast. If Walt Disney were looking for a location for a nature park this would be the ideal place. (They might have to add a number of restrooms, however.)

In a region about the size of Colorado, with an area of 269,178 sq km (103,930 sq miles), Ecuador's geography has been a major factor in the development of the cultures that have resided there. It is also a virtual mosaic or museum of almost every type of terrain, flora or fauna to be found on our planet. There are so many types of flora that many have not even been described or catalogued to date. Ecuador is a very special place which is under increasing stress from human and commercial pursuits.

Ecuador is one of the smallest Andean countries located in the north-western corner of South America. It borders Colombia to the north; Peru to the south and east; and the Pacific Ocean to the west. The mainland is comprised of three unique geographical regions. These areas are referred to as the Costa (coastal lowlands in the west), the Sierra (central mountainous region) and the Oriente (eastern region, also known as the Amazon region, which slopes easterly from the Andes Mountains). There is a fourth geographic zone called the Galápagos Islands or Archipiélago de Colón, lying about 998 km (620 miles) off the Pacific coast.

The Costa and Sierra make up about 60 per cent of Ecuador's land area and the Oriente, the remaining 40 per cent. The Costa and Sierra regions are home to most of the population, with slightly more people living in the Costa. Only about 5 per cent of the population live in the Oriente.

Population

In July 2000, the population was approximately 12.9 million, with about 60 per cent between 15 and 64 years of age and about 36 per cent younger than 14 years of age.

COSTA

The Costa is an alluvial plain on the west coast, as much as 161 km (100 miles) wide in some places and as narrow as 19 km (12 miles) across. Its main rivers are the Esmeraldas to the north and the Guayas to the south, forming a fertile delta in between. This is the food basket of Ecuador, producing crops such as bananas, cacao, rice, sugar, coffee and toquilla palm (from which the inaccurately named Panama hat is made). Petroleum and gold are also produced here. This used to be the centre of oil production but the oil has largely run out and the Oriente is where about 85 per cent of Ecuador's oil is now pumped. Guayaquil, on the banks of the Guayas River, is Ecuador's largest port and a major source of economic capital.

The northern and eastern Costa is covered with tropical rainforest, including lianas, epiphytes, balsa and cinchona trees. Moving south, the rainforest gives way to deciduous and semi-deciduous woodland. Here, palms which provide nuts for buttons and fibre for the Panama hat can be found. The swampy coast and river floodplains were once covered by dense mangroves which have now been cleared for shrimp farms.

The Costa is the most populous region of Ecuador. Most of the country's agriculture production and industry take place in this region, with the focal area being Guayaquil, Ecuador's largest seaport. The Costa also holds a tremendous amount of opportunity for tourism, which has not been fully exploited to date. Much of the original mangroves have been eliminated to make way for shrimp farms. Economics, unfortunately, always seems to rule over conservation. The streams and the rivers in the Sierra flow to the sea through the lowlands of the Costa through its soil, which makes its basins rich for agriculture. My first time in Guayaquil, I remember I was amazed to see mangoes and papayas the same size as large cantaloupes in the United States!

Climate

The temperature is generally high throughout the year here. Temperatures average between 24–32°C (76–90°F). The rainy season (December–May) is warmer and more humid than the dry season.

The Costa's dry season takes place during the second half of the year. Humidity can be quite high and stifling. Much of this depends on the wind patterns and rainfall.

The southern Costa near the border with Peru receives very little rain and is quite arid. The northern Costa, comprising rainforest and mangroves, receives between 1,270–2,032 mm (50–80 inches) of rain annually. Guayaquil receives about 1,016 mm (40 inches) of rain per year. The southern Santa Elena Peninsula is a dry area, with rainfall averaging 101 mm (4 inches) a year.

Every four to seven years, during the rainy season, the infamous El Niño phenomenon may occur, resulting in torrential rains. I have experienced two El Niño seasons over the last eight years and have witnessed the amount of damage they can do. During the 1982–1983 season, there was a huge loss of life and damages amounting to billions of dollars. During the 1997–1998 season, numerous dead blue-footed boobies washed up along the Ecuador coast, about 966 km (600 miles) from their Galápagos Islands habitat. I also heard that Ecuadorian bananas and aquatic reptiles were found in Peru. Deadly floods and mudslides washed away towns and destroyed highways. Unusually warm waters caused coral near the Galápagos Islands to bleach. A terrible drought also hit the Amazon region, resulting in raging forest fires.

SIERRA

The Sierra is the central mountainous region of Ecuador, consisting of the Andean highlands which run north to south along the entire length of the country. The world's highest active volcano, Cotopaxi, is found here, standing at 5,897 m (19,347 ft). The slope to the west is quite steep but more gradual to the east toward the Oriente. There are two distinct Andean ranges—the Eastern and Western Cordilleras. The fertile valley between them is called the Avenue of the Volcanoes. The Sierra has more than 12 peaks which are higher than 4,877 m (16,000 ft), and most are capped with snow. Ecuador's highest peak is Chimborazo (6,310 m / 20,702 ft), an inactive volcano.

Ecuador has a long history of volcanic explosions and earthquakes. Tungurahua, an active volcano, is known locally as The Black Giant. On 10 November 1999, explosions of ash

The Cotopaxi Volcano—a photographer's dream.

and incandescent material occurred some 25–35 times per day from The Black Giant, and loud bangs could be heard as far as 19 km (12 miles) away.

Ecuador's major rivers and streams begin in the Sierra, making deep trenches in the landscape and causing much erosion. This has limited the amount of land available for agriculture in the highlands.

Much of the Sierra feels as if it were in an eternal spring. Temperatures average around 16°C (60°F) and the sun sets at almost the same time every day. North of Quito, on the way to Otavalo, there is a mountain range which makes you think you are in the mountains of Arizona. However, rainfall patterns can be quite varied, decreasing toward the centres of canyons and valleys. The interior plateau and slopes are very dry and cold. The rain here is often very fine, producing misty conditions. Some basins in the Sierra are comparatively arid. Rainfall reaches a maximum during the equinoxes. The rainy months are from October to November and February to May.

Quito is nestled in the Andes Mountains, at an altitude of 2,850 m (9,350 ft). Having limited contact with the outside world until recently, Quito and the other Sierra cities of Cuenca and Loja have developed into bastions of conservative

The Quito skyline on a cloudy day.

Spanish culture. Even today, alongside modern office buildings and apartments stand some of the finest examples of colonial art and architecture in all of Latin America.

ORIENTE

Slowly descending from the Sierra into eastern Ecuador, you will enter the mystical jungle region of the Oriente. Comprising the eastern slopes of the Ecuadorian Andes and the lowland areas of rainforest in the Amazon basin, the Oriente takes up about 40 per cent of Ecuador's land area. There are three principal waterways in the region, with the slow and wide Amazonian rivers and their tributaries—Río Napo, Río Pastaza and Río Santiago.

Fantastically coloured birds, such as long-beaked toucans, noisy macaws and flitting hummingbirds, share this land with exquisite butterflies, 28-foot anacondas and ferocious howler monkeys.

Largely undeveloped, this region is home to only about 5 per cent of Ecuadorians. Most of them are Indians, the largest Indian community being the Jíbaros, who live on the banks of the rivers in the south-eastern jungles. A fiercely independent people, they successfully fought off the Spanish by killing them, abducting their women and setting fire to their settlements. Headhunters and skillful warriors, they can blow poisoned darts with deadly accuracy. Other communities found here include whites and mestizos from the highlands, the nomadic Huarani, the Quichua-speaking Záparos and Yumbos and the tunic-wearing and ornamented Cofáns.

Petroleum and timber and, previously, gold are the major economic resources of the Oriente. Oil was discovered here around 1970. Plantains and cassava are important staple food crops and corn (maize) and oranges are also cultivated. Cattle are left to graze.

The Oriente is very hot all year round and experiences continuous and abundant rainfall. Temperatures range from a high of 29–33°C (84–91°F) during the day to a low of 20–24°C (68–75°F) at night. This region has a poor drainage system because of the low gradient of the topography.

GALÁPAGOS ISLANDS

The fourth geographical region of Ecuador is the Galápagos Islands. American novelist Herman Melville described these islands as such: "Take five and twenty heaps of cinders dumped here and there in an outside lot, imagine some of them magnified into mountains and the vacant lot the sea; and you will have a fit idea of the general aspect of the Encantadas, or Enchanted Isles." These heaps of cinders consist of 13 major islands, ranging in area from 14 to 4,587 sq km (5.4 to 1,771 sq miles), six smaller islands and scores of islets and rocks lying west of the mainland of Ecuador. The islands have a total land area of 8,010 sq km (3,093 sq miles).

The government of Ecuador designated part of the Galápagos Islands a wildlife sanctuary in 1935. In 1959, the sanctuary became the Galápagos National Park. This archipelago is Ecuador's main tourist magnet. When I first visited Ecuador in the early 1980s, it still seemed to be an exotic destination reserved only for scientists and the rich. Now, tens of thousands of tourists arrive every year. The value of the Galápagos Islands tourism to the Ecuadorian economy is estimated to be more than US$ 55 million a year.

An iguana lounges in Guayaquil.

Only five islands are permanently inhabited, San Cristóbal being the most populous. Some 80 per cent of the islanders live on the islands of Santa Cruz, San Cristóbal and Isabela. Many Ecuadorians try to move to the Galápagos Islands to cash in on the tourism. Every few years you will notice efforts by the government to restrict migration to these islands. Tourism and migration places severe pressures on the ecosystem and great care should be taken to preserve the qualities of the Galápagos Islands, qualities which make it such a unique destination.

Underwater volcanoes formed the islands millions of years ago. The first historical report of these islands dates from 1535 when it was discovered by accident by the Bishop of Panama, Tomás de Berlanga, when his ship drifted off course. He did not name the islands but reported tortoises or *galápagos* "so big that they could carry a man on their backs." This was probably what led the Flemish cartographer Ortelius to name the islands Insulae de los Galopegos. A seafaring Spaniard, Diego de Rivadeneira, visited the islands after Berlanga and named them Las Encantadas (The Enchanted Isles) after strong currents threw his ship mysteriously off course, giving the impression that the islands could move out of his reach at their own will.

It was, ultimately, Charles Darwin who drew international attention to Las Encantadas or Archipiélago de Colón as they are known locally. This was where Darwin, arriving in 1836 and staying for five weeks, gathered evidence for his momentous study—the 'Origin of Species by Means of Natural Selection'. His study of the Galápagos finch (or Darwin's finch) gave him evidence for his thesis that 'species are not immutable'.

An Abundance of Life

Numerous species of plant and animal life are endemic to the Galápagos Islands. There are approximately 625 plant species and subspecies found here, of which 36 per cent are endemic. There are approximately 1,000 insect species present (including 50 spider species), and more than 60 species of snails. Some 298 fish species have also been recorded.

One animal endemic to the Galápagos Islands is the famous giant tortoise (Geochelone elephantopus). Whalers and sealers have decimated the tortoise population and now only 15,000 remain. The small-winged flightless cormorant (only 700 to 800 are still in existence), the dark-brown Galápagos hawk with a 4-foot wingspan, the small and scurrying Galápagos rail, the hideous and prickly-pear-eating iguanas, the drab and non-poisonous Galápagos snake and the luxuriously coated Galápagos fur seal are just a sampling of the local inhabitants.

The climate here is influenced by the ocean currents. January to May is the typical hot or rainy season. June to December is the dry or cool season. There is minimal rainfall, which often forms a mist.

Two of the most interesting islands are San Cristóbal and Santa Cruz. San Cristóbal is the easternmost island. The first permanent settlers arrived here in 1869. Many of the cruise tours of the islands begin in San Cristóbal.

Santa Cruz is where the National Park headquarters and the Charles Darwin Research Station are located. A number of tours also begin from this island. The US Navy had a small installation just off this island during World War II.

VEGETATION

Ecuador is one of the richest places in the world for flora. Ten per cent of the world's vascular plant species are located within an area that covers just 0.2 per cent of the Earth's surface. Ecuador houses some 25,000 species of vascular plants. (All of North America only has 17,000 species.) This is largely due to the diverse ecological conditions created by the great altitudinal differences in this small land. The vegetation varies from xerophytic scrub to rainforest.

This land is one of the largest growers of roses in the world. More than 10 per cent of all the orchid species in the world grow here. Forests, from which many exotic woods such as cedar, ebony, cyprus and myrtle are derived, cover much of the country. Other plants include vanilla, cinnamon and chicle. Montane rainforest covers the eastern slopes of the Andes. The soils in the Sierra are porous and there is poor forest coverage except for the eucalyptus, which was imported from Australia. The lower levels of the Sierra are comprised of scrub brush and cacti. The higher levels consist of tufted grass, just before the glaciers begin.

WILDLIFE

Ecuador's wildlife is just as impressive. In the Sierra, llamas exist alongside pumas and jaguars. The Costa and Oriente are populated by many varieties of parrots and monkeys, which you might see for sale on the streets of cities such as Guayaquil. There is a wide variety of rodents, bats, alligators, turtles and iguanas.

If you are a bird-lover, Ecuador is also the place for you! There are about 1,500 species to be found here, a number endemic to Ecuador. In 1998, a new species from the Antpitta family was discovered—a bird which barks like a dog and hoots like an owl! There are also over 115 species of hummingbirds that add a lot of colour to the geography.

Frogs and butterflies are also abundant here. I remember seeing, during my first trip from Guayaquil to Cuenca, places in the lower Andes which were just covered with blue butterflies. There are also more than 450 marine species and 800 freshwater species in Ecuador's teeming waters.

PROVINCES

Understanding the names of places in any country can give you substantial insight into the local culture. The country of Ecuador is divided into 22 *provincias* (provinces). These provinces are divided into *cantones* (regions), which are in turn divided into *parroquias* (parishes). Very small villages, where there may be just a few homes, are called *caseríos*.

A number of places have older names that were changed by the local government. However, the locals continue to refer to the place by the old name, even though it officially has a new name. One example is J Gómez Rendon, a small city, which was originally called Progreso. The locals still refer to it as Progreso despite the fact that, when you go through the town, it is marked J Gómez Rendon. A number of towns are named after saints such as San Miguel de Salcedo. Towns named after male saints outnumber towns named after female saints.

Llamas at play, watched over by the Cotopaxi Volcano.

In the Sierra, many town names were originally in the Quechuan language. A number of town names have aquatic associations, named after nearby bodies of water. Examples are Los Encuentros where two rivers meet or La Bocana which refers to the mouth of a river. A number of provinces and towns have taken on the names of volcanoes. Examples are Cotopaxi and Cotocachi. Towns within certain provinces use names of lesser-known volcanoes such as El Altar and Toacaso.

In the Costa region, you will see names of cities which refer to the elevation of the area or of certain vegetation. Some examples are Lomas de Sargentillo, which refers to the hills, and Zapotal, which is named after the Zapote tree.

Other cities may have used the last name of the founder such as Rivera or Mariano. Some townships use the name of a large land owner or of a ranch. Often a feminine name will be used, as in La Hacienda Mercedes (Plantation Mercedes). Names may also refer to a certain ideal or concept. Examples are El Progreso (*progreso* means progress), La Paz (*paz* means peace), or El Paraíso (*paraíso* means paradise). Houses are often named, no matter how humble. You may also see a home or small home with the name of the female occupant over the front door. An example is Villa Rosa.

GHOST TOWNS

Villages and cities come and go with time. Acts of nature and man contribute to the death and change of communities.

In Ecuador, both earthquakes and volcanoes have a tremendous impact on both geography and societies. A potent combination of lava and ice has caused significant mud and river flooding, aggravated by deforestation. Riobamba and Ambato have been destroyed three times. The most serious earthquakes and volcano explosions have had their major impact in the Sierra.

Humans have also played their part. Many of the initial Spanish settlements in the Oriente were wiped out by Indians. Other settlements such as Tomebamba and Mocha also suffered similar fates. During colonial times, Guayaquil, Manta and Portoviejo were attacked by pirates and their locations shifted. Since many of the earlier houses were built from cane, fires burnt down many towns, especially in the Costa region. Guayaquil burned down a total of three times prior to the 20th century. Babahoyo, Esmeraldas and Vinces have also been damaged by fire.

CHALLENGES IN THE 21ST CENTURY

Ecuador's main challenge in the 21st century is maintaining the balance between man and geography. Planning, discipline and the curbing of greed will be indispensable in keeping Ecuador a beautiful natural location. The country is considered ecologically unique, with an unrivalled variety of ecosystems and diversity of species. Its breadth of ecological variation is largely attributable to the biodiversity on the Galápagos Islands.

The engines of economic development and enterprise (such as petroleum exploration, lumber production and agricultural cultivation) are putting this delicate ecosystem under threat.

The Destruction of the Environment

Unsound environmental practices have contributed to considerable environmental degradation and given rise to grave environmental problems—deforestation, as a result of petroleum exploration and lumber production; soil erosion, as a result of over-grazing, poor agricultural cultivation practices and deforestation; desertification; water pollution; and deterioration of biodiversity.

There is a huge demand for shark's fin around the world, in particular Asia, with its insatiable appetite for shark's fin soup. A bowl of shark's fin soup can cost up to US$ 100 in some Hong Kong restaurants. World Heritage Sites and Marine Reserves, such as the Galápagos Islands and the Cocos Island (in the Indian Ocean south-west of Java), are increasingly raided by illegal fishermen, as shark populations in outside reserves decline. Some fishermen take only the fins, dumping the maimed sharks back into sea, often still alive. At US$ 50

Alarming Statistics

It is estimated that between 250,000 and 300,000 sharks are killed a year in Ecuadorian waters. Sea turtles and sea birds (such as the rare-waved albatross and blue-footed boobies) are also often casualties that sadly get caught in nets that are meant for sharks.

per lb (0.45 kg) for the fins, local fishermen also have no qualms about killing sea lion pups for bait. In 2004, the government issued a decree which prohibits the sale and export of shark fins. However, the Central Bank reported 70,871 kg (156,246 lbs) were exported in 2004.

Sea cucumbers lack an advantage that other sea creatures have, i.e. the ability to scurry or swim away from attackers. Due to their profitable return (up to 25 times their cost), the sea slug is particularly susceptible to over-fishing. Following the alarming decrease in numbers in the early 1990s and an Executive Decree in 1993, all fishing of sea cucumbers in the Galápagos Islands was banned.

The government of Ecuador has committed itself to an environmental agenda called Agenda 21. In accordance with this, there is an urgent need to replace exploitative practices with sustainable development. The aims of Agenda 21 includes establishing a programme to conserve and preserve the biodiversity of the Galápagos Islands; strengthening its system of protected areas; and applying strategies for reforestation. Ecuador must also formulate a legal framework, based on public policies, to address and regulate these suggested measures.

The regulation and protection of the environment in Ecuador is controlled by the Ministry of the Environment and the Dirección General del Medio Ambiente (General Directorate for Environment). The non-governmental environmental organisations and entities that are active here include the Amigos de la Naturaleza de Mindo, EcoCiencia and the Fundación Charles Darwin para las Islas Galápagos.

Galápagos Islands

Most scholars of the Galápagos Islands agree that the human population here has reached unsustainable levels.

The growing number of visitors who have come to witness the natural wonders of the Galápagos Islands have the potential to endanger them. The Park Service has found it difficult to limit the number of visitors to the islands but does regulate the licensing of guides required for disembarkation to the islands as well as the designation of low-impact landing sites. The National Park has to deal with the conservation problems that motor yachts and their rubbish (often dumped in the waters outside Park limits) bring. Although responsible tourism is a sustainable means for preserving the park, its negative effects have to be closely monitored.

THE SOMBRE HISTORY OF A DIVIDED LAND

Several years ago, on a flight from Ecuador, a young American woman sitting next to me commented that she regretted not having read more about Ecuador's history prior to her visit. She felt, as she looked in the residents' eyes and at the colonial architecture, that there was much she had missed.

She was right. History is the golden key that will help you unlock the mind of the Ecuadorian. So we should start by trying to unravel some of the threads of this small country's intricate past.

ECUADOR'S ANCIENT HISTORY

Pottery figures have been discovered that date from 3,000 to 2,500 BC. This indicates that Ecuador was inhabited as early as 5,000 years ago. Apparently, a great variety of tribes (nearly 50) had settled along the coast, in the Sierra and in the Amazonian hinterland. However, unity was not achieved among these Indians. The greatest divisions existed between the tribes of the coast and of the mountains.

Some of the earliest civilisations included the Valdivia, the La Tolita and the Manta cultures, which settled along the Pacific coast.

THE INCAS

The Incas invaded and dominated Ecuador's groups before the Spaniards. They would have a substantial impact on local history, despite reigning supreme in the region for only a hundred years.

The Incas first established themselves in the 12th century in Cuzco, now part of modern-day Peru. Their main period of territorial expansion came during the reign of Inca Pachacuti Yupanqui (1438–1471). They moved south to the Titicaca Basin and north to Quito, ruling over the Chancas, the Quechuas and the Chimús.

Cleverly resettling the locals, the Incas practised the divide and rule principle, making organised revolt difficult. The Inca Topac Yupanqui (1471–1493) extended the southernmost border to central Chile, and his successor, Huayna Capac (1493–1525), northwards to the Angasmayo River, obtaining power in what is now southern Colombia.

Quito became a vital administrative and military centre for the Incas. Huayna Capac divided the empire for his two sons with Atahualpa governing the north (including Quito) and Huáscar ruling the south. Huayna Capac's death set off a struggle for succession, which was still unresolved when the Spanish arrived in Peru in 1532.

At its height, the Incan civilisation controlled about 12 million people in more than 980,000 sq km (380,000 sq miles) of territory. They introduced taxes, the Incan religion and the Quechua language. An extensive network of roads and bridges was laid—4.6 m (15 ft) wide in some places. (This network ironically aided the Spanish conquest.) Llamas were used for transport and runners were used to relay messages, covering hundreds of miles in one day.

Incan society was highly stratified. The emperor ruled with the aid of an aristocratic bureaucracy, exercising authority with harsh and often repressive controls. Indians were at times forced into labour but the Incas did not tax them on the production of their own fields.

Incan technology and architecture were highly developed, although not strikingly original. Their irrigation systems, palaces, temples and fortifications can still be seen throughout the Andes. The economy was based on agriculture, its staple crops being corn (maize), white and sweet potatoes, squash, tomatoes, peanuts (groundnuts), chili peppers, cocoa, *yuca* (cassava) and cotton. They raised *cuy* (guinea pigs), ducks, llamas, alpacas and dogs. Much clothing was made from llama wool and cotton. Practically every man was a farmer, producing his own food and clothing.

The Incan religion combined features of animism, fetishism and the worship of nature gods. The pantheon of gods was headed by Inti (the sun god), and included Viracocha (a creator god and culture hero) and Apu Illapu (the rain god). The Incan religion was a highly organised state religion, but, while the locals were required to worship the sun god, their native religions were tolerated.

> Incan rituals included elaborate forms of divination and the sacrifice of humans and animals. Much of their religious institutions were destroyed by the Spanish conquistadors in their campaign against idolatry.

The descendants of the Incas are the present-day Quichua-speaking indigenous Indians of the Andes. They combine farming and herding with simple traditional technology. Rural settlements are of three kinds: families living in the midst of their fields, true village communities owning fields outside inhabited centres and a combination of these two. Towns are centres of mestizo communities. An Indian community is usually close-knit, and intermarriage within families is common. Much of the agricultural work is done cooperatively.

Their religious beliefs are a form of Roman Catholicism infused with the pagan hierarchy of spirits and deities.

THE CONQUISTADORS

After the discovery of the New World, stories spread about the fabled wealth and riches of the Incan dynasty. A number of Spanish expeditions set out from Panama in search of gold. It is the view of some that it was the Spanish conquest that brutalised the region and put in place a rigid class structure. The area of Ecuador was first discovered by the Spaniards on an exploratory voyage which landed at Esmeraldas in around 1526.

Francisco Pizarro departed from Panama in 1531. He ventured further south, landing in 1532 at Tumbez, on the present-day Peruvian coast. At that time, at least four culturally related Indian groups who possessed gold and jewels: the Esmeraldas, the Mantas, the Huancavilcas and the Punáes, occupied the coastal lowlands. The highland peoples included the Pastos, the Caras, the Panzaleos, the Puruhás, the Cañaris and the Paltas. The Esmeraldas worked with gold and platinum and were hunters. The Mantas lived

south of the Esmeralda and worked with gold jewellery and emeralds. They were extensive traders and sailed up and down the coast.

Pizzaro continued down the coast to what is now Isla Puná (Puná Island), in the Gulf of Guayaquil. He had heard of gold in Tumbez but found it in ruins as a result of an Indian battle. He travelled into what is now Peru to Cajamarca where he planned to take Inca King Atahualpa into custody and hold him for ransom (a common tactic of the Spanish). When he arrived in Cajamarca, he found that Atahualpa was not there but had moved himself and many of the residents to the surrounding hills. The Spanish pressed Atahualpa to visit and he foolishly accepted. He was taken captive and promised his freedom only if he could fill a room with gold. Atahualpa did so once with gold and twice with silver. The Spanish still executed him. It was from here that they tightened their noose around the region. The Inca, weakened by internal division and defenseless against Spanish horses, canons, guns and swords, did not put up much resistance.

One of Pizarro's lieutenants, Sabastián de Benalcázar, headed north with a band of 200 men. Forming an alliance with the local Cañari people, they fought their way along the inter-Andean valley to Quito. Even the great Incan tactician, Rumiñahui, was finally forced out of Quito, but not before razing it to the ground. Benalcázar would initiate one of the first municipal governments and become a lieutenant governor to Pizarro. (Benalcázar's home still stands at calle Benalcázar y Olmedo in Quito.) He conquered most of Ecuador, including Guayaquil in 1533. This was a brutal time when the Indians were basically beaten into servitude.

The half-brother of Francisco Pizarro, Gonzalo Pizarro, was made governor of Quito in 1539. In 1541, with about 200 Spanish troops, some 4,000 Indians, horses and other animals, he made an expedition into the unexplored region east of Quito. The expedition ran into trouble when supplies dwindled. The Indians did poorly in the tropics and died. The Spanish were also not accustomed to such difficult terrain. They had previously obtained supplies by stealing them from the locals but the Indians they encountered in the new areas escaped. Gonzalo's lieutenant, Captain Francisco de Orellana, left with some men down the Napo River in search of provisions. Pizarro waited and waited and waited for Orellana. After his men had eaten their dogs, horses, shoes and saddles, Gonzalo, realising that Orellana and his men were probably not coming back, stumbled back to Quito with the survivors—only to find the city in upheaval. Francisco Pizarro had been assassinated by the Almagristas and another Spanish faction was seeking control of the region. Something good did come out of this expedition, however—the discovery of the Amazon River!

The Spanish Crown was upset with the situation and specifically with the enslavement and maltreatment of the Indians. The Crown ruled that the Indians be set free. It was also declared that the land acquired by the conquistadors was to be returned to the Crown for management after their death. This caused an uproar since many of their widows and children would be reduced to poverty. In 1544, a new viceroy was sent to try to manage the local administration. Blasco Nuñez had a short and violent career. It started with him trying to impose the New Laws of Bartolomé de Las Casas to the letter. He stepped hard on many important toes and either ordered a murder or committed one himself.

Opposition grew against him and he was arrested and packed off home to Spain. On the way home, however, he was killed by troops loyal to Gonzalo Pizarro.

In 1547, the Crown then sent Pedro de la Gasca, a priest and lawyer, to try to calm things down. He succeeded by granting amnesty to the rebels and repealing many of the most hated laws. Pizarro had planned an attack against Gasca, refusing all offers of a peace accord, but he was grossly outnumbered and his troops deserted him, professing allegiance to Spain. When Pizarro was taken into custody, he knew his time had come. Before he was beheaded in 1548, he asked the executioner to make it quick and clean.

COLONIAL PERIOD

The colonial period of Ecuador continued to be a difficult time for the inhabitants. It is important to understand that

Barrio Las Penas in Guayaquil dates back to the 1500s.

Ecuador's history at this time was really one of Peru's. At the same time, it is was during the colonial period that the seeds of nationalism were sown, starting a long but painful gestation that would bear fruit with independence in 1830. This identity crisis explains, to some degree, the persistent problems between Ecuador and Peru and the regional divisions within present-day Ecuador.

In 1563, the northern region acquired the status of *audiencia* and came under the auspices of the viceroy of Lima in Peru. The *audiencia* was the highest tribunal of justice and a general administrative board for the region. The hierarchy of authority was absolute and began with the King of Spain. Under the king and governing the new colonies of America was the Council of Indies established in 1524 and residing in Spain.

Under the council were four viceroys who resided in the new Americas. The viceroy of Peru was based in Lima and was founded in 1544. The area of Ecuador and Quito reported to Lima. The *audiencia* or judicial body of Quito was formulated in 1563. Under the *audiencia* were provinces with a *corregidor* (governor) also appointed by the king. In what is modern-day Ecuador there were five provinces, consisting of Cuenca, Guayaquil, Loja, Quito and Zamora. In 1739, Ecuador became part of the new Spanish Viceroyalty of Nueva Granada, which included Colombia and Venezuela, with its capital in Bogotá (Colombia).

Colonial cities were governed by a city council, its councillors appointed by the king. This was very likely a position for life. The councillors were referred to as *regidores* and would select a city leader or judge called an *alcalde*. In some instances, there could be two *alcaldes*. The management style was quite onerous and the sole reason for the existence of these positions was to handle the king's affairs. Spain had no system in place to handle the conflicts in its new territories. All decisions had to be approved by Seville and answers could take longer than a year to obtain.

While Spain's primary interest was to expand its wealth, it professed a desire to convert the indigenous population to Catholicism. The Church became extremely important in the development of what is now Ecuador and became powerful and wealthy. In many ways, the Church became more powerful than the government organisations. There was much bickering between the bishop and president of the *audiencia* as to who held the higher social status. The people of Quito found themselves constantly battling sickness, droughts, earthquakes and volcanoes.

In the 1580s, there were attacks by pirates along the Ecuadorian coast. In 1591, Spain realised that it needed numerous ships to protect its interests and a tax was levied to raise money for shipbuilding. The residents of Quito were upset with this and felt that the coast and Guayaquil should take care of itself. They revolted. A number of rebels were jailed and troops were sent from Lima. A representative was sent from Spain and a number of people were hung.

Caste System

It was during colonial times that Ecuador developed a strict social or caste type system. These social divisions have endured until today and one's place in society is often determined by the shade of one's skin. The social levels in colonial Ecuador were basically divided into five different levels:

Blacks

Blacks were among the lowest echelon of society. In fact, they were not considered human and had no rights. The clergy made no attempt to convert or care for the blacks. They were originally brought to Ecuador along the northern coast of Ecuador in the late 16th century to work the sugar plantations. However, in present-day Ecuador, blacks are considered a step above the Indians in society.

Indians

Indians provided most of the labour in colonial Ecuador. In general, they were passive and did as they were told. They were usually attached to a large *hacienda* (plantation) and would be called from time to time to work on large public projects. The Church made efforts to teach the Indians to read and to convert them to Catholicism.

Mestizos

Mestizos claimed the next level of society and were often fathered by a Spaniard and had an Indian mother. They had very little access to positions of power or prestige. There was some movement by mestizos into the Church culture.

Criollos

The criollos were of Spanish descent and officially had the same rights as the Spaniards. However, it was the Spaniards who received the best positions and the favour of the courts. There was a great deal of quarrelling and hatred between the criollos and the Spaniards.

Spaniards

The Spaniards clearly held the highest places in society. There were approximately 1,000 Spaniards at that time. Most of the early Spaniards were conquistadors. They believed that the Indians were there to do their manual labour, having a distaste for working with their hands. This is still the case in Ecuador where it is believed that only the lower classes work with their hands.

Some Spaniards married Indian women because there were few Spanish women then. Their children had little opportunity of moving into the higher circles of society and were often relegated to managing groups of Indian labourers. Many became artisans and contributed significantly to much of the beautiful architecture of Quito.

The lower classes had literally no representation at that time and were perceived to exist to serve the higher classes. Greed and ambition existed among the higher classes.

INDEPENDENCE

Ecuador's independence from Spain followed similar lines to the unrest spreading across the South American continent. The first rumbles started in Quito in 1592, recurred in 1765

A soldier in parade dress during an independence parade in Guayaquil.

and erupted in the events which took place between 1770 and the end of the 18th century.

One of the strongest proponents for independence for Ecuador was Francisco Javier Eugenio de Santa Cruz y Espejo, a mestizo medical doctor. A well-regarded scholar, he had a wide range of interests and a grand vision for Ecuador's future. Advocating complete freedom from Spain, autonomous government for each colony and nationalisation of the clergy, he was persecuted, imprisoned and later exiled for his ideals. Eugenio Espejo published the first newspaper in Ecuador (*Primicias de la cultura de Quito*) that was heavily critical of the Spanish government. This newspaper only made seven issues. He died in 1795, but not before he had planted the hope of independence in many Ecuadorian hearts.

The independence of North America, the French Revolution and the invasion of Spain by Napoleon fed existing anti-Spanish sentiments. The Spanish government had tried to dominate all aspects of economic and political life and many locals found its rule unjust and oppressive, bringing more negative consequences than benefits. They blamed the Spaniards for establishing hateful racial, economic and cultural castes; stealing land from those who depended on it for their livelihood; forcing the poor into slavery; bringing with them infectious diseases such as smallpox and syphilis; and stripping Indians of their self-respect.

A group of Quito elites formed a junta on 10 August 1809. Successful for a year, it collapsed due to a lack of support from other Ecuadorian cities. Further plans for rebellion were held in check by the locals' fear of the Spanish Pacific fleet. But the military's abuses caused much of the population to side with the rebels, resulting in riots in 1810. After an agreement for a troop withdrawal, the junta was told it could exist, but only under the leadership of the *audiencia*. The viceroy of Peru opposed this plan. The Spanish remained in control for the next 10 years.

By 1819, the Spanish threat had lost its teeth. Another movement for independence had begun in Guayaquil. Leaders were able to enlist the assistance of Simón Bolívar

Simón Bolívar's monument in Parque Bolívar, Guayaquil.

from Venezuela and José de San Martín from Argentina who were marshalling independence struggles on both sides of the continent. Simón Bolívar (nicknamed The Liberator) had a grand vision of several large independent countries across the continent—Gran Colombia. He had soon entered Bogotá, the capital of Colombia, taking the Spanish by surprise in the Battle of Boyacá on 7 August 1819. In 1821, troops were sent from Colombia under the command of Antonio José de Sucre. The liberators foiled the Spanish troops in Guayaquil and then focused on the Sierra. General Sucre defeated the royal troops in the mountains above Quito at the Battle of Pichincha. Venezuela was freed from Spanish rule in 1821 and Ecuador in 1822.

It was in Quito that Bolívar won Ecuador's independence, and it was also in Quito that he won Manuela Sáenz's heart. Sáenz was an ardent revolutionary who united her life with Bolívar's cause. She saved him from conspirators in 1828 in Bogotá and attempted suicide when he died in 1830. Exiled to the small Peruvian port of Paita, she spent her last days eking out an existence selling sweets and tobacco.

Bolívar's goal at that time was to combine Colombia, Ecuador and Venezuela into the Viceroyalty of New Granada. Bolívar and San Martín met from 26–27 July 1822 in Guayaquil on the banks of the Guayas River, where there is now a statue of the both of them. San Martín's campaign was to liberate Peru but Bolívar wanted it as part of his Gran Colombia. What was said between the two was not recorded but they parted quickly, neither promising aid to the other. Guayaquil was divided and had three options to determine its existence:

- Unite with Bolívar and become a part of Gran Colombia
- Unite with Peru
- Become self-governing

Bolívar made the first point come true, delivering the final blow to the Spanish colonial regime in South America two years later.

As a part of Gran Colombia, Ecuador became embroiled in military campaigns to liberate Peru. Ecuadorians resented the 30 per cent tax Bolívar had levied on Guayaquil's cacao exports to finance his Peruvian campaign.

The Guayaquil elites agitated for self-rule and on 13 May 1830, the independent republic of Ecuador was proclaimed. Juan José Flores was appointed president five months later. Venezuela and Quito both withdrew from Gran Colombia in 1830. Bolívar died of tuberculosis, soon after his dream, in the house of a Spaniard near Santa Marta, Colombia. His last words were "(South) America is ungovernable. Those who have served the revolution have plowed the sea."

BABY REPUBLIC

While Ecuador gained its independence, it in no way lost the tremendous and deeply entrenched culture of Spain. The divisions between the social classes continued, and power remained in a few aristocratic hands. The lower classes had no say and little influence.

The distinct geographical divisions also played a considerable factor in dividing the three distinct regions (Costa, Sierra and Oriente) into one country. The main divide lay between the Sierra's wealthy landowners and the coastal merchants, centred around Quito and Guayaquil respectively. They had contrasting economic and social attitudes. The inhabitants of the Sierra were conservatives, devout Catholics and supporters of Church-sponsored education for all. Their economic interests revolved around the close management of native labour.

In contrast, the coastal peoples were liberals who favoured free enterprise, the development of agricultural exports and other trades. They opposed the Church's involvement in matters of state.

Juan José Flores

Juan José Flores was a general in Simón Bolívar's army. A Venezuelan by birth, he married into an influential Quito aristocratic family and became a national hero during the fight for independence.

Flores was merciless in his pursuit for power. He called an assembly to declare the Republic of Ecuador a new nation and himself president. Flores' autocratic rule, poor administrative ability, his support of entrenched privileges, especially those of the Church, and his perceived favouritism towards the Sierra provinces, fed opposition against him.

Based in Guayaquil, Vicente Rocafuerte headed opposition to Juan José Flores. In 1834, at the close of Flores' first term as president, civil war broke out between Quito and Guayaquil. To quell this dangerous unrest, Flores cleverly installed Rocafuerte as president from 1834 to 1839. Flores retained a great deal of power from behind the scenes, however, by keeping a strong hold on the army.

Vicente Rocafuerte's term in office was a productive one. He promoted civil liberties and established public schools. Many reforms were carried out to protect the rights of native Indians and to advance and secularise education.

Once Rocafuerte's term ended in 1839, Flores resumed control with the support of Venezuelan and Colombian soldiers loyal to him. The tussle between these two strong leaders continued, but with Flores as president up until 1845. Rocafuerte went into self-exile in 1843 in protest against Flores' unsavoury dictatorial practices, including inviting the Spanish to return. A young student, Gabriel García Moreno, made a failed assassination attempt on Flores. The coastal liberals finally forced Flores into exile. Even then, Flores stirred up trouble in Ecuador, attempting to overthrow the government from abroad.

CHAOS AND CATHOLICISM

The period 1845–1860 saw Ecuador in chaos, with a string of weak leaders jostling for power. In 1859, a general controlled Guayaquil, both Loja and Cuenca declared themselves independent and Quito had a provisional government. During this vulnerable time, Peru invaded southern Ecuador and placed a blockade on Guayaquil. There was discussion with Colombia about dividing up the country.

Even as Ecuador seemed to be torn apart politically and wrecked economically, some saw this as a time of emancipation. The first laws to the advantage of the indigenous population were passed at this time, many slaves were liberated and three centuries of compulsory tribute payments by Indians were ended.

Gabriel García Moreno was watching and waiting in the wings. He was repulsed by the chaotic violence that liberalism and self-interested factionalism had brought about. Careful analysis of Ecuadorian society convinced him that the country was hopelessly divided by regional interest, class, race and language. Convinced that the only thing that could unify Ecuador was religion, García Moreno, himself a devout Roman Catholic, saw religion as the only means to create nationalism and foster social cohesion. To achieve this, Ecuador desperately needed a period of peace and a strong government.

In 1859, Peru took possession of Ecuador's southern provinces. Drastic action was needed. Courting the help of the man he wanted dead in the 1840s, García Moreno joined forces with Juan José Flores, forced the Peruvians out and began uniting the country.

García Moreno

García Moreno has been described by liberals as one of history's worst tyrants and by conservatives as a great nation-builder. Ruling from 1860 to 1875, he made Roman Catholicism the exclusive state religion and no other religions were tolerated. Education, welfare and government policy came under the Church.

García Moreno's presidency inaugurated many public works projects. Schools (from primary to polytechnic level) and hospitals were built. Construction started on the Quito-Guayaquil railroad to link the Costa and the Sierra, and roads were built. Eucalyptus trees were even brought in from Australia to alleviate erosion in the Sierra. Agricultural reforms improved production. Cocoa exports grew from approximately US$ 1 million to US$ 10 million annually. Guayaquil developed as the key port for Ecuador and a rising middle class.

The object of countless assassination attempts, García Moreno was said to have had an indefatigable confidence in the future, allegedly declaring: "The enemies of God and the Church can kill me but God does not die." Not long after his third term, his presidency was abruptly ended when he was hacked to death on the steps of the presidential palace.

LIBERALS TAKE THE LEAD

After García Moreno's death, the liberals and conservatives jostled for power. Due to the increasing economic importance of the coast, the Guayaquil-based liberals began to take the upper hand. General Eloy Alfaro, a magnetic liberal hero emerging from the lower classes, became the constitutional president for two terms (1897–1901 and 1906–1911).

Under Alfaro, the affairs of the State were separated from those of the Church. Commercialism was promoted, as was freedom of religion and speech. Divorce was permitted as was civil marriage and burial. The Church title was abolished and many large estates confiscated by the State or liberal leaders. Alfaro continued and completed many of Moreno's road and railroad projects—the Quito-Guayaquil railroad was completed in 1908.

The Downfall of Alfaro

Alfaro was as heavy-handed as his predecessors, making little impact on the impoverished lives of the Indians and peasants. His growing unpopularity and relentless attempts to hold on to power led to his overthrow by a coalition of conservatives and dissident liberals. He and his lieutenants were dragged, dismembered and burnt by a lynch mob in 1912.

DARK TIMES

During World War I and the short boom which followed, power shifted into the hands of the wealthy merchants and bankers of Guayaquil. This clique made attempts to take control of the agriculture of the coastal plain. The 1920s brought economic depression, the devaluation of the sucre and a fungal epidemic which destroyed cacao crops. This precipitated urban discontent, the formation of trade unions in Guayaquil, riots and even massacres conducted by the army. Riots broke out in November 1922, killing hundreds.

The army stepped in and seized power in 1925. They were unable to unite Ecuador, however, and the country entered a period of instability. Twenty-two presidents, dictators or juntas were catapulted in and out of power over the next 25 years.

The 1930s were horrendous for the country. It would not be until the late 1990s that Ecuador would experience such difficult times again. During the 1930s, a number of new political parties evolved and presidents came and went. Border disputes were frequent during this time.

Ecuador–Peru Border Dispute

In 1830, there was a signed agreement with Peru designating the Marañon–Amazon River as the border. However, Peru had continuing and deep disagreements with this accord. During the mid-1930s, Colombia turned over a section of territory that Ecuador had claimed in exchange for Colombia's access to the Amazon River. In the mid-1930s, Peru would continue to contest the eastern border without any success.

On 5 July 1941, Peru invaded Ecuador while President Carlos Arroyo del Río was still trying to work this dispute out diplomatically. With 13,000 Peruvian troops aligned against them, the 1,800-strong Ecuadorian troops in the affected areas in the eastern Amazon and sections of the southern provinces of Ecuador were unable to put up much resistance.

In 1942, a meeting was held among numerous countries in Brazil discussing the entrance of the United States into World War II. The issue of Ecuador and Peru was debated. Ecuador ceded more than half of its territories to Peru and four countries (Argentina, Brazil, Chile and the United States) guaranteed that this new border would stand. In exchange, Peru promised to remove its troops from the southern provinces of Ecuador. This treaty was called the Protocol of Río de Janeiro and was signed on 29 January 1942. Thus far, 400–500 Ecuadorians and just over 100 Peruvians have been killed over this border conflict.

A Chain of Events

An interesting fact about this conflict is that paratroopers were used for the first time in Latin America by Peru. More significantly, the Peruvian invasion and the outcome of the Protocol of Río de Janeiro brought about the political demise of Arroyo del Río. Violence erupted across the country. José María Velasco Ibarra was then president for four years, operating as a dictator.

THE 1940S AND BEYOND

In 1948, Galo Plaza Lasso was elected president. He was an influential landowner from the Cotopaxi region. He didn't have the support of the military but he took some progressive measures. He brought in a number of outside experts to assist in the development of the country. However, Ecuador had limited funds and many of his plans never came to fruition. During this period, agriculture developed and a number of new roads were constructed.

But the presidents played musical chairs and Velasco Ibarra returned from exile and was re-elected. Velasco Ibarra had a propensity towards socialism and kept close contact with Russia and Cuba. However, he never turned down aid from the United States. He made significant promises to the poor but little happened. He only lasted 14 months this time. Velasco Ibarra was president five times but only completed one term of office.

In 1961, the vice-president Carlos Julio Arosemena was made president. He, too, had strong socialist or communist leanings. Fearing a communist takeover, the military took control of the country. A number of the communists were exiled.

In 1964, the government introduced numerous agrarian reforms. However, regionalism remained a constant thread through the 1960s, the people from the coast (costeños) often felt cheated that the people from the Sierra (serranos) received the best share of everything, including the fruits of the costeños' labour. There were numerous riots in 1965.

The military performed a coup in 1972, claiming that it would be better for the military to run the oil deposits for the country so that the elite would not get all the benefits. Money had started to roll in from oil exports by this time. Significant oil reserves were discovered in Ecuador in the 1960s and with it, the promise of changing fortunes. Modernisation programmes began and the debt started to pile up with the belief that oil revenues would make all the difference. A middle class developed and many set up businesses. For example, there were only a handful of automobile parts importers in the mid-1970s but, by the 1980s, there were several hundred.

In 1979, Jaime Roldós Aguilera from Guayaquil became president. He was a technocrat and inherited many of the problems that came with a country deep in debt. He was killed along with his wife and several military leaders in a plane crash in 1981. Ecuador's economy suffered tremendously during the 1980s and much of the middle class disappeared. Ecuador went through a number of presidents including socialist Rodrigo Borja Cevallos from Quito. Inflation went out of control and the indigenous problem continued.

In 1995, Ecuador had a brief battle with Peru again over their border. At that time, I was in Guayaquil and my nephew was called into military service. It was a tense time as many young men from both Ecuador and Peru were placed into action against each other. After dozens of troops were killed and hundreds were injured, a ceasefire was called. Thousands of troops were withdrawn from the Cenepa Valley where most of the conflict was lodged and more than 140,000 troops were demobilised. Negotiations began immediately and lasted for the next few years until a peace accord was signed in 1998. Peru was granted a 48-mile section in the eastern Amazon. Ecuador was granted, in the middle of this area, a 250-acre hill called Tiwintza. Ecuador defended this area during the conflict. A new treaty was drawn up around four major themes:

- Securing a land boundary between the two countries.
- Establishing a commerce and navigation treaty.
- Defining and resolving security issues.

- Providing a comprehensive accord as to the integration of the borders.

I feel that there will be tremendous growth and development over the next 50 years along the border of Ecuador and Peru. There are numerous restructuring projects which have been instituted and planned, including highway connections and human development projects. Two negative aspects of the peace accord involve land mines that remain in the area and the rights of indigenous groups that were not consulted during the settlement process.

The Horror of Land Mines

At least 11,000 of the original 60,000 land mines remain which threaten to maim and kill residents. At least 114 Ecuadorians and Peruvians have been killed or injured from the mines along the border since the end of the war in 1998.

Chile entered into an accord to assist Ecuador and Peru in the removal of these mines over an 8 to 10-year period. Ecuador had 260,000 mines stockpiled of which about 4,000 remain.

In 1996, Abdalá Bucaram was elected president and made many promises to the poor. However, corruption and mismanagement led to him being voted out by congress and exiled to Panama. From the late 1990s to 2000, Ecuador went through several more presidents. It would also suffer its worst financial situation in nearly 70 years. So bad was the situation that between 1999 and the end of 2000, nearly a million Ecuadorians left their homeland for economic opportunity. (*Please refer to* Chapter Three, Ecuadorian Society *for more details on the exodus of the 1990s.*)

There was much dissentient opposition to the government and President Jamil Mahuad in the late 1990s. He had proposed that Ecuador remove the sucre as the official currency, to be replaced by the US dollar (US$). Inflation was at over 60 per cent and the gross domestic product had shrunk at least 7.3 per cent primarily because of low

The care-worn face of an indigenous farmer. Originating from Manabí province but driven by need, he has moved south to Chanduy, an ancient fishing village on the coast south of Salinas.

oil prices. Unemployment had jumped from 12 per cent to 17 per cent. There was much opposition to Mahuad's proposal and, on 22 January 2000, thousands of indigenous people and middle to lower level military members walked into congress (which was unoccupied) and placed a three-man junta in charge of the country.

The United States placed pressure on this group and the committee was disbanded. Vice-president Gustavo Noboa was instituted as president to fulfill the remaining three years of office. Noboa vowed to continue with the dollarisation plan and attack corruption. Now in his early 60s, he is an educator and is viewed by many as intelligent and honest, not appearing to have acquired material wealth for himself. Noboa does not belong to a political party and his priorities are modernising the state and economic reform.

The indigenous community felt betrayed by the military as the government was put back in the hands of those sympathetic to the oligarchy. I agree with Walker Lowry who said in his book *Tumult at Dusk*: "Ecuador means equator. It ought to mean Indian." The Indians are now more organised than ever before and are committed to controlling

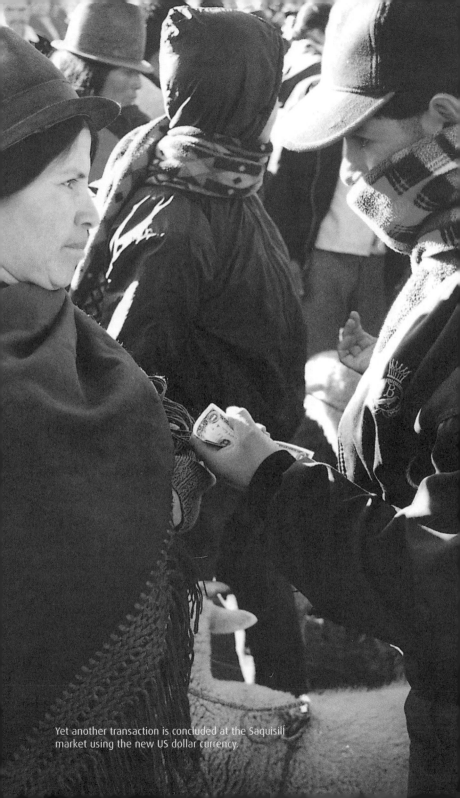

Yet another transaction is concluded at the Saquisilí market using the new US dollar currency.

their destiny and Ecuador's. There has been increasing activism from indigenous groups. The Confederation of Indigenous Nationalities (CONAIE) is leading the struggle for representation in Ecuador. The CONAIE President, as of 2006, is Luís Macas. (Related material can be found on CONAIE's website: http://www.CONAIE.org.)

Here is an extract from a statement by the former President of CONAIE, Antonio Vargas:

'If they want to find the coup participants, they should look for them in the corridors of the oligarchies, the parliament, the corrupt courts and bankers who with their policies and holdups have deepened the misery, the hunger, unemployment, and the migrations from the countryside to the city ... Again historical injustices are repeated. During 500 years of oppression, our towns rose up demanding justice and the respect to the human rights which were cruelly violated again and again. But when there were uprisings, leaders like Rumiñahui, Tupac Amaru, Jumandi, Daquilema, and many others were taken prisoner, tortured and assassinated ... But they must understand that there will be no wall nor any bars that can stop our ideas and

our equitable and deeply participative fight, because with wrath and wisdom of centuries we are up building pressure like our sacred volcanoes to construct Ecuador as a just and participating Nation.'

The deep-rooted contrasts of Ecuador's varied peoples and the divisive powers of external influences have been dominant threads in Ecuador's history. This author feels that Ecuador is on the verge of tremendous change. In thinking about Ecuador's future, I fear that Ecuador could fall prey to ambitious dictators, drug lords or guerrilla groups from Colombia in the next 50 to 70 years. Whatever the outcome, we can only watch anxiously as Ecuadorians forge their unique identity in these tumultuous times.

GOVERNMENT AND POLITICS

Instability is often the norm when it comes to Ecuadorian government and politics. This is partially evident by the number of constitutions (19) which have been instituted since 1830. The longest period of time between new constitutions was from 1978 to 1998. Geographic regions play a significant role in politics and the differences have kept a cohesive front between political parties. No significant leader has yet been able to consolidate power. While democratic principles are espoused, regional issues seem to take precedence over national interests.

There are three main branches of the government, which are comprised of the executive, legislative and judicial sectors. The executive branch position is to manage all sectors of the government. The legislative branch is responsible for running the congress. The judicial branch administers the justice programmes. Voting is compulsory between the ages of 18 and 65 and the president is elected every four years, serving a single term.

The executive branch consists of the president and vice-president. His responsibility as head of the government is to manage the public administration, maintain internal order, public security, present a government plan and inform the congress each year of the government's and country's status. He also coordinates the development of new laws and selects ministers and diplomats. He is elected to take office on 10 August of the year following his election by the people. The president must be at least 35 years old and born in Ecuador. If he becomes incapacitated, the vice president or a designated minister takes over. If both of them are not able to serve, the president of the national congress steps into place until congress selects a new president to serve the remaining term within 10 days. President Gustavo Noboa was elected to office on 22 January 2000 following a coup which deposed President Mahuad. Vice President Pedro Pinto has been in office since 28 January 2000.

The military exercises considerable power in Ecuador, reporting directly to the president. It is known to support labour unions which oppose the privatisation of many of the country's state-owned companies. Many of the leaders in the military are from the Sierra. The military, during the early years of oil exports, took over the government. Profits from petroleum allegedly provide an unofficial source of funds for the military. It was a military-indigenous coup which toppled democratically elected President Jamil Mahuad.

In 1998, a new constitution was drawn up, largely as a response to the deep depression the country was in. Limits were placed on state intervention in the economy and rights were widened to all Ecuadorians, including the youth, Afro–Ecuadorians and indigenous groups.

A Brief Discussion
Here is a brief discussion of a few of the articles that were newly instituted or revised:

- Article 16
  The state has the obligation to respect the rights of human beings guaranteed by the Constitution.
- Article 23
  To protect the civil rights, liberties, and safety of its citizens. Citizens have the right to life, personal integrity, and liberty under the law. This includes the absence of a death penalty, cruelty of punishment, and torture. This includes the state's responsibility of trying to prevent and eliminate violence especially to children, women, and the elderly. Everyone

is to have the same rights without the distinction of age, gender, sexual orientation, colour, religion, political party, state of health, or economic position.

- Article 27

  Voting is to be secret and is obligatory for those from 18 to 65 years of age. For those older than 65 voting is optional. Those that are in the armed forces or work for the government are barred from voting, as well as those who have a judicial order or who have been sentenced.

- Articles 83–85

  These articles specifically address those who are indigenous or black. Their ability to practise traditional medicine and to maintain cultural traditions is protected and this article also promotes the management of the ecological areas of such groups. The intellectual property rights of ancestors are to be retained and the quality of education improved. Their native languages are to be continued and taught.

ECUADORIAN SOCIETY

CHAPTER 3

'Ecuador has a severe inferiority complex.'
—Ecuadorian State Department Officer to author
Tom Miller in an interview for
Miller's book *The Panama Hat Trail*

IDENTITY CRISIS

Ecuador is a country rich in human and geographical capital but appears to suffer from an inferiority complex and an identity crisis. It is this which seems to keep the majority of the population from true social and economic change. There is perhaps a Malinche syndrome in Ecuador. Malinche was the name of an Indian slave girl who belonged to Hernán Cortes in Mexico. She became his lover and was seen by many as a traitor to her Aztec roots. Malinche-thinking is a term I use to describe a Mexican preference for things foreign rather than things Mexican. I feel that Ecuadorians also prefer foreign things rather than their own unique and rich culture. I have found that shop assistants push an imported item over a local brand as if the imported item were automatically superior. I once interviewed a president of a trade organisation in Ecuador who commented that his country always views its products or itself as being inferior.

Tom Miller, acclaimed writer and author of the book *The Panama Hat Trail*, found that many Ecuadorians, especially those from the lower classes, expressed this same sense of inferiority. Some of these identity issues may be caused by the fact that Ecuador's history has been so much a part of Peru's and Colombia's heritage.

Ecuador is also a country of numerous internal cultural differences, which have been magnified by geographical divisions. How, then, was it supposed to establish a clear and consistent sense of identity?

CLASS STRUCTURE

Ecuador's social structures have also been indelibly marked by the caste system from colonial times. Wealth and human rights seem to belong to the upper class or oligarchs and the rest of the country remains in abject poverty. James Orton expressed this eloquently in his book *The Andes and the Amazon; or, Across the Continent of South America*, writing this about the white aristocracy: "This is the governing class; from its ranks come those uneasy politicians who make laws for other people to obey, and hatch revolutions when a rival party is in power."

While Saudi Arabia is not a democracy, a visitor can see that the oil wealth of the country has trickled down to a wide group of the populace and raised the overall standard of living. To my foreign eyes, however, Ecuador's hundreds of thousands of barrels of oil a day do not seem to have an impact on the spreading of wealth. Compared to the United States, there are also limited opportunities for movement to higher social classes. If one is poor in Ecuador, one usually accepts one's station in life and concentrates on the continual struggle for existence.

Much of the rigid class structure, which has been in place for nearly 500 years, still exists. It is almost like going back in time. This hierarchical social structure is similar to that found in other Andean countries, such as Peru and Colombia. Much of Ecuador, until the last century, remained in isolation from other parts of Ecuador and the outside world, due to the rugged terrain and the absence of a good national transportation system. Hence, much of the Spanish psyche lingers on.

REGIONALISM

Another unique aspect of Ecuador is the strong regionalism, especially between the people from the Sierra (Serranos) and the people from the Costa (Costeños). Differences in region and social class can be observed in one's dress, physical appearance, language, title and family name. After some time in Ecuador, you will be able to tell quite quickly where an Ecuadorian is from.

Serranos vs Costeños

Serranos are for the most part mestizo. There are also a few who would consider themselves white and of pure Spanish blood. These will tend to dress more conservatively in the Sierra than in the Costa. I have also found that Costeños are stouter than people from the Sierra.

The original fortunes of the Sierra were made from large landholdings. Few Serranos branched out to the Costa during colonial times, due to its harsh living conditions. Guayaquil, in the Costa, has more of an appearance of a frontier town, with inhabitants of many classes. Guayaquil has been seen as a place to make a fortune and move on. Quito and Guayaquil have developed independently and do not think they need each other. Guayaquil grew into a major shipping and economic centre. Society here is more liberal and the classes less well-defined than in Quito. There is still a divide between the lower and upper classes, however.

THE CLASSES, AGAIN

The family you were born into, in addition to your skin colour, 'classifies' you.

Upper Classes

The whiter members of society are usually from the higher classes. Whiteness seems to mark one out as from among the top tiers of society. This can be seen in the advertisements and the media, which feature white actors and actresses. There is a lower upper class in the smaller cities throughout the Sierra with family names like Riobamba and Ambato.

Middle Class

Ecuador's middle class evolved in the second half of this century when the country went through tremendous growth, largely due to oil exports. The middle class is made up of businessmen, professionals, bureaucrats and military officers. Most middle-class members have at least a high school education and are not involved in any type of manual labour. Working with one's hands is viewed by the middle and upper classes as inferior work. This thinking is a by-product of

Spanish colonial times. As a result, you are unlikely to see people from the middle or upper classes doing any sort of work around the house, even gardening or home repairs. Attention to dress, grooming and manners are also important to the middle and upper classes.

Lower Classes

The lower classes often work as guards, factory workers, small or street merchants and domestic help. In the rural areas, they work as labourers and farm workers.

The lower classes have divisions of their own. Blacks or negroes are usually found in the lower classes, ranked just above the position of indigenous groups. It is believed that the first blacks to enter Ecuador did so with Diego de Almagro, the Spanish conquistador, in about 1534. They participated in the conquest and worked the mines. There are differing accounts as to why the blacks concentrated in Esmeraldas, on the north-western coast of Ecuador, and in El Valle de Chota (the Chota Valley). It is believed by some that there was a shipwreck off the northern coast and that they settled in this area. Other blacks migrated here from neighbouring Colombia. The community of blacks in the

Mother and child tending to their flock of sheep near Cotopaxi.

Chota Valley live in an Afro-Ecuadorian settlement called Chamanal, six hours from Quito and 34 km (21 miles) north of Ibarra, on the Carchi–Imbabura border. This valley was once the principal holding area for slaves brought from Colombia and Panama and is also famous for sugar cane. The Chota Valley is still predominantly black. They have a famous phrase there that states that Ecuadorians go to the Chota Valley to vote (for presidents) and for football players (noting the high number of football players that come from the region).

The blacks have maintained many aspects of their African heritage, evident in their native music, dance and oral traditions. Their music has been their main contribution to the Ecuadorian culture. Laura Hidalgo Alzamora, Ecuadorian literary critic and literature professor, has produced an excellent study of the oral traditions of the *decimas* of the Afro-American culture in Esmeraldas. Her doctorial thesis of 1982 was called *Decimas Esmeraldeñas—Recopilacion y Analisis Socio-Lieterario*. The *decima* are compositions which were passed down orally and are often satirical in nature. Many are also quite comical and have double meanings, including sexual innuendo.

A Favourite Decima

While most decimas contain about 44 lines, one of my favourites, which is shorter than a normal decima, is often used before the marimba and other instruments join in and a dance follows. Here it is in Spanish then in English:

El Hombre:	*!Ay por Dios!*
	Cuando veo a la negrita
	bien vestida y peinadita,
	me dan ganas de abrazarla
	y besarle esa boquita.
La Mujer:	*!Ve!*
	Amores habrás tenido
	como bardolada en playa,
	pero nunca encontrarás
	una negra de esta laya.

El Hombre:	*Qué bonita muchachita,*
	si su mama me la diera
	sólo esta noche y mañana
	se la volviera.
La Mujer:	*Bolívar con su espada*
	conquistó cinco naciones,
	y yo con mis caderas
	conquisto los corazones.
Coro,	
Los Hombres:	*Y vamo' a ver si eso es cierto,*
	y que suene la marimba.

Man:	Oh, my Lord!
	When I see that little black woman well
	Dressed and combed,
	I want to kiss her little mouth.
Woman:	Look
	A lot of lovers you've had like the bardolada plant
	That grows on the beach,
	But you're never going to find a black woman of my kind.
Man:	A good-looking little thing you are!
	If your mother would give you to me
	For just tonight and tomorrow
	I would bring you back.
Woman:	Bolívar with his sword
	Conquered five nations
	And me with my hips
	I conquer all hearts
Group of Men:	And we're going to see if
	That's true—
	Let the marimba play.

Indians

Nearly 25 per cent of Ecuador's population is indigenous but they are at the bottom of the social ladder. However, this group is growing in political power and the Ecuadorian government would do well to take their interests into consideration.

The other Indian groups include the Salasacas, Saraguro, Siona-Secoya and Awá (Kwaiker). While many Ecuadorians superficially take pride in their indigenous culture, there is deep rooted-racism and discrimination against them.

Class Struggles

One of my closest Quechua friends once remarked to me that there was a rich Serrana that wanted to hire her to wash her clothes. She had responded that she was a professor and spoke five languages. The upper class Serrana could not believe it and still persisted that she work for her.

Quechuas

The Quechuas are the largest indigenous group in Ecuador, numbering over 1.5 million. They are located throughout the Sierra and the Amazon. While they share a common language (Quichua), both groups differ in culture and practices. The Quechua in the Andes are primarily small plot farmers and tend to flocks of sheep and cattle. Textiles and weaving are also an important source of income. The Quechuan basic belief system revolves around the cosmos having four floors: Ahua Pacha (heaven), Puyo Llacta (clouds), Cai Pacha (earth) and Ucu Pacha (inner world).

Huaorani

Standing barely more than 1.5 m (5 ft) in height, the Huaorani are also known as Auca and have been little influenced by the outside world. (*Auca,* which means 'savage' in Quechua, is considered a derogatory term by the Huaorani). They are located east of Tena and south of Coca. They often marry by age 10 or 12 years old and the men are polygamous. They are communal in nature and everyone contributes to the group's interests. The men are hunters and use poisoned darts with blowguns. Their lifrstyle has come under great pressure due to the drilling of oil and contamination of their lands.

Jíbaros

The Jíbaros are the infamous headhunters of the Amazon and include the Shuars and the Achuars. They are located in the south-eastern jungle of Ecuador and are about 20,000 strong. Missionaries have influenced some of their lifestyle although they still believe in spirits and magic. They cultivate fruits and potatoes and hunt.

Cofáns

Situated in north-eastern Ecuador, their communities straddle the Ecuadorian–Colombian border. The Cofáns paint their faces with *achiote* (a food colouring used throughout Ecuador) and they often have large holes in their earlobes and noses that are adorned with feathers. When a Cofán wife passes away, she is usually buried in the house, which is never entered again. A new house is built for the remaining members of the family.

Cayapas

The Cayapas homeland is in the Esmeraldas province. They are river people and there are approximately 4,000 remaining. The Cayapas travel by canoe and live in homes made of palm fronds. They also paint their bodies using *achiote*. They are famous for the hammocks they make and grow cacao and fruits.

Colorados

The Colorados reside near Santo Domingo de los Colorados. They are best known for painting their hair using a paste made of *achiote* and slicking it down with Vaseline. The women often paint their teeth blue, believing that it prevents tooth decay. There are just over a thousand Colorados remaining. Quite open to outside influences, the Colorados continue some of their traditional practices, not living in villages but separate houses divided by cultivated fields and forests. Girls will often marry just after puberty.

EXODUS

Ecuadorians began leaving their country in droves in the late 1990s. Friends would ask me for loans of up to US$ 2,000 in their quest to get out. With the recent collapse of the Ecuadorian economy, men and women from all over Ecuador have been leaving legally and illegally for destinations such as Spain and Italy, which have fairly lax entry requirements.

This is a human tragedy in the making. If you are at the airport in Quito, you can often see people crowded outside the fence at the end of the tarmac watching their families take off. They are watching family members leave Ecuador for perceived greener pastures. It is believed that, as of 2001, as many as 1.3 million have left to make new lives for themselves.

Stemming the Flow

In 2005, much of the exodus slowed due to a reduction in the numbers of travel visas to Spain. In fact, Spain has made it difficult to get visas, which was fuelling the influx of Ecuadorians to its country. They have closed their consulate in Guayaquil which now requires applicants to apply for a visa in Quito.

This exodus created a cottage loan industry, based on the concept that people borrow money to leave and then pay it back to the lender. The lenders are often family or friends or a unique network of small businesspeople charging high interest. Borrowers are usually required to place a large amount of collateral, which may be a vehicle or jewellery.

Many of the emigrants who move to Spain from Ecuador work as caregivers, cooks and manual labourers. A number of women have found work as prostitutes. This exodus has taken a human toll on families back in Ecuador and will have a permanent effect on society. The positive effect is an influx of foreign currency, which has helped families and made possible much new investment in homes and land. If a million people are sending US$ 100 back each month to Ecuador it is not hard to imagine the significant boost to the economy that it brings. It is estimated that about 19 per cent of Ecuador's foreign currency is derived from funds sent home from around the world. In fact, on a recent visit to Ecuador, I noticed that business was quite brisk for many companies. Several Ecuadorian residents and expatriates commented that if it was not for the funds being sent to Ecuador from overseas, there would be a massive collapse of the economy.

In the neighbourhood of La Chala in the suburbs of Guayaquil where I visit my relatives every year, I have observed whole families who leave the country. It is hard not to find a family in the middle and lower classes that doesn't have a family member living in Spain or Italy.

I have also had the opportunity to visit numerous Ecuadorians living in Spain. Many who have secured resident status are developing new lives for themselves and certainly have more opportunities there than they had in Ecuador, at least financially. However, there have been sacrifices. Most notably apparent is the separation from one's family and home. There are thousands of families that have broken up due to the stress of being in a new country. There are also numerous spouses who have left their families in Ecuador and have begun new romantic relationships. Most of all, Ecuadorians miss their country and culture. There are a number of Ecuadorians living in Spain illegally and move from place to place and job to job if they can find one. One Ecuadorian I know living there cannot find a job and 'break-dances' in the metros of Barcelona for tips. The name many of his friends have given him is Sinpa, meaning *sin papeles* (without papers).

> One day, I was speaking to a young man in Barcelona who had come from Ecuador. He said "I miss my neighbourhood, I miss my beer, I miss the music, I miss my family."

PROSTITUTION

Although a far cry from other parts of the world, prostitution is an unpleasant fact of life among Ecuador's lower classes. Many women resort to prostitution to survive and many of these women have been abused or abandoned by their husbands. They are forced to take on full-time jobs and work as prostitutes to supplement their meagre incomes.

I once visited a bar in Guayaquil where sex workers had an arrangement with the owner of the bar, who let them leave with his customers. I frequented this bar to drink beer with my friends and because I didn't participate, the women would often jokingly accuse me of being a homosexual. I noticed that the drinking by the women seemed to increase significantly during Christmas. I was surprised at this and could only determine that it was a difficult time for them as they thought of their plight. One night, just before New Year, an older prostitute whom I had seen working in the same bar for years called me over. She took a long drink of her beer and said *"Nicholas, todos somos putas."* ("Nicholas, we are all whores.") This was surprising to me because you will seldom hear a prostitute refer to her1self as a whore. However, I believe what she was saying was much more profound in that most people have a price. There was much sadness in her eyes.

Prostitution is legal in Ecuador. In Quito, there are several entertainment establishments where women are available for sex on the premises. Several of these places cater to the higher end clientele of wealthy businessmen, diplomats and tourists. The cheaper places cater more to the locals. Establishments that provide massages are often just fronts for the sex trade. There are numerous streetwalkers in both Quito and Guayaquil, a number of whom are transvestites. Most towns will usually have a house or street where the sex trade is conducted six days a week. One of these is the infamous and rough Calle 18 (18th Street) in Guayaquil. Another aspect of prostitution is that many prostitutes have sexually transmitted diseases but hold the appropriate permit to work as a prostitute. It is believed that many prostitutes pay off doctors to provide them a clean bill of health so they can continue working.

Sadly, there has also been a recent increase in child prostitutes. After the depression of the late 1990s, many children from the poorer barrios and rural areas were recruited with the empty promise of a chance of a career or training in the city. It is distasteful for Ecuadorians to speak about this but, with more than half of the population living in poverty, this is a real social problem. The US State Department reported in June 2005 that the government does not fund programmes to assist victims and that many raids result in the minors being returned to their families or, if this is not possible, to NGOs. There are also a number of prostitutes in Ecuador that are from Colombia. It is believed that many are part of drug trafficking rings.

RECENT IMMIGRANTS

There are a number of ethnic groups which have settled in Ecuador. The Lebanese have a history of several generations in Ecuador and have become quite powerful in both the economic and political arenas. They have, for the most part, preserved their culture, are viewed as middle-class and often possess significant monetary wealth. They are often referred to as Turcos (Turks). There are also a number of people of Lebanese descent who have left for Lebanon because of the improved political and economic situation.

A Chinese Influence

The Chinese have made their inroads into this society. The original immigrants arrived in the 1800s and were based primarily around the area of Quevedo. They make up the middle class and many have made it good here as middlemen and traders.

About a thousand Jews arrived in Ecuador during the 1940s to escape Hitler's regime. Some Arabs have also moved here. Most recently, many Colombians have immigrated to Santo Domingo de los Colorados, giving rise to the nickname Santo Domingo de los Colombianos!

While there has never been a large immigration of Germans in Ecuadorian history, there was a time when they were removed from society. During the signing of the Protocol of Río de Janeiro in 1942, the issue of the Germans in Ecuador was addressed. A number of Ecuadorians of German descent were identified by the government and were deported to the United States, forced to leave everything behind. There are still a few survivors left in the United States where they were housed for some time in Houston, Texas.

There are thousands of Colombians living in Ecuador both legally and illegally. Many have escaped the civil war in Colombia. Many Ecuadorians resent these recent immigrants, seeing them as taking jobs and conducting illegal activities such as counterfeiting. Nevertheless, there are numerous Colombians who have invested in Ecuador and are making a livelihood. A number of Colombians have been responsible for the rise of exports in the floral industry in Ecuador.

WOMEN'S ISSUES

Ecuador still lags behind most of Latin America when it comes to the advancement of women's rights. Generally speaking, up until the last 10 to 15 years, a woman was raised to find a husband and play a subservient role. Today, except in the higher-middle and upper classes, even marriage is not the norm. The upper and middle classes often marry both in a civil ceremony and a church-sanctioned wedding. However, in the lower classes, many women are abandoned by their 'husbands' and find themselves raising children by several fathers. This is especially the case in the coastal provinces.

The female's role in the marriage is commonly the running of the home and the raising of her children. Walker Lowry in his book *Tumult at Dusk* depicts the situation of Ecuadorian women as such: 'So little by little she gives him up, little by little she turns to another love, to the love of her children. She busies herself with the management of their affairs. She plots and prays for them. And the prayer in her heart is that somehow life for them will be better, more gracious and more glorious. For herself she has fallen into middle age and its endless, trivial bustling about. She is forever busy with the demands, the servants she must manage, the husband she must placate, the friends she must entertain.

'Her secret thoughts, when she has time for them, are mostly memories, memories of being seventeen with the world at her feet, memories of a dress or a kiss, of a few moments of adoration, flattery and a sense of importance, memories of her wedding day. The years lie ahead but her life, when she comes to think of it, is mostly behind her.'

Ecuadorian poet Jorge Carrera Andrade expressed it more beautifully:

Mi madre, revestida de poniente,
guardo su juventud en una honda guitarra
y solo algunas tardes la mostraba a sus hijos
envuelta entre la musica, la luz y las palabras.

My mother, clothed in the setting sun,
put away her youth in a deep guitar,
and only on certain evenings would she show it to
her children,
sheathed in music, light and words.

Nowadays, women have moved ahead and there are many who are educated, have careers and have become an integral part of this male-dominated society. I have met many women who will not tolerate the practice of infidelity or physical abuse, which is still prevalent and largely tolerated in Ecuador's lower classes. For the most part, however, the Ecuadorian woman still desires to please her children, spouse and employer. This is part of her heritage that has been honed for nearly half a millennium.

MACHISMO

A common complaint Ecuadorian women voice about the men in their lives is that he is *muy machista* (very macho).

Machismo runs deep in the Ecuadorian man's soul. It affects both relationships between men and women and men and men, especially if there has been any slight to his manhood, which seems under constant threat. This behavioural pattern was introduced by the Spanish conquest when Spaniards dominated the Indian population. Prior to that, it is said to have originated with the Moors who invaded Spain.

One of the strongest traits of machismo is a sense of male superiority manifested in refusing to back down from an argument and dominating one's wife and children. Machismo also includes being gallant and

Ecuadorian men can be very charming until they have made their conquest. You will even hear a woman referring to the man she has fallen in love with as having conquered her. It is almost as if she is his property and below his status.

involves sexual conquests, the more the merrier, in an attempt to prove his masculinity.

Both men and women may refer to men who don't demonstrate machismo traits as homosexuals or as weak. Machismo behaviour also tends to place women into black-and-white roles as good or bad, especially if the woman in question decides to have more than one relationship. A European woman once remarked to me that she has had to be careful about her relationships with men in Ecuador. She believed that if she had a short relationship with a man that included sex, she would be perceived as being promiscuous, whereas this would not be the case in her home country in Europe. She said that she would never marry an Ecuadorian man because of the *machista* attitudes.

CHILDREN

When a woman is pregnant in Ecuador, friends and family will refer to the unborn child as a *luz* (light). A common question is "*¿Cuando va a llegar el luz?*" ("When is the light going to arrive?") Children are regarded by most Ecuadorians as special and are given much attention. For the most part, they are doted on and coddled and may be considered by

Indigenous children near Cuenca.

foreigners as somewhat spoiled. However, they are taught to obey their elders and to show a deep respect for their parents and other family members, more so than in the United States. When they are young they can seem quite rambunctious, especially in public restaurants.

A Mother's Love

I noticed when visting Ecuadorians through the years how common it is for a mother to help a child do his or her homework. Actually, mothers often do most or all of the homework. Even with the advent of the computer, some things don't change. On a recent visit to Ecuador, I was making my regular visit to an Internet café on a Sunday evening. I was amused at how crowded it was and noticed a large number of mothers with their children. And there they were, on the computer helping their children do their homework.

Most children remain at home until they marry, especially in the case of girls. Boys have more freedom of movement than girls. Being the father of three boys with an Ecuadorian mother, I must say that they are a joy and have inherited some of the finest Ecuadorian traits, most especially the enjoyment of dancing.

DANCING

One aspect of Ecuador's society, which permeates all social levels, is dancing. Ecuadorians love to dance as much as they like to eat. Most social functions, whether a baptism, birthday party or dinner party are an excuse to celebrate life through dance. An old gringo (a common Ecuadorian term for an American) friend of mine who has lived in Ecuador for nearly 30 years, commented to me that dancing 'is part of the package of being Ecuadorian.'

After attending hundreds of festivities over the years, I have noticed that Ecuadorians enjoy music and sway unconsciously to the rhythm of whatever is playing on the CD player. People of all ages can dance and there is no feeling of embarrassment or self-consciousness. Richard Poole, in his book *The Inca Smiled*, summed this up perfectly in his description of an Ecuadorian party: "At gatherings such as these everybody dances all evening. There is no division between the ages, no self-consciousness and no respite. It is a function as natural as breathing, and it embraces everyone—even babies are brought along."

Several years ago, at the height of the recession in Ecuador in the late 1990s, my Ecuadorian wife and I took two of our sons to visit her family. The neighbourhood had decided to have a party in the street. There was laughter, drinking, fighting, hugging, kissing and most of all dancing! It was a moment of living life to the fullest. My boys still recall this experience vividly and comment that they wished there were parties like that in the United States. I now understand why my children are such fun at parties and can dance so well. It must be their Ecuadorian blood!

HUMOUR

Ecuadorians possess a wonderful sense of humour. Their jokes cover all aspects of life in society and they often poke fun at themselves. Many people will tell jokes about *pastusos*.

A young girl enjoying an orange at a rodeo in Salitre.

A *pastuso* often refers to an idiot or clown. The name derives from Pasto, Colombia. The nearest equivalent are the Polish jokes which are popular in the United States.

Ecuadorian Jokes

Below are three jokes, a *pastuso*, a political joke and a joke which pokes fun at Ecuadorians. Many jokes in Spanish do not translate well into English, and the humour may be lost.

- A *pastuso* called a travel agency and asked, "How long is the flight from Tulcán to Tokyo?" The secretary said, "One moment." The *pastuso* replied, "Thank you very much," and then hung up the phone.

- When President Bucaram (often referred to as *loco*—crazy) was in office, he visited the White House when Bill Clinton was president. He was amazed when he rang the doorbell and it sounded out "Clinton, Clinton". When he returned to Quito he asked someone on staff if they could make a doorbell like Clinton had. The staff member said yes and had one installed. One day Bucaram told his wife, "Honey, come and ring this doorbell." She went over and touched the bell at which time it rang out *"Loco, loco."*

- Once, residents of the countries that border Ecuador were complaining to God about all the things Ecuador had. "God, why do they have the ocean, the mountains, the jungle, gold, oil, and beauty in such a small place?" God responded, "Don't worry, I put Ecuadorians there."

FITTING INTO SOCIETY

CHAPTER 4

'We look like you, sometimes we talk like you,
but we do not think like you.'
—Colonel Borja from the book,
Tumult at Dusk: Being an Account of Ecuador
by Walker Lowry

RELIGION

The Catholic Church arrived with the Spanish conquistadors. It played a critical role in Spain's conquest; as an excuse to abuse the Indians in the guise of converting the indigenous population to Catholicism and, more beneficially, as a foundation for the development of educational institutions. The Catholic Church became one of the largest landowners in the country and was closely allied with the Government, especially the political power in the Sierra.

After independence, the Church continued to have a close relationship with the Government but continued to spark debate between the conservatives in the Sierra and the liberals on the Costa. When Eloy Alfaro seized power in 1895, it marked the beginning of the separation of the Church from the state.

While the Catholic Church is still the dominant religion in Ecuador, it has lost some of its power over the last 25 years. One of the earliest groups to enter Ecuador was the Christian group HCJB. This Christian organisation began in 1931 and has one of the largest radio stations on Earth, broadcasting its Christian message to the world. Mormons, Jehovah's Witnesses, Baptists and Pentecostal groups have all made inroads. Much of this progress has been due to the increasing poverty of Ecuadorians. I remember seeing few other churches than those of Catholics and Mormons in the early 1980s. Now, numerous churches abound, especially in the Costa. The Protestant groups now account for about 10 per cent of the population and the Catholics are about 90 per cent. There is also a smattering of other religions in Ecuador.

Shamans and Herbs

One word that is loaded with mystique for visitors to Ecuador and much of Latin America is the word shaman. It is believed by some that the word originated from Russia and means 'someone who has powers over an individual's soul'. Shamans play an active role in the medical field in Ecuador, using both the physical and spiritual world to treat maladies. They are also consulted to settle issues and provide solutions to problems. Many refer to themselves as medicine men.

Numerous tools such as dolls, beads or other items may play a role in the shaman's efforts to help an individual. Dead animals and their body parts are sometimes also used. Shamans pass down their art from father to son. They are also highly skilled with the use of herbs which play a major part in Ecuadorian medicine.

The Power of Manzanilla

I was never a believer in herbs until one day I had a nasty stomach upset and my Ecuadorian wife pulled some ugly twigs and dried flowers out of a bag. She used them to brew a tea, which was very soothing. Within half an hour my stomach was much better. Since then, I have turned to this tea rather than modern remedies for stomach upsets. Some of you might have heard of it. It's known as *manzanilla* in Ecuador and camomile in English.

Godparents

Godparents play a very important role in Ecuadorian society. As Ecuador is primarily a Catholic country, the role of godparents is considered an important responsibility in helping to guide a child's spiritual life. Parents will choose a married couple as godparents who, in effect, become coparents with the female becoming a comadre and the male a compadre.

The godparents play an active role in the child's baptism with the godfather providing a gift to the child. The mother and father incur the cost of the baptism while the godfather will also provide small gifts to the altar boys. The godmother will provide the dress for the godchild and small gifts for the people who attend the ceremony. These gifts are small ceramic pieces with the child's name inscribed on them. Such items are available in many party shops, which can be found at most of the major shopping centres. After the baptism, there is usually a large party at the child's home. There will be loud music with lots of dancing. Baptisms are often video taped by professional cameramen to record the start of a lifelong relationship between godparents and godchild.

Godparents will usually give the child a gift on his or her birthday, first communion, graduation, Christmas, New Year and any other important event in the child's life. The godchild also has an obligation to visit the godparents at least on New Year's Day. The godchild should also send an invitation or announcement of his or her first communion and wedding to his or her godparents

Godparents—the Extended Family

Godparents also play the role of an extended family to the child. I once was with a friend in Quito when he received a call from his goddaughter in Guayaquil who was on a school excursion. She had become ill and didn't know what to do. He was there within a half-hour to check on her.

First Communion

The first communion often begins with a breakfast with the family, sometimes a new set of godparents and maybe a few close friends. After the ceremony, there will usually be a party at the child's home, beginning at about 5:00 pm and ending not too late in the evening. Acceptable gifts may include a bible, CDs or cassette tapes of classical music, a crucifix, rosary beads, watches or jewellery. The child is obligated to provide a small gift or memento of the occasion to the priest who conducted the ceremony.

WEDDINGS

Many marriages in Ecuador are formalised both by a civil ceremony and a church wedding. The civil ceremony is required for a marriage to be considered legal. The chief of the civil registry oversees civil marriages. Civil registries are located in the capital of each province. In rural areas, the Teniente Politico, who is the local police head or official, oversees the marriage. Two witnesses are required, who must provide identification and proof of voting. The couple getting married should provide their birth certificates. The civil ceremony usually takes place prior to a church ceremony.

When a couple decides to get married in Ecuador, the parents of the man need to seek the permission of the woman's parents. This practice is known as *pedir la mano* (to ask for her hand). If both sets of parents know each other fairly well, they will invite the prospective bride's parents to their home for dinner. If they don't know each other well enough, they will visit the woman's parents with her suitor to seek their permission for the marriage. If a commitment is made, the bride and her mother will visit the groom's parents' home within three days.

If you are invited to a wedding, you are obligated to attend and to provide a gift. Many couples will have a gift register at one of the better department stores in Ecuador, such as Casa Tossi or De Pratti in Guayaquil. Your gift should be delivered at least three days before the wedding to the home of the bride or groom, depending on whom you are closer to. You shouldn't bring your gift to the wedding. Cash gifts are traditionally given only by the families of the bride and groom. However, a cash gift (averaging about US$ 40) is usually appreciated by the couple and is increasingly the practice. The bride's family is obligated to purchase most of her necessities for the wedding. This includes the banquet after the wedding and the flowers for the ceremony and banquet. Her family will pay for the invitations as well as the cake and wedding mementos. The groom pays for the ceremony including the services of the church and the priest. He also incurs the cost of the wedding rings and the honeymoon. Both rings will be inscribed inside with the names of the bride and groom and the date of the wedding.

In coastal areas, most weddings take place between 6:00 pm and 7:00 pm and in the Sierra region, at about noon. After the ceremony, the party proceeds to a banquet and dance. After dinner, the bride cuts the first slice of the cake. The bridesmaids then cut the rest of the cake for the guests and the waitresses serve it.

Champagne is served and the toasts begin. The following people make toasts: the groom, the best man, a close friend of the family and the father of the bride. Women usually do not make any toasts. After the cake and toasts, a dance will start. The bride and groom will have the first dance together. Dancing usually lasts until midnight and it is considered rude to leave before the bride and groom.

FUNERALS

Ecuadorian law requires that corpses be buried within 24 hours after death. Many Ecuadorians still adhere to several basic funeral customs. However, many of these customs have been relaxed over the years.

While many *velorios* (wakes) are conducted in *sala de velacion* (funeral parlours), it is just as common for the wake to take place in the home of the deceased. A wake in the home is the norm if the deceased passed away in his or her home or if the family doesn't have enough money for a funeral home. If there are not enough funds for a casket, a collection is often taken up. In the home, often all the furniture is moved against the walls and windows are often shut. Many valuables are put away, including pictures and mirrors.

If the body of the deceased is lying in a funeral home, someone will stay with the body around the clock until it is buried. The wake will usually be in full swing by 10:00 pm, with the older people in the main living room and the others in the adjacent rooms.

Appropriate flowers for funerals include lilies and marigolds. *Rosquillas* (pastry shaped like horn shells) are usually served to the friends and family, who will also be offered *chicha* (corn beer) or cognac. Turkey or chicken broth is also served around midnight. People take this time to sit around and remember the deceased with fondness and respect.

The wake may last all night. The body is buried the next day between noon and 5:00 pm. The most common practice is a procession accompanying the casket to the graveyard. The priest will usually have a small mass in the home or the funeral home before the burial. Family and friends will then offer prayers for the deceased for nine days. Remembrance masses are held one, six and 12 months after the funeral and are often announced in the newspapers. After the first 12 months, a mass is usually held once a year.

Mourning or *luto* (grieving) is a very important part of Ecuadorian society. The general rule is that the spouse will mourn the deceased for two years. The mourning for children or grandparents usually lasts six months. Aunts and uncles are mourned for three months and cousins for three months.

Very young children wear white for mourning. Adults wear black and white clothes and black shoes. A black tie is appropriate. When half of the mourning period is over, subdued colours such as grey or burgundy are appropriate.

If you are told about the death of someone only after the funeral, you should stop by the home a few days later with a card, conveying your condolences. The remaining spouse will not socialise or visit others for about three months and they should not attend parties or dances.

CUSTOMS AND ETIQUETTE

Understanding Ecuadorian culture will require some adjustments and study. Those who think Ecuador is like all other Latin American countries are very mistaken. While there are resemblances, Ecuador has its unique cultural mores. You will no doubt make blunders in your communication no matter how good your intentions. This section will introduce you to some of the intricacies of Ecuadorian life, customs and etiquette. I have had to make some generalisations and beg your forgiveness if some of my observations are not always

accurate. I do hope, however, that they will lead you a short way into the maze of communicating in this country.

Asi Es La Vida

Ecuadorians are by nature optimistic and positive in many of their attitudes to life. There is a feeling within the Ecuadorian spirit that one should not fight one's fate but make the best of a bad situation. Common expressions may include 'Asi es la vida' which translates to 'Life is so' or, more literally, 'What can I do? What happened, happened. So let's start all over again!' Another popular expression is 'Si Dios quiere' which means 'God desires it'.

Many Americans, in contrast, believe that their destiny is in their own hands and that they can control the outcome. Ecuadorians concentrate more on being content with their station in life. But this doesn't mean that they are static or rest on their laurels. For example, millions of Ecuadorians left their country in the late 1990s to seek better financial opportunities abroad.

Courtesy is the Best Policy

Ecuadorians prefer to converse in an indirect way, as opposed to the American style of frankness and directness. Ecuadorians tend to be very good at paying compliments and showing respect to get what they want. They will often tell the listener what they want to hear and not necessarily what they intend to do. The language used is often courteous and diplomatic. Being straightforward is considered being rude in most situations. This also applies to telephone conversations.

The Art of Diplomacy

One Ecuadorian who has lived in the United States for many years provided the following example: A committee from the Ecuadorian Ministry of Health was trying to introduce sex education in schools. When they were making the 'pitch' they stated: "Well, we have something that you will find fascinating, it won't cost you anything. You will find it so useful, especially for the beautiful young women in your school." My friend tried to get them to get to the point as she had to rush off for another appointment. The presenters then became offended and annoyed with her.

Criticism

A person's dignity is of utmost importance in this society, no matter what their social or economic status. Relationships are often based on developing a state of trust, which may grow over many years. You will find that many Ecuadorians will not be confrontational in their opinions and that to tell someone they're wrong may cause a very serious break in your relationship.

This is especially true in a public situation. I once criticised a new security agent at a check-in counter at the airport for discarding my tourist visa. It happened to be her first day on the job. When the agent didn't respond, I realised that I had made her lose face in front of her colleagues and superior. Her manager responded very delicately and acted as if it was not important, in an effort to restore her dignity. One needs to be patient and to maintain calm at all times. Yelling in public or raising your voice is also considered ill-mannered and inappropriate.

Gestures

There is a lot more handshaking going on in Ecuador than in the United States. But in Ecuador, handshakes are not as firm, are almost expressionless and last between two and three seconds. Almost always you would shake hands with someone when greeting them or parting with them. Also, the man will initiate the shaking of a woman's hand not vice versa. The handshake between a man and a woman is less firm than that between two men. Handshakes from indigenous people are often very soft and almost a brushing of the palms.

Ecuadorian men familiar with each other will often hug and pat each other on the back, especially if they are good, old friends. A familiar greeting between a man and a woman and a woman and woman is a light kiss on the cheek.

Pointing at someone or a group of people with a finger is almost always considered rude. Many Ecuadorians will sometimes make a pointing gesture by puckering their lips and will slightly raise their chin in the area they are making reference to. Pointing at objects is not offensive.

Another rude hand gesture is to give the height of someone with the palm down. This is only used when giving the height of an animal. If you were giving the height of a person or child, you would turn your palm sideways at about a 90° angle.

Waving or beckoning to someone to come over to you by using your forefinger or wrist with your palm up is not done. Instead, Ecuadorians make a motion of waving with the palm down, their fingers towards their bodies.

Whistling may also be used to get the attention of a person such as a waiter or porter. But, while this is practised, it is considered poor manners.

Yawning in public is considered rude.

Personal Space and Queuing

The personal space between Ecuadorians is much closer than what most North Americans are accustomed to. Queuing can be quite frustrating for the non-Ecuadorian.

Space within Ecuadorian homes is often cramped as large families are common. In many middle- and lower-class homes, extended female family members will often be entertained in the mother's room. My Ecuadorian wife, when visiting her mother, will often sleep with her in the same bed.

This different culture regarding personal space can become quite frustrating especially when standing in a queue. I have to consciously control my discomfort. There also doesn't appear to be much respect for queues. Social status might indicate who can cut a queue and often people who are white, considered to be of a higher social class, or those more senior in age, may take a place in front of others or are given preferential treatment. In place of queuing, people tend to bunch up next to a counter, no one knowing whose turn it is next. Friends of the counter staff are often better taken care of. This happens quite often at airports as domestic flights are often very crowded.

Remaining calm and trying to move up is the best way to handle this situation. Yelling, making a commotion, getting irate or complaining will work against you, especially if it is an elderly person who moves in front of you. Employees or counter staff might sometimes procrastinate in direct relation to how hard you push.

Time

Time is seen as being quite open-ended in Ecuador and is referred to as *hora ecuatoiana* or the 'Ecuadorian hour'. There is a *mañana* (Spanish for 'tomorrow') attitude and few people arrive on time for appointments and parties. Half an hour to one hour late is the norm.

When attending a party, if the appointment is 9:00 pm, you should not arrive at the person's home at 9:00 pm sharp. You will find your host still preparing and maybe not even dressed. It would be safer to arrive a half hour to 40 minutes after the stated time. Going out for the evening usually gets started later in Ecuador too. If you're going to dinner it would not be abnormal to eat at nine or later and stay out until two or three in the morning.

Ecuadorians are more punctual for work and business engagements. My experience, however, is that most appointments with business people, especially if it is an owner of a small- or medium-sized company, will not start before 10:00 am, and that the latest appointments will probably not exceed 6:00 pm. The provision of services is, also, not as prompt as what I am used to in the United States.

It is one thing for the Ecuadorian to be late but if the foreign business counterpart is late, it might be perceived by the Ecuadorian that you are not taking them seriously. I once had an appointment with a buyer in Quito who was already a customer for the company I represented. I wasn't too worried about being on time, and in fact, missed the appointment by a day. I was embarrassed to find, when I met him, that he was far from amused with my untimely manner. My speculation is that the reason his perception of time seemed different was because he was educated in Germany. Ecuadorians often use the phrase 'German time or Ecuadorian time', German time being on the time stated and not later.

Which Time?

I once was in a photography studio and a client was told his film would be ready in an hour. The customer asked "German time" and smiled when he said "or Ecuadorian time".

Working Hours

Generally speaking, in the Sierra, most offices will be open from 9:00 am to 6:00 pm. Lunch is usually for two hours, starting at noon. Working hours are generally the same on the Costa but lunch may last for two to three hours, especially during the hot months of December through to April.

Banks are generally open from 9:00 am to 1:00 pm. Many banks have longer hours than posted. Most banks have branches in the major shopping centres that are usually open as long as the shopping centre is and even at weekends. Most shopping centres close by 8:00 pm.

Gifts

This is an important part of Ecuadorian society, both for social and business reasons. Here are some guidelines:

- Gifts when visiting a home may include chocolates and sweets. Ecuadorians love chocolate.
- Flowers, such as roses or a small bouquet, are always welcome. However, if they are for a business associate's wife, be sure not to pay her too much attention. Never give artificial flowers to anyone.
- If you know the gift-recipient well, something to decorate the home would be appreciated.
- Perfume is always a nice gift especially if you know the person well. I always carry small bottles of perfume with me and present them to secretaries and staff. They will always remember you for that and it also becomes easier to work with them afterwards.
- Appropriate gifts for men include cologne, soap, books (self-help or business in Spanish) and alcohol. I also purchase small bottles of Chivas Regal and other well-known brands of alcohol that only cost a few US dollars. They don't take up much space and are always appreciated.
- CDs always make nice gifts, especially jazz ones.
- If you're going to a home with young people, take along pens, pencils, decals (transfers) or small rubber stamps as I always do.
- Postcards are appreciated as well, especially to show locals where you are from.

In business, women need to be very cautious about what they present as a gift to men. A book on a business subject is considered acceptable.

Visiting

If a woman enters the room, men will stand and greet her after extending a handshake and a small brushing kiss on the cheek. When a man enters a room, women often remain seated.

You should also acknowledge each and every person in the room with a hello and handshake, especially if it is a small group of people. I have even been to large parties and functions where a new person entering the party will introduce himself to every person. If you enter a room and have been introduced, you shouldn't make a quick exit. It is considered courteous to stay and talk for at least a while.

Service

For the most part, a high level of service does not appear to be the norm in most retail establishments here. Sales assistants are generally not well-paid and many establishments are family-owned. One tip about paying your bill is that Ecuadorians often refer to it as *cancelar* or literally 'to cancel'.

Window Shopping

Both sales assistants and merchants frown upon window shopping. You may even be treated rudely if you say you are just looking. But this may not always be the case in more tourist-oriented establishments.

Before you pay for an item, many establishments require a sales assistant to write a ticket for the item. He will hold on to the item while you go to a window to pay for it. You will then pick the item up from another sales assistant or window before leaving. However, this system is changing in most large or modern establishments where you go to a checkout queue. When entering some establishments, including grocery shops, your briefcase or other items will be checked as you enter. Your property will be placed in a cubicle and you will be given a claim ticket.

Social Status

One's educational accomplishments, family name and titles count for a lot in Ecuador. People are treated differently depending on their gender, age or social status. Titles are used even in conversation. (*Please refer to the titles section of* Chapter Eight, Language.)

Palanca

The phrase 'it's not what you know but whom you know' is a predominant aspect of the Ecuadorian culture. While this is true of any place on Earth, it critical to operating in Ecuadorian society at all levels. *Palanca*, which means 'lever' in Spanish, is the use of connections to obtain favours, employment and business deals.

If you think having the lowest price and even a higher quality product is going to get the sale, you may find yourself mistaken. I learned this the hard way. I represented a manufacturer of universal joints that were new to the market and identified a distributor who could purchase a substantial quantity. My initial contact at the company identified himself as the general manager and buyer for the firm. He seemed quite interested in the product and liked the price.

However, he said they had been happy with their supplier but would be interested in a lower price. After several visits, he said that if we would make a concession of 5 per cent they would place a sample order. I left happy, thinking I would get an order and a commission cheque. After getting the ok for the discount, he told me that they needed more of a discount to make a purchase.

I made a visit with the sales manager from the United States. We made another price concession and the manager said to wait a few minutes. After a long wait, the manager returned and said that he was checking with his superior. I realised then that a sales manager is not always a decision-maker and that the real decision-maker usually has his own office. Upstairs, we met the owner of the business who was very polite and considerate but explained that they had a long relationship with their existing supplier who had agreed to meet our prices so they would not be changing suppliers. Having the best product and the lowest price didn't help at all.

I strongly suggest that if you're new to Ecuador and trying to develop *palanca* that you join several organisations as soon as possible. One excellent group is the Rotary, which is quite ubiquitous throughout Ecuador and has numerous high-ranking business officials as members. Joining the Ecuadorian/US Chamber of Commerce is another viable alternative.

The Importance of Friends

Relationships take time to develop in Ecuador and they need to be cultivated. It is also a good idea to make as many friends from both the Sierra and the Costa. If you live in the Costa you will always been seen as a *costeno* by your customers in the Sierra and vice a versa.

Bribes

Ecuador is often referred to by international organisations as being one of the most corrupt countries in the world. While most Ecuadorians denounce bribes, culturally speaking, this is a grey area and payoffs, especially for services at the lower levels of government and in business, are a part of daily life. The longer you are in Ecuador it will become evident that what many North Americans call bribes are seen by Ecuadorians as a means to smoothen situations to obtain what one needs. Many Ecuadorians will blame corrupt politicians for the cause of the country's ills and in the next breath conduct such a transaction.

I was once in a heated conversation with an Ecuadorian who was criticising the *politicos* (politicians) for having their hands in the till. When I then asked him if he would pay

a traffic officer to get out of a ticket, he smiled and said "Of course" with a large smile. I then asked him where the practice of paying bribes started. He responded frankly, "That is the problem."

The art of paying for services is deeply rooted in the Ecuadorian psyche and is well documented since the Spanish conquest. Politicians will often espouse their intent to eliminate graft but often find themselves participating in it. A case in point is ex-president Bucaram who appeased the poor with promises of improving their position but who was accused of stealing from the public coffers. One of his ministers was caught, after the fall of Bucaram's government, trying to leave for Colombia with suitcases filled with millions of dollars.

The government continues to try to tackle the problem, having set up the Comisión Anticorrupción or Comisión de Control Cívico de la Corrupción (Commission of Civic Control of Corruption), which tries to make inroads. You can read about them and their efforts at:

http://www.comisionanticorrupcion.com.

This author would never recommend that you do anything illegal. It is important, however, to understand that there is such a system. One of the ways to understand payoffs in Ecuador is that it is not always seen as dishonest behaviour but a tip for a service. Bribes are also seen as a way for lowly paid government workers to keep bread on the table. However, they pervade all levels of government. The judiciary is notorious for its corrupt practices. One attorney I know well says it makes it very difficult to practise law without paying bribes to judges and states "Justice is politicised in Ecuador." One example is, if you are arrested and your case does not call for the normal bonding requirements, a bribe of between US$ 300 and US$ 1,000 is usually given by the attorney to the judge's secretary. The more serious crimes require a larger amount, especially for drug charges. Another bribe would then be required for a reduced sentence. Several Americans I have visited in prison for drug charges and who have not been released prior to trial indicated they kept paying and paying but there would always be something else coming up and then their money would run out.

You should never allude to someone that a payment is a bribe. Any proposition for a payment would be dealt with in a very discreet and unobtrusive matter. I hope the examples below will demonstrate how such a system works.

My Own Experience

The first time I encountered such a situation was when I was getting married. I needed a letter from the police department in Ecuador to state that I was offence-free. My fiancée and I approached an officer standing outside the station and asked him what to do. He took my information and said it would be ready tomorrow.

However, if I wanted it in several hours I could have it. There was no specific verbal clue but my wife-to-be explained to me that I needed to ask how much the service would cost. He told me US$ 10. I returned in several hours and I got my clearance. I wondered if they had even checked if I had a criminal record.

When I first moved to Ecuador, I was in severe need of a *casilla* (post office box). I went down to the main post office and inquired about this. The clerk was very pleasant and said there were none available. He said to return next week. I returned the following week, anxious to get my box. However, he explained he was sorry but that there were none. This went on for about a month until a family member told me he could get me one within a day. I was upset that he hadn't told me this earlier. To my surprise, I found out I could have it the next day but it would cost me US$ 200. I thought he was kidding. He took me to a grungy old building where we walked up several flights of stairs and entered an office that looked like it was out of an old detective film. There were several people typing away on old Royal typewriters. My relative introduced me to a gentleman who said that he would be happy to secure a box for me. I handed him US$ 200 and of course I didn't ask for a receipt. He then told me to return to the post office the next day and a gentleman would be at the window to provide me a post office box. I returned the next day to be greeted by the same fellow who had told me there were none available, except this time he was smiling. He handed me a key and had me sign a few papers and I got my box! I have kept that box for the last 20 years even though I don't use it personally.

Traffic police, especially in Guayaquil, are notorious for graft when it comes to traffic violations. Several years ago, during the Christmas season, I was in a friend's car with two of my sons when we came across a roadblock set up by the police known as vigilantes. The officer came up to the window and instructed my friend to drive his vehicle just down the block. My kids were anxious to know what we had done wrong. We parked and my friend got out of the car and approached the officer. He returned to the car, took out some papers and returned to the officer. Our friend's back was turned to us as he handed the officer the papers. When our friend returned, he said his papers were in order and that he had given the officer something for Christmas. Traffic officers are respected, feared and hated here. Female officers should never be offered a bribe as they are considered above reproach.

My most revealing moment of understanding the payment system in Ecuador came many years ago. On that day, I must admit I actually appreciated the 'something-for-a-cola' system. In my early days in Ecuador, I would often ask others how bribes were conducted. I was always told that there would be no outright request for money but that the person asking for a payoff for a service would comment "How about something for a cola." I didn't believe this until one day I had the chance to buy some Ecuadorians a cola and was happy to do so.

Just a Little Something for a Cola

My family had suffered through the wet heat in Guayaquil for six months while I attempted to open a sales agency. I had imagined difficult times but had not anticipated some of the worst rains and floods in the history of Ecuador. It was during the January of 1983 and I had never imagined that we would be living in a mosquito net for eight to 10 hours a night. Even with the netting, my family would wake up with large, quarter-sized bites, which made me fearful that they would catch dengue fever, or worse, malaria.

The climate was terrible but the economy was worse. I was a self-employed sales representative but could not make a sale. I could not believe that this was the same country where, a year earlier, I had sold US\$ 50,000 worth of car parts in one week. Worse, I was broke and concerned about making my meagre savings last.

Some months later, my wife and I decided to throw in the towel. If I was going to be poor, the United States was the place to be, not Ecuador. We were depressed as both of us wanted to remain here. My wife's dream was to be with her family in Ecuador. My dream was to go to some exotic land, build a fortune, wear Indiana Jones hats and smoke Cuban cigars, while my employees worked my large banana plantation. I went to bed that night knowing tomorrow I would have to start making plans to get back to the US, broke. I thought, 'What a hero, my friends will call me Indiana Loser'. I was hoping a large mosquito bite would wake me from the reality of this terrible nightmare.

The next day, I went to see my Ecuadorian attorney about my visa. My tourist visa had expired and I was trying to obtain a permanent working visa. The permanent visa was as yet unavailable since my attorney had not paid off several bureaucrats to obtain it. She advised me that immigration would understand my predicament and I would have no problems at the airport. Boy, was she mistaken. I left her office shaking my head. I never understood this game of paying people off to get things which should be available through regular channels to the masses. My wife had explained to me many times that this was the way of life in her country and public servants supplemented their meagre salaries in this manner. It was viewed as a tip for faster service.

We decided to leave the following week. We arrived at the airport and waited through the long line of people making the trek to Miami. After saying our good-byes to friends and family, we exited through the security gate to leave. My wife and son presented their documents and were signalled by the immigration officer to pass. I then presented my passport and began to walk through the second security clearance gate when the officer yelled, "¡Alto!" The officer had a grin on his face as though he had caught a thief. He explained to me that my tourist visa had expired and I could not leave the country. I was told I must report to the immigration office on Monday to clear up the matter. Of course, it was Saturday and Immigration was closed. I pleaded with him to no avail.

At that moment, I suggested to my wife that possibly this matter could be resolved with some type of payment. It's funny how one's perspective changes when one is in a serious predicament. We decided that she would conduct the negotiation since they might put me in jail if I was suspected of trying to bribe a public official.

My wife got the attention of the officer who seemed to sympathise with our plight. She offered him US$ 60. He went to the sergeant and we watched as they discussed our fate. My heart dropped to my shoes when I saw him start shaking his head at the offer. At this point, I thought I could hear the plane's engines revving up to depart. I looked around a pillar and saw the door on the plane close. I told my wife to offer more money and to beg the junior officer. My wife handed her passport to him, who then handed it to the sergeant. The junior officer returned and gave my wife back her passport.

The sergeant then contacted airline officials and told them to open the door for three more passengers. I couldn't believe it. We were running like crazy as security officials rushed us to the tarmac of the waiting plane. I could hear people laughing but did not know why until I realised that my Sansabelt slacks had drooped to my knees, exposing the rear portion of my anatomy. It was moon over the Guayaquil airport. At that point I didn't mind being the butt of laughter.

As we were running towards the plane, the junior officer accompanied us. I began to shake his hand to thank him for his assistance. He then looked me in the eye and asked, "May I have a little something for a cola?" Clearly he was paying me a compliment by knowing that I understood his culture so well that I would not be offended. He explained that the cola money we previously supplied was only for the sergeant. I reached into my pocket and only had twenties. At that point only US$ 20 separated me from home. This was no time to be budget conscious or to ask if he had change. I handed over a twenty and told him I hoped he enjoyed the cola and to drink one for me. I had a feeling it would be some wonderful Ecuadorian cold draft. He smiled as he shook my hand and felt the bill pass to his. He then said that he hoped I had a good trip and to return to his country.

As I buckled my seatbelt, sweat pouring down my face, I took my wife's hand and yelled, "Yes!" My wife asked me what had happened with the officer. I told her that I had just contributed to the officer's emergency fund. She smiled and congratulated me, saying that I was now officially Ecuadorian.

As I reran the recent events through my mind, I could not believe the whole event had taken place. Was I wrong in paying or was I simply following the rule of a culture different from my own? I could even rationalise that I was being fined for my visa having expired. Whatever had happened, I was glad I had followed the cultural norms that day. I reclined in my seat and started to drift off to sleep when the stewardess came by and offered me a cola. Coca-Cola would never taste the same again.

ECUADORIAN VIEWS OF EACH OTHER

Like people all around the world, Ecuadorians are just as fond of making broad generalisations of each other. People from the Sierra and Costa, especially, have many stereotyped ideas of each other. These distinct regional groups do not have a lot of affection for each other. Here are some examples:

What people from the Costa say about people from the Sierra:

- They are tightwads.
- They are crybabies and are often referred to as *chichihueros*.
- They are hypocrites.
- They think they are aristocrats and won't admit that they are mestizos.
- They always want more after an agreement has been made.

What people from the Sierra say about people from the Costa:

- They are monkeys.
- They spend all the money they make and party all the time.
- They can't keep a secret.
- They don't do what they say they are going to do.

These divisional differences are important to keep in mind if you're assigning representatives to the country or hiring.

I know of an operation based out of Quito which hired an office manager from Guayaquil. After looking at the situation, I understood why. Clearly the office staff didn't like the fact that she was from Guayaquil and not one of them. However, being from Guayaquil himself, the manager figured that the office manager's loyalty would probably be with him and that she wouldn't team up with the staff. She was also good-looking, and that was good for business. Many Serrano men find women from the coast particularly alluring.

If assigning an agent in Ecuador, one should try to have representatives both in the Costa as well as the Sierra.

Many manufacturers will assign dual representation in Ecuador despite it being a relatively small market for most products.

SETTLING IN

CHAPTER 5

'Lodgings were scarcely to be had for money,
and services were difficult to secure.'
—Edward Whymper when arriving in Ecuador in 1879

ECUADOR IS STILL NOT AN EASY OVERSEAS ASSIGNMENT, although things have changed since 1879. Stresses are increased by language, cultural, societal and geographical differences. Nothing happens in a hurry in Ecuador, except when you don't want it to. You will have to consciously adjust your patience level. The information provided in this chapter should significantly increase your learning curve and hopefully soften some of the shocks you might face. For the most part, many assignments will take place in Quito or Guayaquil and you will find that many of the same systems exist in much of the country. The Resource Guide chapter at the back of this book will provide you with alot of contact information to help you settle in and smooth your transition into Ecuador.

ACCOMMODATION
Choosing where to live in Quito or Guayaquil is an important, significant decision. Both cities are metropolises and are subject to the same problems any large city might have. Choosing the best neighbourhood you can afford is important. Many of the better neighbourhoods will have access to supermarkets and pharmacies. Rents are typically less expensive in Quito, compared to Guayaquil.

When selecting your residence, it is best to live as close as possible to work and school. Distance is important, as driving in Quito and Guayaquil can be a horrendous experience. Try to cut down on commuting time. Before selecting a residence, it may be wise to settle in an apart-hotel, which can accommodate you for a short- or long-term stay. Apart-hotels in Ecuador are typically a hotel-type operation with suites varying in size, usually including a kitchen and maybe a dining room. This will allow you the freedom to explore the different neighbourhoods before signing a lease. Taking your time to locate the most appropriate housing for your needs is advisable. It is also possible to rent rooms and live with families where no lease is involved. Be prepared to take a month to several months before you find appropriate housing.

In Quito, you will find a number of differing architectural styles to choose from, both colonial and modern. There is a fantastic use of wood, much of which is native to Ecuador. The city is divided into four sections: south, north, historical and valley. The best neighbourhoods in Quito for expatriates are Bellavista, El Batan, El Bosque, El Condado, Gonzalez Suarez and Guapulo. The Gonzalez Suarez area close to the Hotel Quito is among the nicest in Quito and there are a number of nice apartment buildings in this area. Some expatriates have found a number of suburban areas attractive. Valle de los Chillos and Valle de Tumbaco have numerous housing options and services available. They are both about 15 to 20 minutes outside of Quito. Do remember that as areas grow, commuting time will increase to and from Quito. Just a few steps down in quality are the neighbourhoods of El Inca, Granda Centeno, Jipijapa, La Floresta and La Granja.

While Guayaquil has similar rental and buying systems for real estate, there are not as many options as in Quito. Rents in Guayaquil are also generally more expensive than in Quito. There also appears to be little negotiating when it comes to price. The best areas for expatriates are Los Ceibos, Puerto Azul, Santa Cecilia and Los Parques. Urdesa may still offer options, although it has become rather commercial and less residential of late. My favourite is El Barrio Centenario. It is located in the south of the city and for years was the poshest neighbourhood of Guayaquil. Its residents are rather well-to-do and the area is kept immaculate. The biggest drawback is commuting time into either Guayaquil or the northern

Apartment sprawl in Guayaquil.

part of the city. There are also a number of apartments in this area. Entre Ríos is an up and coming suburb of very wealthy residences.

There are several ways to locate your residence. The major newspapers run advertisements in the classified sections and the best day for this is Wednesday. In Quito, there will be numerous places that may display rentals or have access to individuals who know of rentals. Major schools that cater to expatriates would also be a good option. A number of Spanish schools also have apartment listings, as does the South American Explorer's Club. Another source would be your country's embassy or consulate. Using rental agencies is another way to obtain your housing requirement. However, they usually receive one month's rent from the landlord as their commission. Some may be rather pushy and few seem to speak English.

The rental contracts are quite standard in their wordings, covering duration, monthly rental amount, deposits (guarantees), any annual increase as a cost of inflation, the condition the residence should be in prior to departure, responsibility in the event of damage, prohibitive activities of the tenant and reasons for early termination of the contract. Most rental agreements will require a one- or two-year lease. You are normally required to pay for all the utilities.

A landlord may terminate a contract if you fail to pay the rent for two months, use the premises for illegal purposes, use the residence for purposes other than what is in the contract and sublet without the approval of the owner. The owner must notify you three months in advance if he intends not to renew the contract for some legal reason. A rebuttal to this would have to be handled in a tenancy court by your attorney. However, this seldom happens.

Rental Agreements

Deposits range from one to three months. If you're renting a furnished residence, make sure there is a list of all items and the condition they are in. Have both parties sign this and attach it to the contract. The chances of receiving your deposit back are very slim unless you return the flat in an immaculate condition.

In Guayaquil, the expression *'lagarto que traga, no vomita'* ('the alligator that swallows doesn't vomit') can be accurately used here.

Electricity

Ecuador uses 110 volts, 60 AC, compatible with North America but incompatible with Britain and Australia. Plugs have two flat prongs, as in North America. Be prepared for numerous blackouts in Ecuador. Many businesses and residences use generators as backup. Also, it is a good idea to have surge protection equipment for your computers. Electric bills are delivered to each home and you can pay the bill at any of the offices printed on the back of the bill. Some banks offer debit services to pay electricity bills.

Rubbish

The municipality takes care of rubbish collection. Pack your rubbish in plastic bags and they will usually be picked up outside the front of the house (there are no back alleys here). In Quito, there are receptacles outside some homes where you can place these plastic bags. Rubbish disposal is billed yearly on the property tax bill. Depending on where you're staying in Quito, rubbish collection will usually take place three days a week, i.e. every other day except Sundays.

Sewage

The sewage system in Ecuador is poor and the water pressure is too low to accommodate toilet paper. To avoid clogging bowls and to prevent overflows, no matter how unpleasant this sounds, please remember to place toilet paper or tampons in the receptacle next to the toilet. There are a few major hotels, which don't request that you do this. Most do, however, and this should be adhered to. Clean public bathrooms are almost non-existent. Once I arrive in any area of Ecuador where I am to stay for a while, I always scope the area out for hotels with lobbies or restaurants, such as Burger King, in case I need a toilet.

Temporary Digs

Making the transition to a new residence can be very stressful. It is therefore important to have a short-term place to stay whilst you are looking for your permanent housing or getting it set up. I have found the Latin America Reservation Center (LARC) a good reservations site. The booking office can

be contacted at 1-800-361-7003 or http://www.larc1.com. LARC staff members can attend to residential needs in Latin America, Australia, and New Zealand.

In Quito, I recommend La Colina Suites as an excellent housing alternative for either short- or long- term stays. It is a small establishment with 22 suites of which all are quite modern and very elegant. Popular with embassy personnel, it is dedicated to a high level of service and can assist you in almost any of your needs in Quito. The suites all have a dining room and kitchen and sufficient space for families. It is also the only hotel in Quito that will accommodate pets. It is also one of the few hotels in Quito that carry an insurance policy and that provides treatment if you require emergency care at the hotel in the event of an accident or illness. In the event that you need more serious treatment, the hotel will make sure you get safely to a doctor or hospital. Prices are even negotiable for longer stays. The hotel is located at La Colina N26-119 y Av. Orellana. Its website s:

http://www.lacolinasuites.com.

Accommodation Advice

Another option for a short- or long-term stay is the Apart-Hotel Antinéa located near Avenida Amazonas. It has a number of 'French-style' hotel rooms and suites, and eight apartments.
Address: Juan Rodriquez 175 y Diego de Almagro, Quito, Ecuador
Website: http://www.hotelantinea.com

(*For further information, please refer to the list of hotels in* Chapter Seven, Enjoying Ecuador.)

Domestic Help

Another key to comfortable living in Ecuador is domestic help. As with housing, you should take your time in selecting suitable domestic staff. Many household employees are from very humble origins and are often from the countryside. Many may have as little as a third-grade education and speak only Spanish. It is wise to obtain recommendations from your embassy or consulate staff. Part of the selection procedure is

to conduct an interview and secure letters of recommendation from former employers, not just friends or family. (The same methods mentioned in the section about finding a residence will also suffice.) There are also employment agencies that specialise in domestics. Many domestics prefer to work for expatriates as they are thought to pay and treat household help better than Ecuadorian nationals.

Live-in maids are still a common practice in Ecuador. Many residences have maid's quarters which will include a furnished room with a bathroom. The employer may also provide uniforms and personal items. Uniforms in Quito may be purchased at El Uniform in the shopping centre Quicentro and their main shop at 6 de Diciembre in the Plaza Argentina (tel (02) 239-616). In 2000, the average complete uniform (two sets) including shoes cost about US$ 40. Make sure that your agreement covers salary (salary in 2000 was about US$ 200 per month) and days off. (Sundays are normally the day off for domestics.) Standard duties include cleaning the entire residence. Live-in maids will also prepare and serve most meals and should eat as well as your family.

There are a number of labour laws protecting domestic workers that are important to keep in mind. There is a minimum wage. (On top of this, experience and special skills such as cooking may demand a higher price.) If the employer wants to dismiss the employee there should be a 30–day notice given to the employee. She must also be given at least two hours a week off to find another position. If your maid becomes ill, she can ask you to provide an illness document, which would entitle her to medical care at an Ecuadorian Social Security facility.

Ecuadorian law also requires employers to pay additional bonuses. Payable in December, this is called the 13th salary since it is an additional one-month salary. The 14th salary consists of two minimum wages, paid between 1 and 15

Tips On Relating to Your Maid

- Respect the privacy of a maid's quarters and try to communicate with her when in the common work area.
- Address maids with the polite form of you—'usted'. Some North Americans falsely believe they should be addressed with the 'tú' form. Only if a maid is very young is 'tú' an appropriate form of address.
- Maids should be kept at a proper social distance but be treated in a polite manner. Saying 'thank you' and 'please' are common courtesies.
- Maids don't eat with the family.
- Don't set the table, clean dishes or sweep. This may often be perceived as a way of telling them they don't know how to do their job.
- If you're a guest in a home, it's inappropriate to be too sociable with the maid.
- In most cases, don't pay too much attention to the maid's children.
- In most instances, don't introduce your maid to your guests.

September. There is a 15th salary payable in April. A 16th salary is payable every month and is one-eighth of the paid salary.

Depending on the size of your home and number of children, it may be appropriate to have a nanny as well. This can be an excellent experience for your family and children. Ecuadorians dote on their children and this will probably be true with your nanny. The children will grow close with her and learn Spanish from her.

Lawn Man

While back yards, such as those in the United States, are not the norm in Ecuador, you may have a small area of garden or yard that needs maintaining. You can request for a lawn man to tend to the plants and upkeep the house. He will probably have other customers and will come to the house only on an agreed schedule or on a need-to basis.

EDUCATION

If you have children, I think you will be happy with the various school options here. The schools are often close-knit groups where your children will get the chance to mix with both

local and foreign students. The private schools tend to attract children of diplomats, executive expatriates, missionaries and wealthy Ecuadorians. The environment in the schools, whilst more demanding, seems to be generally more wholesome or innocent than schools in the United States. Discipline problems and drug use don't appear to be as much of a threat here, unlike in US schools. Many of the children speak two or more languages and this is an environment that fosters cross-cultural learning and interaction.

The Ecuadorian Ministry of Education must approve the schools' curricula. School curricula vary and schools have different operating permits.

The private schools, which cater to international students, operate on the US school calendar. Ecuadorian public and some private schools run on the Ecuadorian school calendar. Schools in Quito run from October to the end of July. Schools in Guayaquil operate from May to January. The cost of private schooling here is comparable to the United States and many of the schools are computer-equipped. In fact, the Inter-American Academy in Guayaquil was using computers and web pages before many schools in the United States.

Schools

There are several school options listed in the Resource Guide at the back of the book. It is advisable to contact these schools as far in advance as possible, and be equipped with references and academic records. Costs are comparable to US private schools.

SAFETY

Ecuador has become a much more dangerous place in which to live for nationals and expatriates over the last few decades. This is partly due to the lack of employment. Petty crime, such as pickpocketing, has always been a problem in the larger cities and along the coastal areas. The last several years have seen a dramatic increase in the number of violent crimes against individuals and businesses. Kidnapping has become a cottage industry. Security should be considered in your travels through Ecuador.

There are a number of security companies operating in Ecuador. Please do check that they are qualified and that the company's documentation is in order. They should have permission from the Minister of Police and the Ministry of Defence. A security company needs to have authorisation to operate from the Commander of the Armed Forces and the Superintendent of Companies. If security is your priority, you can expect to pay about US$ 350–US$ 400 a month for protection. I would advise checking the company out with your embassy and I recommend companies that have contracts with large organisations such as airlines.

One of the most frequent comments among travellers to Ecuador concerns safety. I often overhear them advising each other to stay away from dangerous places, not to act foolishly and to use common sense. This may be naive, however, as something that makes common sense in your homeland may not make common sense in a foreign land.

I have found the following tool, used by the police, very reliable in increasing your chances of not being victimised while travelling in Ecuador. Being aware of your environment is critical to your safety. But what level of awareness is necessary? Let's think of different levels of awareness in terms of colours. White constitutes you not being aware of your surroundings due to distractions, being tired or assuming there is no risk of danger. A yellow state of alertness has you in a relaxed state but observing what is going on around you. You are not expecting a physical attack but are aware that it may happen. An orange level of alert is when you are aware of an impending problem that may escalate. This is a very volatile situation but you have a plan of defence. You may not need to physically protect yourself but should have a plan of how to get away from the threat. The most intense state of alert is red. This is a situation where, if there is trouble, you need to take immediate action and your whole sense of purpose is to protect yourself by all reasonable means.

There will be times when you shift between all four colour levels. While it would be nice to live at the white level all the time, you will be asking for trouble if you do. Examples of different scenarios with different levels of alert may include the following:

- White—Bars on the windows, full-time security guards and alarms may provide such an environment. Choosing a nondescript home may also provide you with some protection. In certain shopping centres in both Guayaquil and Quito, you may feel quite safe, as there is greater security for customers. However, even in such an environment, you may find yourself going into yellow mode especially when leaving a shopping centre.

- Yellow—When in public areas, you should be at least in yellow mode. Walking down the Malecón in Guayaquil or Avenida Amazonas in Quito you should always be aware of what is going on around you. This may include walking closer to the buildings, making yourself less of a target by holding your rucksack, briefcase or handbag on the side closest to the building. You might wish to shift your gaze from left to right and occasionally glance behind you. As of late 2000, Avenida Amazonas has become significantly more dangerous at night. A source indicated to me that it is actually off-limits to US military personnel in the evening.

- Orange—Walking along Avenida Amazonas you are in the yellow height of awareness when a small group of children run up to you and start holding their hands out to ask for money. This is a perfect time to shift into orange alert. While the children may be harmless, you must prepare for trouble from any angle. It is here that you may have a plan in place such as making sure your briefcase or bag is closer to you. You could also look for a business establishment to enter.

  A woman once approached me as if she was going to ask me a question. It is very uncommon for a woman here to approach a strange man in public. I immediately went into an orange mode of alert and then to a red by shouting at the woman, delaying her approach and attracting the attention of passers-by. I then dashed into a shop. This allowed me to disarm a situation that was most probably a setup for theft.

Orange status should always be your *modus operandi* when entering or leaving banks or using ATM machines. I advise using ATM machines in major shopping centres. Many criminals have become more sophisticated and are better dressed. One scam along Avenida Amazonas is that an attractive and well-dressed woman will drop something in front of you. When you bend over to help her, her accomplices will come up from behind and rob you. Be cautious if you are a male and if a lone female approaches you in public. There is a good chance you are being set up to be robbed.

- Red—In this mode, your safety is at risk and you must react immediately. Your adrenalin is running at 100 per cent and you must take control of the situation. While I have never found myself in a true state of red in Ecuador, I have had a number of situations where I was on the highest level of orange about to go to red.

The first situation was when I was walking at night along Avenida Amazonas. At night, this area becomes another world with numerous small groups of young people out looking for trouble. You should be on constant alert and probably not be in this area at all at night. The second situation was when I entered a very rough neighbourhood filled with prostitutes in Guayaquil. My camera attracted so much attention that there were as many as 50 people following me thinking I was from a newspaper. Luckily, I had a good friend with me. I adopted a confident stride and a non-confrontational manner to those on the street and didn't stand in one place for any more than a few minutes.

Types of Crimes

Here is a small summary of some types of crimes that take place in Ecuador and some places to be cautious of.

Car theft is a very significant problem in Ecuador. It is highly organised with well-equipped gangs. Many gang members are armed and have false identification papers. They are very good at obtaining false papers for the cars that they have stolen.

A new type of crime has been quite prevalent in Quito and Guayaquil. Called the 'robo express', people are often carjacked and forced to ATMs to empty their bank accounts. Also, there have been a number of carjackings where the victim is taken to his home behind security gates and waived through by the guards who think the people in the car are friends of the victim.

Buses travelling through Ecuador are at a high risk of being attacked. Bus companies take no responsibility for protecting their passengers from assault. This is actually stated on the back of most tickets. The owner of a bus company mentioned that, in July 2000, five of his buses were attacked.

The most dangerous routes are in the northern part of the country sharing a border with Colombia and certain sections of Guayas province. The route north from Guayaquil through Daule and on to Velasco Ibarra (El Empalme) is the most at risk. Also included in Guayas are the routes from Nobol to Pedro Carbo and south from Guayaquil to La Troncal and the alternate route between Boliche and Puerto Inca.

Many of the assaults are by passengers. You are not required to provide a photo ID when purchasing tickets. Often the aggressors purchase three to five tickets and will use an attractive female as a decoy. Guns and knives will be smuggled onto the bus underneath trousers or inside a basket or a fruit such as a watermelon. The highest number of assaults in the Guayas province occur between 6:00 am and 9:00 am. This is true for buses in Guayaquil and for buses travelling between different cantons of Guayas. Some of the other dangerous routes in the country are the ones from Guayaquil to Riobamba and from Guayaquil via Durán to de Milagro, Jujan and Tres Cerritos.

The border with Colombia is considered quite dangerous. Guerillas from Colombian groups such as FARC and the ELN have made significant inroads into northern Ecuador, especially in the Sucumbios province. The selling of exotic animals is illegal. It is also illegal to purchase or export the hides of various animals, e.g. turtles. The situation between Ecuador and Colombia has become quite tense.

Jungle lodges have become targets of criminals due to the influx of foreigners. Caution should be taken in the Lower Rio Napo and Cuyabeno National

Reserve. Check with travel providers as to what safety steps they take. The Sucumbio and Orellana provinces may be dangerous for travellers due to civil unrest and oil workers are at risk of attack and/or kidnapping. Landmines are still a problem along the Ecuador Peruvian border (a result of the 1995 war).

Protests and civil unrest are a constant problem in Ecuador. University areas are often sites for unrest and road blockades are common.

Crimes of violence are another increasing problem among young people in Ecuador. Gangs are called *pandillas*. In Guayaquil alone there are at least 300 gang members. Gangs in Guayaquil go by names such as Los KK de Perro, Los X-15 and La Muerte. They are often dressed in a similar fashion as gang members in the United States, with extra long trousers that hang very low on the waist. All black or red are common gang colours. Gang members are usually armed with knives and revolvers. A unique gun made locally is called a tube and uses 22-calibre ammunition. It is called a *rambo*. A number of gangs from the Guayaquil area have now made inroads into less populous areas due, in part, to lack of police protection. Manta was specifically noted in newspaper reports in 2005 as having an increase in gang activity imported from Guayaquil.

The local newspaper, *El Universo*, stated in a special report in 2000 that 50 per cent of gang members are from homes which suffer from domestic violence. Seventy per cent are from lower-middle-class homes, 28 per cent from middle-class homes and 2 per cent from upper-class families. Between January and June of 2000 there were 728 crimes committed by minors in the province of Pichincha, which includes Quito. This included 458 robberies along with 213 assaults. The province of Guayas, including Guayaquil, reported 700 crimes by juveniles with 266 robberies and 149 assaults. Guayaquil placed a plan, called More Security, into effect in August 2000 to address increasing crime rates.

There are times in Ecuador when civil rights are suspended so that security can be increased. During 1999, this happened as the banks failed and the economic crisis deepened.

Ecuadorian policeman at a road block in rural Ecuador inspecting a driver's papers.

Fifteen agencies and groups were involved with the common objective of keeping an eye on crime and acting against it and corruption.

Ecuadorian Police
There are numerous police organisations in Ecuador. You will see many types of uniforms and colours. Here is a listing of some of the police units in Quito, their assigned duties and the colour of their uniforms:

- National Civil Police—They are charged with public safety and order. Their uniform includes olive-green trousers, olive shirts, olive jackets and white helmets.
- Regimiento Quito Número 1—They are riot police with similar uniforms: olive-green trousers, shirts and jackets.
- National Transit Directorte—In charge of traffic and signals. They wear blue trousers and light blue shirts.

There are a number of other police units in Quito. Although officers are armed in Ecuador, there was an increase in police deaths in 2000.

FINANCIAL MATTERS
Thirteenth September 2000 was 'D Day' in Ecuador when the United States invaded. That is, the US dollar invaded.

This date marked the official replacement of Ecuadorian sucres by the US dollar (US$) as the official form of currency. Since then, the sucre is no longer used and has no official monetary value.

It was not until late 2000 that the new coins started circulating. Today, US coins, minted in the United States, are also in circulation and accepted. The new Ecuadorian 1-, 5-, 10-, 25- and 50-cent coins resemble the US currency but are not the same. They bear images of famous Ecuadorian rather than famous American figures. You can't take a new Ecuadorian coin and spend it in the United States but you can use the Ecuadorian paper currency.

Be careful not to confuse the old 50-sucre coin with a US 50-cent piece. Individuals may try to pass the old coin off as a new Ecuadorian 50-cent piece to an unsuspecting person. Fifty-cent pieces seem to be more common in Ecuador than they are in the United States.

Most vendors also examine notes for counterfeits. At first this may offend you but counterfeit money is a chronic problem in Ecuador. Employees are held responsible if

they accept a counterfeit note. Between October 1996 and September 1997 it was estimated that US$ 34 million counterfeit notes were in circulation. Ones, fives and 10s are the most common counterfeit notes; US$ 100 counterfeit notes are also present.

Government authorities believe that many of the illegal notes are produced in clandestine facilities in Colombia.

Spotting Counterfeits

There are several clues for identifying legitimate notes:

- First, feel the note for a change in texture, especially the picture of the person on the note and his clothing. You will feel a small raised surface.
- Second, on US$ 100 notes you will observe watermarks by holding the note up to the light.
- Third, all US$ 20, US$ 50 and US$ 100 notes since 1996 have a security thread which can be seen by holding the note up to the light. I carry with me a pen, which can be purchased in most stationery shops, that helps to detect if a note is counterfeit.

Many people are still adjusting to the dollar conversion. If you visit markets in rural areas you will probably find more people offering you a price in sucres. The last official sucre rate for the US$ was 25,000 sucres to US$ 1.

Having many smaller denominations is still recommended for paying for inexpensive items. Dollar notes in 20s, 50s or 100s could prove difficult when trying to negotiate for change. The smaller the denominations you have, the fewer the hassles you will have. One of the most frustrating aspects of conducting transactions is the lack of change available from many shops, individuals and vendors. This had been a problem in Ecuador even with the sucre. It is not uncommon to purchase an item only to find that the cashier does not have enough change, and he conveniently keeps the balance. It is a common phrase that 'a man in Ecuador with hundred dollar bills is like a man with no money' referring to the change and counterfeit problem. Many individuals, and even banks, will not even accept US$ 100 notes because of the risk of counterfeit notes.

Banks

Banks in the late 20th and early 21st centuries are seen by many as the culprits for Ecuador's financial woes. Numerous banks failed and many of the country's residents lost their money when the banks were unable to meet withdrawal demands. Banks are creeping back into operation and locals are beginning to use them, but only sparingly.

Many of the better-known banks have branches in the major shopping centres. This may prove convenient in that they have weekend opening hours. Banks are generally open from 9:00 am to 6:00 pm on weekdays. In some cities, banks may be open on Saturdays, especially if it happens to be market day. *Casas de cambio* (currency exchange bureaus) are usually open from 9:00 am to 6:00 pm weekdays and until noon on Saturday. In Quito and Guayaquil, the international airport and major hotels have exchange facilities that stay open for longer. Long queues are always a problem at most banks.

Most banks have ATM machines. Many display the logos of banks, such as Cirrus or Star, that they have affiliations with. If you are using a card from an unaffiliated institution there may be an additional service charge. There is no notification of service charges at some ATM machines, as is required in the United States. I have noticed I am often charged US$ 2 per transaction for withdrawing funds from my US account. Wiring money from abroad to Ecuador sometimes involves a small fee paid in Ecuador and in the country from which the money was sent. (Western Union is the bank I use for this.) Ecuadorian ATMs accept foreign credit cards, such as Visa and MasterCard. (Only MasterCard is accepted in the Galápagos Islands, however.) This will be indicated by the logos on the ATM machines. For foreign credit cards, you might have to pay high interest rates on cash withdrawals. To get around this, obtain a debit card in the form of a credit card from your bank. All the major towns have ATMs that

Be advised that if you are using a debit card from your home country there may be charges from that institution for withdrawals. I found in October 2005 that I could only draw out US$ 90 at one time. The Ecuadorian bank charged US$ 1.50. I then found out online that my home bank was charging me US$ 5 for each withdrawal.

accept Cirrus (MasterCard) or Plus (VISA) cards.

Most banks have a US$ 100 withdrawal limit per day. You also can take out as little as US$ 1 at some institutions. It is not permitted to use your mobile phone while inside a bank. This is to deter bank robberies and crimes against patrons. I know of one scam several years ago when a bank employee, after helping a customer make a withdrawal, got on his mobile phone and called an accomplice outside who robbed the customer leaving the bank.

When opening bank accounts, you will usually be required to provide your passport, identification and letters of reference. People, generally, still do not trust banks with large amounts of money. Many in Ecuador practise a form of banking called *colchon bank*, which means 'hiding your money in your mattress'.

Another concern includes ATM machines that have been known to make duplicate withdrawals on an account. In 2001, a number of consumers had complained that there were double or ghost withdrawals from their accounts via ATMs. Customers had reported that they would make one withdrawal and then find the same amount debited twice from their accounts. It has also been reported that a customer would fail to withdraw money at an ATM but later find on their bank statement that their account had been debited for that amount. It is highly recommended that you keep all receipts for your ATM transactions and that you check your statements.

Edward Whymper, the great mountaineer, commented about banks in Ecuador in his book *Travels Amongst the Great Andes of the Equator*, first published in 1892. He was referring to the problem he experienced with changing his money if it was not in perfect condition. He noticed that the arithmetic the banks used 'differed from that in common use when transacting business.' Referring to how the banks would not accept the notes they issued after they became worn, he explains that this was a handsome way for the banks to earn money and that seemed to 'be accepted by the people with perfect resignation ...' He continues with great insight that this practice contributed heavily to 'the universal mistrust of each other and of everybody that is exhibited throughout the country.' How little things have changed since then.

CLOTHING

Ecuadorians judge others by their clothing and are class-conscious about the way they dress. For example, you will not find many upper-class Ecuadorians wearing Panama hats. Like people everywhere, Ecuadorians are also quite brand-conscious. Polo and Tommy Hilfiger are popular here.

A general rule is that people in Quito dress more conservatively than people from Guayaquil. This is, in part, due to the climate. Quito is colder and requires heavier clothing. Dark colours are advised, such as blues and greys. Wool is often used. Many businessmen also wear suits in Guayaquil. There are a number of options available. Ralph Lauren, for example, has shops here.

The problem for the expatriate is if you have a large build. It is difficult to find trouser sizes of 38 or larger and shirt sizes of 17 and above. Ecuadorians have smaller physiques than many expatriates and this is also true with shoes. Finding a size 11 or 12 is difficult. As a solution, you may choose to make clothes and shoes locally. The tailors and shoemakers are good here, especially in Quito.

Shoes should always be well polished but this shouldn't pose a problem with the army of shoeshine boys vying for business throughout Ecuador. Women's sizes don't appear to be as difficult to find except for the very tall women with large-sized feet. In business, women especially, should dress conservatively.

Shorts for both men and women in the highlands are not the norm. Shorts are more common in Guayaquil but should be worn with discretion. Shorts and next-to-nothing bikinis are the norm, however, at the beaches. Men should avoid T-shirts but wear polo shirts or long-sleeved sport shirts instead. Fanny packs or bum bags should also not be carried as they make you stand out as a tourist and an easy target for thieves.

Traditional dry cleaners abound in the larger cities and prices are largely comparable with the United States. One Hour Martinizing is one of the more popular establishments in most major cities.

COMMUNICATIONS

Ecuador possesses most of the communication facilities available in most developed countries but reliability seems to be an issue, especially when it comes to telephones.

Telephones

Obtaining a telephone is a very expensive and onerous task. Remember, when renting or buying, to make sure the phone is included in the purchase or rental cost. Andinatel (mainly in the highlands and Oriente) and Pacifictel (mainly in the coastal lowlands) are the main telephone service providers in Ecuador. Both maintain a large number of public phones available in select locations. Calls made from these booths are very inexpensive and the quality is good. In November 2005, average calls to the US were US$ 0.10 a minute.

Cellular or mobile phones have invaded the country, and people of all classes use them. Private companies in Ecuador provide mobile telecommunication services such as mobile telephones, pager and message services, conventional radio communications, trunking services, teleport and satellite communications. Today, Ecuador has two main mobile service providers, Porta and Movistar. The telecommunications sector is still underdeveloped and has a huge potential to grow. As a result, prices have dropped substantially since the early 1990s, except if you are using prepaid cards, rates are about US$ 0.50 a minute. There is no charge for incoming calls, therefore, you will find many landlines are blocked from calling mobile phones. Mobile phones are a status symbol in Ecuador. Both Movistar and Porta have prepaid cards which are available at grocery shops, pharmacies and small markets. Some hotels also rent out mobile phones to tourists. However, if you are there for almost any length of time, phone cards are available in several denominations and usually start at US$ 3. When purchasing a card you need to let the sales assistant know if you want a card for your mobile phone or a *cabina* (phone booth). The cards for Movistar and Porta can only be used in their booths. Porta and Movistar booths don't accept coins. These cards are especially good if you are travelling within Ecuador and need to make local or international calls. (AT&T, MCI and Sprint provide international calling services from the US via satellite links.) *Cabinas* are available throughout much of the country and the reception is very good.

In the past, merchants would rent out their phones and you could see this on most major streets in Quito and Guayaquil. However, it is a practice that has passed.

Calling Codes

The country code for Ecuador when calling from abroad is +593. Local numbers have seven digits and area city codes have two digits. If you're in Ecuador and calling a mobile phone locally you will dial 09 and then the number. There is a charge both from the dialling phone and the receiving mobile phone. Many local phones are blocked from calling mobile numbers. Be aware that hotels charge anything from US$ 0.20 to US$ 0.50 a minute for local calls.

Use the following area codes only when calling from outside these provinces:

Azuay (including Cuenca)	07
Bolívar	03
Cañar	07
Carchi	06
Chimborazo (including Riobamba)	03
Cotopaxi	03
El Oro	07
Esmeraldas	06
Galápagos	05
Guayas (including Guayaquil)	04
Imbabura	06
Loja	07
Los Ríos (including Babahoyo and Quevedo)	05
Manabí (including Manta and Portoviejo)	05
Morona-Santiago (except Palora 03)	07
Napo	06
Orellana	06
Pastaza (including Puyo)	03
Pichincha (including Quito)	02
Sucumbíos	06
Tungurahua (including Ambato)	03
Zamora-Chinchipe	07

The emergency and service numbers 911 (police), 101 (police), 102 (fire departments in Quito, Guayaquil and Cuenca), 105 (national operator), 116 (international operator) and 104 (information) will not be affected.

- To call mobile phone numbers in a local area, place a 09 before the seven digit number e.g. (09) 920-1740
- When calling a landline from overseas:

Pichincha (Quito)   011 593 (2) 2566-566
Guayas (Guayaquil)   011 593 (4) 2566-566

- When calling a mobile phone from an international location: 593 (9) 9566-566

All the major carriers in the US provide their own phone card service to call the US or other countries. If you are using Andinatel, dial: 999 119 (AT&T); 999 171 (Sprint); 999 170 (MCI WorldCom). Dial 1 800 999 170 if you're using Pacifictel lines. It is not possible to use a card from these companies from public phones.

Television Services

There are two major companies that provide cable and satellite TV services—Direct TV and TV Cable. Direct TV is a franchise of Galaxie, an American satellite company, while TV Cable is an Ecuadorian company that provides cable TV services and is part of a consortium of companies that includes Satnet and Americatel.

Direct TV is available in most of the country (Dial 1 800-888-999). There is an installation fee and a monthly charge depending on what programme is ordered

Cable TV is widely used throughout Ecuador. The major supplier is TV Cable http://www.tvcable.com.ec/inicio.php.

Post

The national postal service is a continual problem in Ecuador. Many companies use private postal courier services for mail between their Ecuador office and corporate offices back home. DHL, UPS and Federal Express are quite commonly used but not cheap. A normal letter costs about US$ 21 for a two-day delivery to the United States with these services.

There is no regular door-to-door postal delivery service. Obtaining a casilla (post-office box) is necessary if you're planning to receive post from outside the country. If you go to the post office there probably will be none available. It usually takes special connections with the post office staff to secure a post-office box. (*Refer to the section Bribes in* Chapter Four, Fitting into Society *for my story on opening a casilla.*)

Internet

The Internet has taken Ecuador by storm and is becoming more popular every day. There are literally hundreds of Internet cafés throughout the country, especially in Quito. In March 2000, it was not uncommon to be charged about US$ 5 per hour of use. In November 2005, most Internet cafés appeared to be charging about US$ 1 per hour. Most of these cafés permit smoking, which can be annoying for non-smokers. Also, bandwidth is in shortage in Ecuador and most computers run much slower than what you may be accustomed to in the United States. However, it is much better than five years ago. Most Internet cafés also have facilities for you to make long distance calls. The old net phone service has virtually disappeared due to the low cost of calls available today.

PASSPORTS AND VISAS

You will need a passport which does not expire within six months of your stay. Bring this everywhere with you as you might be asked to produce it, your visa or tourist card.

If you are from the United States and visiting Ecuador for fewer than 90 days, you don't need a visa. If you are a tourist and a national of any of the following countries you do need a visa: Algeria, Bangladesh, Costa Rica, Cuba, El Salvador, Guatemala, India, Indonesia, Iran, Iraq, Jordan, Lebanon, Libya, Nicaragua, Nigeria, North Korea, Pakistan, Palestine Authority, Panama, People's Republic of China, Sri Lanka, Syria, Tunisia and Vietnam. These regulations are subject to change and you should obtain the most current information from your local Ecuadorian embassy or consulate.

If you are a foreign national planning to stay in Ecuador for more than 90 days, you will need to apply for a visa and must present the following documents. When applying for this type of visa in the United States you must also present a valid US visa/green card:

- Valid passport for more than 6 months
- Police certificate with criminal record, if applicable, from the state where you reside
- Medical certificate

- Return ticket (for air, land or sea travel)
- Two photographs
- Application form
- Proof of economic means to support yourself while staying in Ecuador. (In more than 20 years of travel here, I have never been asked this question but it's good to be prepared.)

When dealing with the embassy or consulate staff, always remember to be very polite whether in person or via the telephone. Always ask for the name of the person you're speaking with as this may help in future correspondence. If sending documents to the consulate, remember to include a return envelope with paid postage. I also strongly recommend that you send your documents or return envelope as registered mail.

The airplane crew will distribute Visa 12-X forms before arrival. It is short and straightforward and is both in English and Spanish. When you arrive, present it and your passport to immigration. Many of the officials don't speak English. They will ask you how long you plan on staying in Ecuador and what address you will be staying at. I usually request a week or two more then I anticipate staying, in the event that my plans change. If I don't know exactly where I will be staying, I will usually name a well-known hotel.

The most important thing about this tourist visa is not to lose it. I staple it or secure it to my passport. It is very small and can be overlooked until the time comes when you try to leave and can't find it. If you misplace it, you will be required to go back to the airline check-in area and request a new one from the airline. It is up to the discretion of the immigration officer to let you go without the tourist visa form. It is also important to remember that you cannot change your tourist status in Ecuador nor take up employment. A number of years ago, I had applied for a visa to reside in Ecuador. While under the tourist visa, I was informed that I would have to return to Miami to pick up my resident visa. The official stated that he could send a fax stating that I was ill and could not return to Miami at the moment and the resident visa could be secured. Off the record, I do not think that this is something a bribe or 'cola' could not get you. ((*Refer to the section 'Bribes' in* Chapter 4, Fitting into Society *for a story on colas).*

Other than the tourist visa, there are other non-immigrant-type visas. Student visas are a type 12-V and required by all educational institutions in Ecuador. You will also be required to demonstrate financial worthiness to cover your expenses while in Ecuador. It is usually sufficient to provide a letter from your bank or a letter from a relative guaranteeing that your expenses will be taken care of.

If you're required to work in Ecuador or are a government representative, your employer or government agency must also show that you will be financially supported. Also mandated is a labour contract, legalised by an Ecuadorian labour court. Highly technical or specialised employees will need to obtain a work permit from the Ministry of Labour. Managers, officers of a company or a legal representative will need to obtain a certificate from the Superintendency of Companies. The duration of this visa will be set according to your personal requirements.

Religious visas have several unique requirements. The religious organisation where the visa applicant is to work must supply a letter explaining why he/she is needed and what he/she will be doing. The organisation must also provide a letter from the government of Ecuador permitting the organisation to operate in Ecuador. A so required is a copy of the organisation's rules and a statement identifying the legal representative of the organisation in Ecuador. This visa is usually valid for only two years.

Cultural exchange visas are for teachers or students involved in exchange programmes here. An application from the Ecuadorian authority that is sponsoring the visitor is required. This application must include a statement that the visitor will not receive any Ecuadorian funds for the work done.

If you are going to Ecuador for tourism or business, you can receive a visa for more than 90 days and up to 180 days. The main requirement here is that your consulate is to receive a document verifying that you have sufficient funds. This may include a statement or letter from your bank.

If you are planning on emigrating to Ecuador, there are six types of immigrant visas. They are:

- Annuitant (10-I) is an immigrant who will live on income from abroad. Usually this is a person who is retired and can demonstrate an income of at least US$ 8,000 a year.
- Real Estate (10-II) is an immigrant who will invest capital in purchasing real estate or securities. In most cases, the amount must be equivalent to 350 minimum Ecuadorian monthly salaries. Plus 100 minimum salaries per dependant which may be specified by the consular officer in the United States. It is usually a minimum of US$ 15,000.
- Industrial (10-III) immigrant will invest capital in agriculture, export trade, industry or livestock. The sum of capital must be equivalent to 600 minimum monthly Ecuadorian salaries or what the consulate office in the United States specifies. Normal minimum amount is US$ 25,000.
- Administrative or technical immigrant is considered a general agent status (10-IV) and is usually someone who has been requested to work for an Ecuadorian company. This also applies to foreign local agents of companies who possess unlimited power of attorney to represent the company in Ecuador, provided that 80 per cent of the company's local personnel is Ecuadorian.
- A professional immigrant (10-V) is designated for those with university degrees who desire to practise their profession in Ecuador. Should the applicant's profession not exist in Ecuador, the degree must be locally certified. The applicant must also fulfill the requirements for such practice, e.g. the bar for lawyers.
- A dependant immigrant (10-VI) is a spouse or blood relative who will receive support from another person.
- An HIV exam is required now for many Ecuadorian visas.

If you have been granted a visa, it is necessary to present your documents to the General Directorate of Alien Affairs to register. This is normally done within 30 days of registration.

Remember that you are only allowed to stay as long as your visa states. It is possible to change the status of a visa by applying no later than 30 days before it expires.

If you have emigrated to Ecuador, you must renew your census card annually in the immigration office. As an immigrant you are required, when leaving the country, to obtain a departure permit from the immigration office. You must present your passport with the visa, your Ecuadorian identification card, payment of a departure tax and military permit (for men aged 18 to 55). This departure permit is valid for a year. Minors under the age of 18 and going to live with one parent are also required to have an authorisation from the juvenile court.

The exit permit can sometimes be obtained from the travel agent you purchased your airline ticket from. Some travel agents will also handle a minor's permit, if he/she is travelling with only one parent. In the event of a divorce, both parents may need to present themselves to the juvenile court for authorisation. There is usually an additional fee for this service.

TRANSPORTATION
Getting to or around Ecuador is fairly straightforward, except during festival and holiday periods.

Air Travel
From the United States, the major carriers to Ecuador are American Airlines and Continental from Houston, Miami and Newark. Most flights arrive late at night. Other carriers from the United States are Avianca and Copa from Los Angeles. KLM and Iberia have flights to and from Europe. The main domestic carrier is TAME (an airline run by the Ecuadorian Armed Forces). Prices are comparable, so choose the one whose schedule best matches your own.

Internal flights are comparatively cheap and there is a two-tier pricing system on some flights, foreigners paying more than Ecuadorians. A foreigner would pay about US$ 50 for a one-way flight to or from Quito and an Oriente town (e.g. Macas, Lago Agrio and Coca). Locals would be charged about half that amount. A roundtrip from Guayaquil/ Quito to the Galápagos Islands would cost around US$ 350 for foreigners, depending on the season. This is double the rate for Ecuadorians and four times that for islanders. Entrance to the park costs US$100 and many tours include the price of the flight. Flights between Guayaquil and Quito cost around US$ 57 one-way if bought in Ecuador. Getting to Manta and Esmeraldas in the Costa takes approximately 20 minutes and to Lago Agrio in El Oriente approximately 30 minutes from Quito.

If you're going to visit Ecuadorian cities, it is best to purchase your tickets while in Ecuador. There is no reserved seating for the flights between Quito and Guayaquil. Flights run on the hour between about 6:30 am until early in the evening. The flight time is about 30 minutes.

Airports

Both the Quito and Guayaquil Airports have improved considerably and new airports are under construction. There are airports in Quito, Guayaquil, Machala, Manta, Loja, Cuenca, Macas, Pastaza, Portoviejo, Esmeraldas, Tulcán, Lago Agrio and Coca.

You can reserve seats for the other destinations in Ecuador. It is advisable to purchase your ticket direct from the TAME counter or their local offices. It has been my experience that tickets sold by travel agents are sometimes not confirmed. Airlines fly to the Galápagos Islands for Ecuadorian citizens and residents and you must provide documentation in order to purchase a discounted ticket.

Coming from abroad, after the plane lands, you will enter the terminal and join the queue for immigration. In the last two years, this process has been computerised and your passport will be imprinted via an electronic printer. You will then dash to the baggage area and pray that your luggage has arrived. (Airports here are known to have problems with the theft of luggage.) If you require a baggage cart it costs

US$ 1. There is a clerk who will take the dollar and give you a small receipt.

When you exit the airport there will usually be a swarm of people trying to assist you with your bags. It is a good idea to try to have someone meet you at the airport to help negotiate the crowds. This is especially true in Guayaquil. There have been cases where gangs will await visitors, watch you leave the airport and rob you a short time later.

If you are catching an international flight, I think it's best to be at the airport at least three hours in advance. There have been efforts in the last year, however, to improve the check-in process at the airport. Both in Guayaquil and Quito, only passengers are allowed to enter the ticketing areas. This has helped smooth the check-in procedure. Bags are no longer x-rayed in the counter area and a contract employee views them in a separate area. If he sees something that looks fishy, Interpol is called in. An agent of the airline will then go into the boarding lounge and ask you to go with him to the luggage loading area where they have drug-sniffing dogs. If you don't know what is happening it can be pretty scary. The agent or Interpol officer may ask you a few questions and have you open up the luggage.

Your carry-on bags are checked twice before boarding: when you pass through immigration and as you enter the boarding lounge. Before boarding or walking to your plane on the tarmac, passengers may sometimes be asked to queue up with their hand-held bags on the ground in front of them as police make one final sweep with their dogs.

One last piece of advice. If you have an onward ticket when arriving in Ecuador, you should confirm your seat on the flight with the airline at least 72 hours in advance. I have always had trouble getting through on the telephone numbers provided. Therefore, I visit the airline's office at least half a day or several hours in advance to reconfirm my seat. Going in person means that the staff are forced to look at your ticket and verify that you have a seat and you can actually see the clerks keying this information into the computer. That makes me feel more confident that there will be a seat waiting for me. American Airlines now has an office at the Policentro Mall in Guayaquil which can confirm tickets for you.

Airport Tips
- If you're landing in Quito on an international flight, be prepared for a hard landing. A pilot told me that they have been instructed, when making their approach, to get the plane down fast because of the short runway and the high altitude.
- If you have forgotten to purchase gifts, both Quito and Guayaquil airports have a number of nice shops once you have passed Customs.
- The airport in Guayaquil will almost always smell of insecticide due to spraying for mosquitoes.
- Some veteran travellers will often not get up right away when arriving in Quito to adjust to the high altitude. It can take your breath away when walking to the terminal from the plane.
- Try to get through immigration as soon as possible to get your baggage to prevent losing your luggage to thieves.

Driving

Ecuadorians are generally not considered good drivers. You should always be at least on orange alert. The less you drive in Ecuador, the better. Traffic accidents are among the top killers in Ecuador every year.

Ecuadorians, for the most part, don't heed traffic rules or courtesies. In 2000, the government made it a law for drivers to wear seat belts. The police strictly enforced this law, especially with taxicab drivers. However, most backseats in cabs still lack seat belts.

You will notice a lack of road signs or markings, especially on bends on the various highways and main roads. Drivers seldom heed blind curves. Assume that drivers will pass you no matter what and that drivers from the opposite direction also overtake on blind curves. Stop signs and traffic lights are not followed, especially at night. This is partly in an attempt to avoid robberies.

An Unfortunate Episode

There was an accident in March 2000 when a utility vehicle was speeding over the bridge that connects Guayaquil and Duran. The vehicle crashed over the wall of the bridge and landed in the Guayas River. Investigators surmised that the driver was speeding to avoid thieves as the vehicle was carrying some supplies for a company outside of Guayaquil.

Many of the streets in Quito and Guayaquil are one-way. Several years ago, one of my sons, with limited Spanish skills, asked me why all the streets in Guayaquil had the same name. He was referring to the signs and markings on the walls of the street indicating one-way traffic—*una via*.

Here are some basic guidelines when driving in Ecuador:

- Few roads have shoulders or safety lanes.
- Many towns that have a highway or main road going through them will have speed bumps. These are often very high and can cause severe vehicle damage if taken at high speed. Be sure to slow down when entering towns or small villages.
- Drive only in the daytime. You will substantially increase your risk of injury or death by driving or taking the bus at night. More crimes take place at night and many drivers drive without lights. This is supposedly to prevent the battery from wearing down.
- When driving in the country be sure never to leave your vehicle.
- Depending on which neighbourhood you live in, you may spot a section of a residential block where numerous cars are parked at night. In many middle- and lower-class neighbourhoods, car-owners will park their car with others and pay someone to guard their vehicles.
- When driving, be sure not to have your arms or hands hanging outside the windows or to have the windows wound all the way down. Thieves can steal watches and rings this way.
- Make sure doors are locked and that purses or briefcases are laid down on the floor, hidden from the view of thieves who may attack while you are at a traffic stop.

- Few Ecuadorians use turn signals.
- Ecuadorians are loud drivers. They are known to honk at almost anything.
- If taking a day trip or longer, make sure your vehicle is properly equipped with safety equipment and supplies. Also, make sure you take toilet paper with you, as you will find petrol stations sadly lacking. Public bathrooms are not usually well-maintained.
- Parking lots are hard to find in both Guayaquil and Quito. You might notice that, in front of many establishments, there will be someone who appears to be guarding cars. He may wave you into a space.

  You can ask him to watch your car and pay a small tip for his services upon your departure. There are also those who wave cars in and want the fee up-front. Be wary of them as they have been known to wave you into a no parking zone and by the time you return, your car might have been towed away.
- There are tollbooths on the outskirts of Quito. If you're driving a car, enter the lane with the sign that says *Livianos*.
- I advise you to drive 5 to 10 miles below the speed limit, especially when on highways or main roads. The roads are not well kept as maintenance is erratic so there are many potholes, especially during the rainy season. There are also usually numerous animals crossing.
- Many highways have a gutter running along the road for water runoff. Be alert to these as it is very easy to get stuck in one, causing severe vehicle damage.
- There are few, if any, safety lanes and having to stop along a road for an emergency is very dangerous. If you don't have flares, place debris or tree limbs several yards behind your vehicle to alert drivers of a stranded vehicle.

Fuel

Petrol is sold in gallons and is sold at petrol stations. Texaco is a popular brand. Many petrol stations were constructed in the late 1990s and petrol is now about the same price as in the United States.

The attendant will always pump the petrol. Extra is equivalent to regular leaded. Super is the highest octane available and is also leaded. Diesel is widely available and the cheapest fuel available. You will see credit card emblems displayed, if they are accepted. But not all stations accept credit cards, especially if the credit cards are not local.

Automobile Club de Ecuador

If you're going to be in Ecuador long term it may be advisable to join an organisation such as Automóvil Club del Ecuador (ANETA). ANETA is similar to Triple A in the United States and offers a variety of services such as towing in all parts of Ecuador. It claims to be available 24 hours a day and 365 days a year.

ANETA

ANETA has an office located in:

Quito at Avenida Eloy Alfaro 218 y Berlín

Tel: 593-2 250-4961, 1-800-556677

Website: http://www.aneta.org.ec

Accidents

Accidents can be a very traumatic experience in Ecuador. To add to an already stressful situation, the rules in Ecuador are prohibitive.

Pedestrians are at the mercy of drivers. You must be on your guard as a pedestrian. Vehicles will seldom stop for you, even if you have the right of way. However, once a pedestrian is hit, he suddenly has all the rights in the world. It becomes the immediate assumption of the authorities that the driver is at fault. The driver is obliged to obtain and pay for the victim's medical attention. Expect to go to jail for a while if you hit and kill a pedestrian or a passenger in your car. Your vehicle will also be moved to the transit division.

In the United States, more often than not, people will react unemotionally when involved in an accident, as the less said the better, legally. However, if you hurt someone or run someone over in Ecuador, it is important to show your concern and compunction for the injured party/parties. Not doing so might result in more strident claims from the victim or his family.

In all automobile accidents, you should contact the authorities immediately. Be sure not to move your vehicle until they arrive. A police report is mandatory if you expect your insurance company to make any payment. Make sure that you obtain names, addresses and licence plate numbers of all vehicles involved. Also request for the names of their insurance companies.

However, many Ecuadorians don't have insurance and it can be difficult to get insurance companies to pay. Be careful not to take blame for the accident unless interrogated by a police officer. Don't sign any documents unless they are from your insurance provider. Go over the police report and verify the facts. You will also want to get the policeman's name and identification number and make sure he obtains all the names of the witnesses.

Many people do a hit-and-run in Ecuador to avoid being jailed or facing the financial responsibility. I have heard of a situation several years ago when a US citizen had a drunk walk in front of his car. Before the US citizen knew it, several people had surrounded him and someone even drew out a gun. The streetwise US citizen got the drunk to the hospital, took care of the bills and contacted an attorney. No police report was made. He then left the country and worked through his attorneys until the drunk was compensated adequately.

Another possible scenario in Ecuador is the development of a mob mentality when a car hits a pedestrian. The angry crowd may actually set the car on fire. I have witnessed a crowd chasing a vehicle to set it on fire after it hit someone. Driving in Ecuador is serious business, so beware!

If you're a tourist in Ecuador you are permitted to use the driver's licence from your own country. An international driver's licence may also be used. If you're going to stay long-term in Ecuador, you will need to obtain an Ecuadorian licence. In Quito, this may be secured at the transit authority at José Herboso Calle y Avenida Occidental. The required paperwork includes details of blood type, two passport-sized photographs, passport, eye exam (taken at the transit authority listed above), and your driver's licence. You are originally granted a 30-day permit, which is extended for a total of 90 days before your permanent licence is issued. If you don't have a licence you will need to take a course which is available from the ANETA.

Cabs

Cabs are an integral part of Ecuadorian transportation for the masses. During 1999, taxicab drivers were among the hardest hit by the severe recession. With the change in dollar exchange, few drivers were able to maintain their vehicles, let alone support a family. This caused a very severe situation when there were massive strikes in Ecuador in 1999 by all transport workers.

Meters are used during daylight hours by many of the taxicabs in Quito. Rates are reasonable, thanks to the government's petrol subsidy. In Quito, however, drivers don't use meters at night or during holiday periods and I have never seen meters used in Guayaquil. It is always advisable to negotiate the price before using a cab.

If you're on a strict budget and you don't have a lot of luggage, you might try walking across the street from the airport in Quito to take a cab. It's a very short distance and you're likely to get a better price. The rate from the

airport to most parts of Quito or Guayaquil should be in the US$ 5–US$ 10 range.

In Quito, if you have a question about rates you might ask for the list of tariffs, which all drivers belonging to taxicab organisations should have. I once had a driver who tried to charge me four times the going rate for an excursion in Quito. When I told him that the tariff list stated that the going rate was US$ 3 an hour, he immediately asked me what I wanted to pay. I ended up paying US$ 10–US$ 15 for several hours of sightseeing.

For the most part, cab drivers are reliable and honest when it comes to charging. It is important to get into a marked cab, usually yellow or yellow and black. If the driver doesn't seem to understand where it is you want to go, I would be hesitant to take the cab, especially if your Spanish is not very fluent. It is unusual for a cab driver not to know a location. The exception to this would be in Quito, where the city tried to change the address system being used and most drivers still use the old system.

One rule when it comes to using a cab is to never slam the door. Even if you think you're not slamming the door, you might be by Ecuadorian standards. *(Please refer to the* Resource Guide *at the back of the book for more information.)*

Ecuadorians are survivors by nature. Because of economic stress, taxi drivers have had a rough ride. To cut down on the high cost of fuel, literally thousands of taxi drivers have converted their vehicles over to LPG fuel. And because of the high cost of conversion, many drivers have used cheap systems that are not adequately installed. Therefore, there have been a number of taxis exploding and its occupants burned.

Buses

When I first moved to Ecuador in the early 1980s, buses for travel throughout the country and within the cities were a substantial part of the transportation system. This is still the case in the early 21st century. However, being older and a bit wiser, I avoid them when possible nowadays, although they can be a wonderful way to see Ecuador. This is because bus travel in Ecuador can be very dangerous, especially at night.

Buses can get extremely crowded during holidays and the security risk on highways multiplies.

Buses have become increasingly popular with middle-to lower-middle-class Ecuadorians as air travel is not the bargain it once was. There is virtually no city or hamlet that is not connected by bus and fares are relatively inexpensive. There are different levels of service from chicken-carrying buses to ultramodern sleek buses with films and hostesses on board. Buses come in two types: city buses that offer transport within a city area and inter-provincial buses which offer services to various destinations within a province or another province.

Most cities have a least one bus hub for inter-provincial destinations, usually referred to as *terminal terestre*. Quito and Guayaquil have large terminals where you can catch a bus to virtually any destination in Ecuador. The Quito terminal is located near the Old Town at Cumandá Square. One of the better-known bus lines is Panamericana which serves long-distance routes especially to Guayaquil. Panamericana has locations at the main *terminal terestre* and

A city tour bus in Guayaquil.

another one about 15 minutes away at Colón 852 y Reina Victoria. This facility may be considered a little safer than the *terminal terrestre*. They use large comfortable buses which they call *ejecutivos*.

A number of companies advertise bus services to international destinations such as Colombia and Peru. I think it wiser to take a bus to the border, then to cross the border at immigration, then to purchase an onward ticket to either Colombia or Peru

There are also a number of buses available for intra-provincial travel in Pichincha at the Plaza La Marin which is located near Pichincha and Chile. In Guayaquil, the main bus station is located just outside the airport (cab is recommended to reach this). It is a huge facility that reminded me at first of a sports complex. It is also reminiscent of large bus stations in the United States from the 1950s or even an airport. There are literally hundreds and sometimes thousands of people at the facility in Guayaquil. All types of shops and buses depart from the second level. When using buses I will usually go to the terminal a day or two in advance and look at all of the different companies and check prices and availability. It is usually wise to purchase your ticket for such a trip at least a day before. If you're in a small town the bus hubs are not difficult to find and seldom have any offices. You simply look for a bus which has the names of the towns and cities on its route painted on its side.

Quito and Guayaquil have substantial intra-city routes which are usually called *collectivos*. In my early days in Ecuador I used them but have found them dangerous. Cabs are usually a better bet if you don't have your own vehicle.

Electric Trolley

In Quito, another form of transportation is the electric trolley, known also as *el trole*. This is an amazing piece of transportation specially designed for the inhabitants of Quito. You will have to try it for yourself to find out why!

It runs north to south of Quito and has two main terminals. In 2000, the charge was US$ 0.15. Millions of passengers have used the electric trolley and there are facilities for handicapped riders. While it is a viable transportation mode, there are problems with theft as with any public mode of transportation. Many people use the trolley to connect to buses that run to destinations beyond its reach, further north or south.

Trains

Trains, for the most part, are now non-existent in Ecuador, a stark contrast to the early 1980s. It is a real shame that there is no more need for railways now that highways have basically connected the entire country.

I was very lucky in 1981 to get to ride the train from Guayaquil to Riobamba, which is one of the most beautiful yet hair-raising train rides in the world. However, there is now no more need for this line and the authorities have not maintained it— it could have been a tremendous tourist attraction. Two years ago, it was still operating on a limited schedule. I made my early morning jaunt over to Duran after the manager of the station promised me the train would be running. However, when I arrived at 6:00 am, he said he was sorry but there was no fuel. When the El Niño rains hit, that pretty much put the lines in disrepair.

There is a limited service train at weekends that leaves in the morning from Quito to Cotopaxi, which is a very fun trip. Another line that I missed before it closed two years ago was the line from Ibarra to San Lorenzo. This was another hair-raiser from over 2,438 m (8,000 ft) in the Andes to the small town of San Lorenzo on the Pacific coast. The line shut down when a new highway was constructed. Previously, San Lorenzo was accessible either via train or by sea. Some tourist companies claim to have tours from Quito to Riobamba on that train but the service is so irregular that it would be best to inquire at some of the larger agencies, such as Metropolitan Tours, about its service times before making any plans.

It is a shame that Ecuador has not maintained its train lines, unique engineering marvels that they are. If you are a railroad buff, it is worthwhile visiting the old station in Duran (Guayaquil) where you will see nearly a hundred old cars, dating as far back as the 1930s, rusting away. This is also a great opportunity for photographers. However, many of the trains have now been scrapped for their metal.

BUDGET GUIDELINES

Ecuador is often listed as one of the least expensive places in the world. However, with the economic collapse of the late 1990s, inflation was nearly 100 per cent in the year 2000. Therefore, it is important that you have a real sense of what is needed to live in Ecuador and the costs involved.

To help you work out your costs, I have made some estimates of my own, and conducted numerous interviews. The following prices are on a per month basis. The cost of groceries has increased significantly over the last few years.

Singles	US$
Rent	200–500
Groceries	100–400
Electricity	30–70
Telephone (includes cell phone and a few long distance calls)	10–$ 50
Transportation	100–150
Dining Out	50–250
Entertainment	70–150
Maid	200
Cable	50
Internet	50

Family with Two Children	US$
Rent	400–750
Rent deposit	300–1,250
Groceries	375–700
Electricity	30–60
Telephone	10–0
Transportation	25–130
Dining Out	100–500

Family with Two Children	US$
Entertainment	50–400
Maid (may include a nanny and a gardener)	200–300
Cable	50
Internet	50
Private school (per year per child)	5,500–9,000
Refrigerator	250–700
Stove	200–600
Basic furniture	1,000–3,500
Washing machine and dryer	1,000–2,200
Automobile (used)	5,000–10,000
Automobile (new)	15,000–40,000

LEGAL ISSUES

As with any place in the world, there are legal issues to deal with. In Ecuador's paternalistic and bureaucratic society, this is especially so. There are just so many forms to be filled out, and when you think you have done them all, you find that you're missing one that some clerk hadn't even noticed before.

One thing is clear—drugs are illegal in Ecuador and the legal system is lethargic and slow. You are assumed guilty and must prove your innocence. I visited a women's prison in Quito several years ago. There were approximately seven women from the United States in custody awaiting deportation. Some of them had been there for several years and were all there thanks to drugs. Several indicated that some men they fell in love with used them and planted the drugs on them. I have received reports that drug use is on the rise, especially amongst the young. Don't feel secure about drug use just because you are around friends from Ecuador who are using illegal drugs. Your embassy has very limited means to help you in this case. I have also visited Americans in the men's prison in Guayaquil. They all agreed that it is much worse than they had imagined. If you have no money or access to money, you will be in the most squalid conditions.

Everything costs money and the guards are as corrupt as the inmates. For a price, everything is available, according to the inmates I spoke to—guns, mobile phones, etc.

If you spend any time in Ecuador you may find yourself in need of a notary. This is a very high-level position in Ecuador. Basically, any legal document filed or signed in Ecuador involves a notary. There are very few in Ecuador and usually only law firms use their services.

SOME SERIOUS MEDICAL STUFF

'After the arrival of the Spaniards,
the scanty coastal population along the coast was
decimated by the spread of diseases, such as malaria,
yaws, intestinal ills, tuberculosis, smallpox, and measles.'
—John Leddy Phelan, author of *The Kingdom of Quito* (1967).

Ecuador is generally safe but it is wise to be on your guard against any potential health risks you might face. A number

of medical issues have increased here, largely due to disorganisation in the public sector and lack of funds to fight off certain diseases. For example, in the late 1990s, malaria became a severe threat due to decreased spraying because of financial constraints on local governments. Poor sanitation and food handling have also contributed to significant health risks in the country. Most children and adults in Ecuador, for example, carry worms or parasites in their bodies.

Diseases to be Aware of
Chagas' Disease

Chagas' disease is named after the Brazilian physician Dr Carlos Chagas who first described it in 1909. It has also been called a poor man's disease. This is because the bloodsucking bugs (part of the assassin bug family) which carry the disease (*flagellate protozoan Trypanosoma cruzi*) make their homes in the crevices of walls and roofs of poor houses. The victim is infected through the faeces of the bug, which defecates into the wound whilst sucking the victim's blood. This disease can also be transmitted through infected blood transfusions.

This bug (*Triatoma megista*) is called *chinchorro* in Ecuador. It is oval in shape, brown and about 2 cm (0.78 inches) long.

It was first found in Ecuador in 1923. It usually attacks the face at night while the victim is sleeping and feeds for about 20 minutes. Many victims will rub the wound, which pushes the parasite's faeces into the blood system. The faeces may also enter via the mucous areas of the mouth and nostrils.

What to Watch Out For

Children usually manifest the most obvious symptoms, developing fever, inflammation around the bite, swelling of the lymph glands or an enlarged liver and spleen. With children, it can result in rapid death.

In two-thirds of cases, there are no symptoms, and the victim appears healthy. For the unlucky rest, if an acute infection occurs, the patient may develop heart disease 10 to 30 years later. This, sadly, usually leads to death. There is currently no effective treatment available. A serological test is required to determine infection.

Dr Angel Gustavo Guevara, a leading authority on Chagas' disease in Ecuador, usually takes three tests before giving a diagnosis. While there is no known cure, he will treat it with antiparasitic drugs such as Benznidazole. The provinces most affected are El Oro, Guayas, Manabí, Morona–Santiago, Loja, Orellana, Zamora–Chinchipe and Sucumbios.

Poor housing and a lack of insecticide are primary reasons for the spread of this disease. While rural areas are at a higher risk, the movement of large population groups to urban areas have had an impact on the spread of this disease. There is currently no preventive drug. There are some precautions one can take, however:

- Try not to sleep in huts. *Chinchorros* reside in palm-frond roofs and in the cracks of walls.
- If you are staying in older or budget hotels, be sure to check for hidden insects in mattresses, drawers and dark areas such as closets. Insect repellent may help. Spray under your bed and in cracks.
- If handling insects, be sure to use gloves.
- Mosquito nets may be helpful.

- Blood banks in both Quito and Guayaquil screen for the parasite. (However, outside of those two metropolitan areas it is doubtful that screening takes place.)

Dengue Fever

In the coastal and tropical areas of Ecuador, you will notice that the newspapers are full of articles about dengue fever. It affects thousands of people and can be fatal. A viral infection, dengue is transmitted by mosquito bites. It is endemic in rural and urban areas of Ecuador.

You will normally notice symptoms between 5 to 8 days after infection. The victim will experience sudden high fever, severe headaches, joint and muscle pain, nausea/vomitting or a rash. One may be ill for about a week. However, lasting effects of depression and fatigue may persist for weeks or longer. The Aedes female mosquito is the culprit. The malaria-carrying mosquito usually feeds at night whereas the dengue-carrying mosquito usually attacks during daylight, especially during the early morning and late afternoon.

The Perils of Stagnant Water

I remember one day in 1999, during the height of El Niño in Duran (a suburb of Guayaquil), coming across swarms of mosquitoes around a large stagnant pool of water. You will notice, especially in the coastal areas, pools of water that just sit for days and days. Many people store water in large rubbish-bin-sized receptacles for their personal use but most of the stagnant water is due to environmental conditions and poor drainage.

The dengue fever infection can be diagnosed by a blood test. It is treated with bed rest, lots of fluids and medication to reduce fever. There is no vaccine available. Avoid mosquito bites by remaining in well-screened or air-conditioned areas. Apply mosquito repellents to clothing and dress protectively to cover as much skin as possible.

Malaria

The female Anopheles mosquito carries a disease of a different sort—malaria. Malaria is a significant problem, especially in the coastal and tropical areas of Ecuador. It is referred to here as *paludismo* and affects thousands of people each year, especially during the rainy season of November through to May. Poor and rural communities are the most badly hit.

In 1999, the government reported that the number of malaria cases had nearly doubled, from 40,000 in 1998 to 80,000 cases in 1999. The destruction of sanitary infrastructure in much of the rural areas during the 1998 El Niño contributed heavily to the surge in cases. A combination of lack of funds for cleaning areas where water collected and lack of fumigating areas contributed to as many as 3,500 new cases of malaria a week.

The goal of the female Anopheles mosquito, like the rest of her kind, is to feed on your blood. Blood provides her the protein that she needs for her eggs. The malaria-carrying mosquito does not hum or linger like an uninfected mosquito. You will not feel it when she bites you. This femme fatale usually attacks during the evening hours and especially between midnight and dawn. She uses a stylet, which contains a duct connected to the salivary glands. Before the feeding she injects her saliva which works like an anaesthetic so you don't feel the bite.

The symptoms of malaria usually develop about 8 days or up to several months after infection. Early diagnosis is paramount to successful treatment. Delay may lead to coma, fluids in the lungs, kidney failure or death. Symptoms are flu-like and include pain in the joints, fever, chills, cough, diarrhoea, nausea, profuse sweating and shivering and even convulsions and coma. If you have any of these problems after being in an infected area you should consult a physician. Be sure you tell him/her the areas you have visited. A serological test should be conducted to rule out the presence of malaria. Assuming it is only flu may prove dangerous.

The provinces of Esmeraldas, Manabí, Guayas and Los Ríos are the most susceptible to malaria. Most cities in the Sierra including Cuenca, Quito and most of the highlands are risk-free. However, there are sections of provinces in the Sierra just below 1,524 m (5,000 ft) where malaria exists. This group includes Cotopaxi, El Oro, Manabí, Morona–Santiago, Napo (now Orellana), Pastaza, Pichincha and Zamora. The Galápagos Islands are risk-free.

How to prevent malaria:

- With your medical professional or local health officials discuss an appropriate anti-malarial regimen. Make sure you do this at least six weeks before your planned departure.
- Window and door screens are mandatory. Make sure they are as tight-fitting as possible and that the mesh is as small as possible. Air-conditioning will minimise the threat of mosquitoes.
- Mosquito nets should be used. Twenty-six holes per square inch are recommended. However, the tighter the mesh the hotter you will be. You might also wish to treat the mesh and your clothes with permethrin insecticide. Permethrin is often sold as Duranon and Permanone.
- Wear long-sleeved shirts and long trousers once the sun goes down. Avoid using cologne or perfume.
- Repellent is mandatory and OFF is a good brand to use. Apply repellent to exposed areas of the skin as well as thin clothes. Avoid the eyes and mouth. DEET, the active ingredient, keeps the mosquitoes away but doesn't kill them. Repellents may damage plastic items such as sunglasses so use them sparingly.
- It is probably wise not to use repellents with greater than 30 per cent DEET on the skin. This is especially true with children and for pregnant women or nursing mothers.
- The brand Raid (with pyrethrin) will kill mosquitoes by attacking their nervous centre. You can spray nets, baseboards, walls, corners, furniture, behind pictures and inside closets. Spraying under sinks is also a good idea.

Most local health agencies can advise what medication to take. Malaria is chloroquine-resistant in Ecuador. Larium is often recommended by health professionals. Larium, in many cases, is well endured without major side effects. However, this author highly recommends that you discuss the use and possible side affects of Larium or any other anti-malarial drug with a doctor. It is recommended that individuals should not take Larium if they suffer from heart disease, epilepsy, liver, kidney or psychiatric disorders. Children under 13.6 kg (30 lbs) , pregnant women and pilots are also advised to refrain from using Larium.

Take Note
Several years ago, during El Niño, I began a regimen of medication with Larium. The side effects were horrendous and took a substantial time to diminish. The drug cannot be taken long-term. Be sure to discuss the other medical options with your health care professional.

In October 2000, the Centre for Disease Control reported that Malarone had been approved in the United States as an anti-malarial drug. It has also received good results as a preventive drug and does not have the possible psychological effects noted with Larium.

High Altitude Sickness

If you choose to live or travel in the Andes area of Ecuador, the high altitude may affect you. Between 2,438 m and 4,267 m (8,000 ft and 14,000 ft) is considered high altitude. Above 4,267 m to 5,486 m (14,000 ft to 18,000 ft) is considered very high altitude. Anything above this is called 'extreme altitude'.

Local slang for high altitude sickness is *soroche*. Caused by the lack of oxygen, some simple planning may help you deal with the change of altitude. I remember my first trip to Quito after living at sea level for most of my life. It took me some time to make the adjustment. I had a splitting headache in the temple region and felt fatigued. Insomnia, vomitting, rapid breathing and increased urination may also occur.

It is hard to anticipate who will adjust well to high altitude. The afflicted may be disoriented especially if fatigued, and may need help to descend. Those who appear quite healthy may react poorly. Children seem to adapt easier to high altitudes. The solution is the same for all: descend, descend

descend! Other cures include rest, deep breathing, adequate fluid intake and mild painkillers such as aspirin or Tylenol to alleviate headaches. There has been at least one study, which shows Ginko biloba, a plant native to China, may lessen the symptoms of high altitude sickness.

The worst form of high altitude sickness is high altitude cerebral edema (HACE). Symptoms include blurred vision, disorientation, dizziness, changes in levels of consciousness, seizures and paralysis. Loosen any restrictive clothing and the afflicted person might have to be carried down. Medical attention may be necessary; give oxygen if available.

Ecuadorians suggest '*chupa el caramello*' ('suck on candy') to treat *soroche*. Many believe that a small amount of sugar via a piece of candy or a sweet helps alleviate high-altitude sickness. Some Ecuadorians also believe that a part of sugar cane, called *panela*, also helps. Several doctors have told me that this does assist the sufferer. *Panela* is very sweet and you only need to put a small piece in your mouth.

Medical Tips

Precautionary measures include gradual ascent, avoiding high fat and high protein diets and drinking lots of water. An excellent online resource is http://www.high-altitude-medicine.com.

Cholera

This can be a real problem in Ecuador. Cholera is a very strong intestinal bacterial infection common in areas where sanitation is not very good. Symptoms can be mild but one in 20 people have it bad: profuse watery diarrhoea, vomitting and leg cramps. Rapid loss of fluids leads to dehydration and shock and can result in death within hours.

Infection is usually acquired by consuming contaminated food or water which contains the vomit or faeces of infected individuals. Some lettuce and other food products in Ecuador are fertilised with human faeces. Raw or uncooked shellfish are also potentially dangerous.

The illness may be treated with antibiotics and lots of fluids. The vaccine that was available in the United States

(Wyeth-Ayerst) is no longer being sold. Cholera can be treated by replacing fluids and salts lost through diarrhoea. Patients can be treated with oral rehydration solution—a prepackaged mixture of sugar and salts, mixed with water and drunk in large amounts. Severe cases require intravenous fluid replacement. With prompt rehydration, fewer than one per cent of cholera patients die. Antibiotics shorten the course and diminish the severity of the illness, but they are not as important as rehydration.

Cholera: Preventative Measures

To prevent contracting cholera:

- Drink only water that you have boiled or treated with chlorine or iodine. Other safe beverages include tea and coffee made with boiled water and carbonated, bottled beverages with no ice.
- Eat only foods that have been thoroughly cooked and are still hot or fruit that you have peeled yourself.
- Be careful when eating undercooked or raw fish or shellfish, such as *ceviche.*
- Make sure all vegetables are cooked and avoid salads.
- Avoid food and beverages from street vendors.
- Do not bring perishable seafood back home.

Water Conditions

Water in Ecuador should be considered contaminated. Tap water is called *agua potable.* Bottled water is a big business in Ecuador and there are numerous brands available in markets. Bottled water is delivered to homes and businesses. You should also be cautious about ice, which can be contaminated. There are establishments that provide ice which has been made out of purified water. It is better to be cautious and not use ice in most cases. You also need to be careful about the water you use to brush your teeth. I always use bottled water plus a peroxide mixture. I also use mouthwash with alcohol. Be careful not to lay your toothbrush down on the sink without it being protected by a plastic cap.

Intestinal Problems

It is very likely that you will suffer some type of intestinal ills while in Ecuador. Expect that you are going to have a change in your bowel movements, which may be caused by dietary change. I have learned, after some 20 years here, that simple precautions in what you eat and drink may save you several days of discomfort and make all the difference to your visit.

Things to Avoid

- Food from street vendors
- Nonpasteurised milk. There are numerous brands of powdered milk available.
- Fruit you haven't peeled or washed yourself
- Raw fish
- Raw vegetables
- Salad: most salads in restaurants have not be cleaned properly.

Imodium A-D anti-diarrheal caplets may be beneficial if your stools get loose. Pepto-Bismol caplets have been shown to help protect one from getting traveller's diarrhoea by taking two tablets a day. Some side effects are black stools and constipation. It is also related to aspirin, which can cause problems if you're allergic to aspirin or taking anti-coagulants. Drinking plenty of fluids is also important to help prevent dehydration.

If you have a sudden burst of watery diarrhoea you may have contracted a form of bacterial diarrhoea. Other indicators may be a combination of nausea, cramps, fevers and blood in the stools. Three drugs often used to treat bacterial diarrhoea are Ciprofloxacin, Norfloxacin and Ofloxacin. Remember these are antibiotics and have side effects, some quite serious. You should always consult a physician before using them.

Onchocerciasis

Onchocerciasis is also known as 'river blindness'. Originally found in Africa, it was brought to South and Central America through the slave trade. It is debilitating but not fatal. It is transmitted by the bite of the female black fly, which is found near rapidly flowing rivers and streams. Found especially in the province of Esmeraldas, it is referred to in Ecuador as *onco*.

Juan Carlos Vieira from the Hospital Vozandes has been involved in a programme to eliminate this illness. There is still a small area in the Cayapas River region where *onco* exists. He only knows of one case where a foreigner has contracted this illness. Short-term visitors are usually at low risk. However, no vaccine is available. Avoid black fly habitats and protect yourself against insect bites.

Yellow Fever

Yet another mosquito-transmitted disease, yellow fever is a viral disease transmitted between humans. Vaccinations are given by most government agencies and are usually good for ten years or more.

Protective measures, as mentioned above with malaria, should also work here. Symptoms of yellow fever may be confused with malaria, typhoid or leptospirosis. There are two phases of the disease. The first phase is characterised by fever, muscle pain, headache, shivering, nausea/vomitting and sometimes a slow pulse. After three or four days, patients appear to recover. Fifteen per cent enter a 'toxic phase' within 24 hours. Fever is followed by jaundice, abdominal pain and vomitting. The mouth, nose, eyes and/or stomach may bleed, and blood may then appear in the vomit and faeces. The kidneys deteriorate and these patients die within ten to 14 days. It is believed by some sources that the death rate may be as high as 60 per cent for those not vaccinated. So please get vaccinated!

Leishmaniasis

This is a parasitic illness that threatens hundreds of millions of people in 88 countries around the world. Luckily, only 10 per cent of the world's cases occur in the Americas, Asia, the Middle East and Africa. It is transmitted by bites from sand flies in the tropical and subtropical areas of Ecuador and was first reported in 1920. It is referred to as *sarna brava* or *charra brava* and can manifest in a cutaneous skin form (97 per cent of cases in Ecuador) or visceral or internal form (3 per cent of cases in Ecuador) which can damage internal organs.

The symptoms of cutaneous infection may appear several weeks to several months after infection. The exposed areas of the body are the most susceptible. The visceral form normally develops after several months but may lay dormant for years after infection.

The markers for *cutaneous leishmaniasis* are sores, which may be open or closed and sometimes scab over. These sores may sometimes be painful. *Visceral leishmaniasis* will give rise to fever and loss of weight. The spleen and liver may also be enlarged and blood counts low. If not treated, death may result.

Cultures and blood tests are usually taken to determine if *leishmaniasis* has been contracted. In Ecuador, Glucantine is usually administered in over 21 injections. This is one of the drugs in Ecuador where there may be counterfeit brands. The illness can cause severe disfiguring and may return after many years, even after the patient thinks it has gone. If you return to your home country and notice some symptoms, consult a doctor and inform him where you have been.

Most cases transpire in rural areas and can be found in the following provinces: Azuay, Bolívar, Cañar, Chimborazo, Zamora–Chinchipe, Cotopaxi, El Oro, Guayas, Esmeraldas, Imbabura, Loja, Manabí, Morona–Santiago, Orellana, Pastaza and Zamora.

Sand Flies

Humid forests are a favourite habitat for sand flies, which can be found on trunks of trees and are usually not active during the day. However, they can bite during the day even though the most dangerous time is from dusk until dawn. They are very small and quiet and it only takes one fly to infect you.

Leptospirosis

The number of cases of *leptospirosis*, a bacterial disease, increased significantly during the El Niño rains in 1998. Humans and animals become infected after being exposed to water, which contains urine from animals carrying the bacteria.

Food or soil containing urine of infected animals may also transmit this disease.

The illness sets in between two days and four weeks. The victim will normally have a sudden onset of fever with flu-like symptoms. Some people recover for a time but become ill again later with even more severe symptoms, including liver and kidney failure or meningitis.

There is no indication that it travels from human to human. It can be treated with antibiotics such as *doxycycline* or penicillin, which should be taken early on. To avoid this illness, stay away from bodies of water or soil which may have been contaminated. Even swimming or wading in such water puts you at risk.

Sunburn

The sun is quite strong in Ecuador. Sunburn and damage to the skin is a strong possibility. Whether in the highlands or the coastal areas, it is important to protect yourself with sunscreen and appropriate clothing. Sunscreen with an SPF of 30 or higher should provide adequate protection.

Rabies

In many parts of Ecuador, dogs are often left unsecured and may bite humans. This is especially true in rural areas where dogs are also used to guard homes and shrimp farms. Bats and other wild animals may present a risk of rabies. Vaccination prior to your visit to Ecuador is advisable. There is often a shortage of rabies medication throughout the country.

Typhoid

Typhoid fever is an infection, which infects the victim with the bacteria *Salmonella typhi*. It can be deadly. Contaminated food or water usually transmits this illness. Symptoms may reveal themselves between 10 and 14 days after exposure. These include a sustained fever as high as 39°C to 40°C (103°F to 104°F), flu-like body aches, loss of appetite, weakness in the body, a persistent dull headache and a rash of flat, rose-coloured spots. There may also be a fever as well as a rash with pink spots on the chest and abdomen.

Typhoid is treatable with antibiotics such as *ampicillin*, *trimethoprim-sulfamethoxazole* and *ciprofloxacin*. If left untreated, 20 per cent of people will die from resulting complications.

There are oral and injectable vaccines available, which last about five and three years, respectively. The vaccines have shown to be effective in 50 per cent to 80 per cent of recipients. It may be better for pregnant women, as people with HIV, to refrain from taking the vaccination as well.

Tuberculosis

This is an increasing problem in the last few years. A number of drugs to combat tuberculosis (TB) have proven to have a high rate of resistance in Ecuador. The World Health Organisation reports there are over 100 cases for every 100,000 people in Ecuador and place the country in the highest risk category.

TB is spread by germs in the air which can be spread to others by sneezing, shouting, laughing or coughing. If you are near an infected person you can breathe the germs into your lungs. Hopefully your immune system will fight off the bacteria and keep you from getting sick. Those most at risk are those with weak immune systems, such as babies and young children. The germs usually attack the lungs, but can also spread to your brain, kidneys and spine. A TB skin test will show if you have been exposed to the bacteria.

Sexually Transmitted Diseases

Sexually transmitted diseases (STD) are a real part of Ecuadorian society, as in many countries. Many myths still abound as to who may have a sexually transmitted disease. For example, many Ecuadorians still believe that HIV is the disease of someone who is gay and that someone from an upper-class position in society cannot be infected. Condom-use is more prevalent than in years past but social values still disdain their use, for the most part. Reasons for lack of use may in part be due to the country being largely Roman Catholic. However, there are other social implications. Women still feel that the use of a condom implies that they are a prostitute or that, as a male, you are questioning their morals, implying that they may be promiscuous. Male and female prostitutes are quite active in the major cities and the incidence of STDs, including AIDS, is increasing among them.

Condoms are not manufactured in Ecuador but are available in pharmacies. They may be of a poor quality, however, and you might consider bringing your own. The use of condoms minimises but does not eliminate the chance of contracting an STD.

Hepatitis A

It is strongly advised to obtain a vaccination for Hepatitis A. This is transmitted through contaminated food and water. The risk is higher in rural areas as well as restaurants with poor sanitation. A suggested counter measure is an immune globulin injection.

Pharmacies

Pharmacies may dispense medications in Ecuador without written prescriptions from physicians. While this may sound advantageous, it may be dangerous to your health. It is recommended that you see a doctor if you fall ill in order to get a correct diagnosis and appropriate drug therapy. Many of the people working in smaller or rural pharmacies may not have been professionally trained. Also, there may be a stronger possibility of picking up counterfeit drugs in smaller or lesser known pharmacies. This has been a problem in Ecuador, especially with rarer prescription drugs. Also, there are many drugs available in Ecuador which have not been approved by other government authorities. Of the non-aspirin pain relievers, Advil seems to be the most popular. In large cities, pharmacies often have a rotating schedule to remain open for 24 hours and this is announced in most newspapers. However, a number of pharmacies are open 24 hours all year round. FYBECA is the largest chain in the country and appears to be operated professionally. It offers a discount card for a small charge. *(Please refer to the* Resource Guide *at the back of the book for more information.)*

Medical Services

Finding medical providers in Ecuador can be a challenge, especially if you don't speak Spanish. In the Resource Guide at the back of the book, I have provided the names of some doctors who speak English or who have had some training in the United States. I have also included the names of the better reputed and more modern hospitals. One doctor advised me that anyone travelling to Ecuador should obtain insurance covering transportation costs home in the event of a medical emergency.

Also, you should check if your insurance will cover medical or emergency services while in Ecuador. For extra security, I advise you to obtain a policy that will cover travelling to, or residing in, Ecuador. If you're working for a foreign company or government, such a service may already be covered. Medical expenses in Ecuador are, for the most part, much cheaper than in developed countries.

In 1998, my son received a very severe insect bite at the weekend. I took him to the emergency room at Clinica Kennedy in Guayaquil. There was no formal procedure in

place. The woman at the check-in counter said that they wouldn't look at my insurance card unless the bill was over US$ 100, which was my deductible. We walked into the emergency room and were quickly attended to. Luckily it was not severe but required the doctor to drain the bite. We were there for about two hours and the total bill came to US$ 30. *(The hospitals listed in the* Resource Guide *accept major credit cards and local cheques.)*

If you are a resident, Humana is highly recommended in Ecuador for health insurance.

Email: humana@humana.med.ec

Medical Kit

It is advisable, if living or travelling in Ecuador, to maintain your own kit of medical supplies. Here is a list of necessary items to start you off:

- Antibiotic ointment
- Anti-diarrhoea tablets
- Anti-fungal cream
- Antihistamine

- Antiseptic
- Aspirin or paracetamol
- Band-Aids (wide assortment of sizes)
- Calamine lotion or aloe vera
- Cold and flu tablets, throat lozenges and nasal decongestant
- Gauze pads
- Hand sanitiser
- Insect repellent
- Lip balm
- Medication which might not be available in Ecuador
- Mosquito net
- Scissors
- Syringe kit
- Snake bite kit
- Sterile kit
- Sunscreen
- Thermometer
- Tweezers
- Water purification tablets or iodine

You might also consider bringing a copy of your medical records, especially if you have some serious medical conditions. I would also recommend having that translated into Spanish.

Immunisation

While no shots are required for travel to Ecuador, you should consult your physician four to six weeks before your trip to discuss health precautions you may wish to take, such as:

- Booster doses for tetanus-diphtheria and measles
- Hepatitis A or immune globulin
- Malaria tablets, if you are travelling to the jungle or the mainland coast
- Rabies vaccinations, if you are travelling to farms in the Andean highlands
- Typhoid, particularly if you are visiting developing areas in this region
- Yellow fever vaccination, if you are travelling to the jungle

> **Further Information**
>
> For more specific information, a good website to visit is the Centre of Disease Control at http://www.cdc.gov/travel/.

FINAL NOTES

If you are currently taking prescription medication, make sure you bring enough to last during your trip. All medication must be clearly labelled, and bring along a copy of the prescription for the medicine. Medicine should be divided into two different pieces of luggage so that if one piece is lost or stolen your medicine is still available.

If you are carrying syringes for medical reasons, a medical certificate of explanation should also be carried.

Due to the high elevations, if you are flying in or out of Quito, if you have high blood pressure or a heart condition, you should check with your doctor about any medical precautions before flying. You might prefer to fly in and out of the port city of Guayaquil rather than Quito.

Please take out a medical-insurance policy, no matter how healthy you are. This is necessary in case of an accident, even if you don't fall sick.

CUY, CALDOS AND CHICHAS

CHAPTER 6

'I like hamburgers for a change.
But to eat, to really eat, soup of cow's foot.'
—Maria Cristina Carrillo in *El Sabor de la Tradición* (1996)

WHILE THERE ARE SIGNIFICANT DIVISIONS in Ecuador's society, food is one thing Ecuadorians can agree on. Ecuadorian food is truly unique. Learning the cuisine and consuming the food of Ecuador will be one of your most interesting and enjoyable experiences in Ecuador. Many of the dishes are a result of the blending of indigenous and Spanish culture over the centuries, although ingredients and preparation methods have remained much the same over time. While numerous North American fast-food franchises have moved into Ecuador (often a great relief to those who are suffering from culture shock), Ecuadorians take great pride in their local cuisine. It's a strong part of their national identity. I have often heard Ecuadorians conversing on the return flight home about how they can't wait to get back to eat.

BREAKFAST
A typical Ecuadorian breakfast may include *pancitos* (small rolls) with butter, jam and coffee. Ecuadorian coffee is often very thick and not very good but is considered a delicacy because it is expensive. Most Ecuadorians drink instant coffee. Hot chocolate is often part of the breakfast along with various juices. Larger breakfasts are not the norm.

LUNCH
Throughout Ecuador, most people will eat three meals a day. Ecuadorian dishes are often referred to as *platos tipicos*

and can be generally described as hearty fare, substantial and very starchy. Lunch or *almuerzo* is the main meal of the day. This is probably one of the most enjoyable moments in the day for an Ecuadorian. It may last up to two hours and people often eat at a very slow and leisurely pace. Even when you see Ecuadorians eating in a fast-food restaurant, they may often stay for an hour or more, especially if they are enjoying the company of friends. However, modern living has shortened this tradition. Familiar fast-food friends can all be found here: Taco Bell, Pizza Hut, McDonalds, Baskin Robbins and Burger King, but they are considered expensive by local standards.

Another aspect to eating in Ecuador that has changed, especially among the lower and some of the middle class, is that many families find it cheaper to eat out than to purchase groceries because the cost of groceries has increased substantially. However, don't assume they are eating out at upscale restaurants. Many of these establishments would be classified as almost the 'soup kitchen' variety.

Many restaurants offer an *almuerzo*, which is often a set meal at a fixed price. It is usually very inexpensive and a

way of life for Ecuadorians. Usually the restaurant will have a signboard reading '*Almuerzo*' and listing the menu. You can be sure that an *almuerzo* will begin with soup. Soups are so popular in Ecuador you would think that someone named Campbell started a soup company there.

Generally, there are two styles of soup in Ecuador, known as *locro* and *caldo*. *Locros* are usually a heavy type of soup, which will always contain potato and often pig skin. There is a children's riddle which goes, 'How do you say soup of potato (*soupa de papas*) without pursing your lips?' The answer: 'Just say *locro*!' *Caldos* are more like a broth. Soup of cow's foot is called *caldo de patas*. This broth contains chunks of cow's feet, knuckles and ingredients such as *mote* (corn). This is really tasty and considered a delicacy by locals.

The main lunch dish is referred to as *seco*. In most cases, this will include a portion of meat (beef, chicken, fish or lamb) with potatoes or another vegetable. Rice is often the staple but if you are eating in the Sierra, you may find more potatoes on the plate than rice. Many working Ecuadorians buy their lunch from small stands and have them packed in small pastel-coloured plastic containers.

DINNER
Dinner may also be called *merienda* and is often a smaller version of *almuerzo*. For working-class families, leftovers from lunch are often used for dinner.

TYPES OF FOOD
This is a sampling of the food you will find during your stay in Ecuador:

Achiote
This is a seed also referred to *anato*. It provides much of the colour and flavour found in Ecuadorian food. The Colorado Indians use this for colouring their hair.

- *Ají* sauce: There is not a table in a home or restaurant in Ecuador that doesn't have some type of *ají* sauce. This is made of red peppers and is not as hot as hot sauces from Mexico. *Ají* sauce from the Costa is usually made with onion, cilantro and tomato. The *ají* sauce in the Sierra is usually thicker, with tomato as the primary ingredient. You may see *ají* sauce served either in a bottle or in a cup on the table in a home or restaurant. *Ají* sauce is available at grocery shops. The chillies on the coast of Ecuador are often pickled with carrots, onions and cauliflower in *encurtido* (banana vinegar). Chillies are also used in a sauce named *agrio* combined with local *chicha* (corn beer), cloves, spices and chives to be served with roasted *hornado* (pig).

- Avocado: Throughout history, avocado thas been heralded as an aphrodisiac. There are festivals that revolve around the avocado and the avocado tree is revered by many of the indigenous population. Avocado is often prepared in a blender and made into a fluffy sauce, served with boiled potatoes or on plantain chips. It is also often cut in half and peeled or scooped out of its shell and added to soup.

- Beans: An integral part of Ecuador's cuisine, corn and beans are often consumed together in the Andes. They are legendary for giving a satisfied fill. You can still see many of these combinations in the Indian markets. Michelle O Fried, a nutritionist in Ecuador, refers to some of these combinations as ancient fast food. Many beans are sold

Another fresh fish catch for the Chanduy markets.

in huge baskets. They are often combined with scallions and cilantro and served on pieces of newspaper. Some combinations include corn on the cob with fava beans and corn nuts with lupini beans.

- *Bebidas gaseosas*: These are soft drinks, often served without ice. International brands such as Coca-Cola, Sprite and Fanta are available. Some Ecuadorians believe that you can catch a cold by drinking this with ice.
- *Ceviche*: Another important national dish, this is usually raw or cooked fish or shellfish (including shrimp, lobster, mussels or oysters) served in a cold soup with small pieces of popcorn on top. It has been said to cure a hangover. Cilantro, lemon and onions are often part of the recipe. Exercise caution, however, as improperly prepared *ceviche*, especially *de concha*, may become a primary vector for cholera and other nasty bacterial infection.
- *Cuáker*: This is a drink made with Quaker Oats and is fantastic for breakfast. To be served very cold.
- *Cuy*: One of the most exotic foods of Ecuador, and deemed by some as one of the most disgusting foods in the world, is the legendary guinea pig (known as *cuy* in South America). The *cuy* is an important part of the Andean diet and culture. It was probably domesticated in about 5,000 BC and also plays a role in medicinal and religious

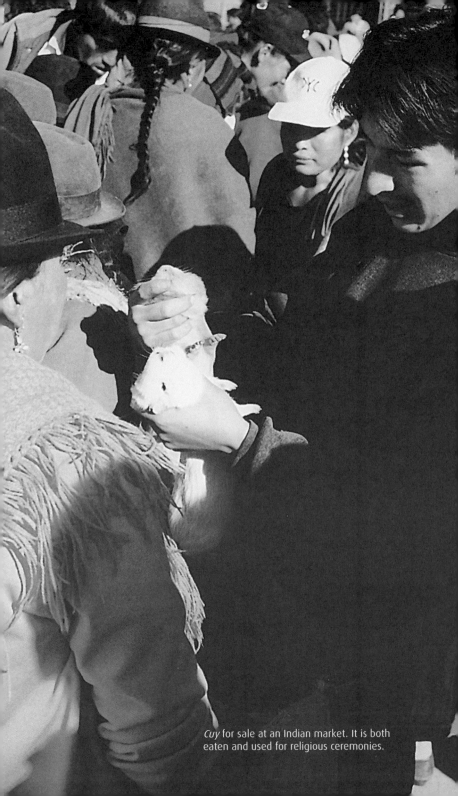

Cuy for sale at an Indian market. It is both eaten and used for religious ceremonies.

practices. Two religious or festival purposes of the *cuy* include the *ashanga* (whole roasted pork with *cuy* and rabbit) and *castillo* (a large, tall pole from which *cuy*, beer, fruit and potatoes are hung). In Latacunga, there is a huge basket of food that is offered to the city. A roasted pig is placed into a basket and roasted *cuy* tied to the pig. The basket is carried down the street as onlookers applaud. Roasted *cuy* is often sold on a stick by street hawkers.

- *Empanadas de Morocho*: This is a white flour-fried tart filled with meat and rice.
- *Empanadas de Verde*: These are plantains not yet ripe, stuffed with cheese and fried.
- *Fritada*: Fried pork. Typical rural dish cooked in a large brass pan.
- Fruits: Ecuador is a paradise for fruit. You are in for a treat if you have only tasted papaya or mangos in the United States. When I first sampled these fruits in Ecuador, I couldn't believe how large, sweet and juicy they were. One my favourites is *mora* (blackberry), but you need to make sure it's well-boiled when prepared. It is also a great flavouring in some local ice cream. Other fruits include *babaco, maracuya* (passion fruit), *granadilla* (a local and

Numerous tropical varieties of ice cream can be found in Ecuador.

IBARRA
ALTITUD 2210 mts.
A QUITO 173.1 Kmts.
A
SAN LORENZO 200 Kmts.

FERROCARRILES
ECUATORIANOS
ESTACION IBARRA

Vegetables for sale at the old railroad station at Ibarra

sweeter type of passion fruit), *guanábana* and *ovos*. You can also enjoy a large variety of delicious *jugos* (fruit juices), such as *naranjilla* (similar to a bitter-sweet orange) and *tamarillo* (tree tomato).

- *Guineo*: Banana
- *Hornado*: A mouth-watering rural dish, this is a slow-roasted, whole pig. Ecuador's main dish for festivities, it is usually served with a sour/vinegary sauce and a choice of garnishes.
- *Humitas*: This is a wonderful combination of sweet corn off the husk, mixed with grated cheese, eggs and butter. The grated cheese and corn are wrapped in a corn husk and then steamed.
- *Fanesca*: This is a special soup which is made at Easter and is a combination of 12 different types of beans and cod. There always seem to be numerous articles published during Easter about the cost of *La Fanesca* and the role it plays in Ecuadorian culture.
- *Llapingachos*: This is a very famous dish from the Sierra. It is a fried pancake made up mashed potato and cheese. It is sometimes served with a fried egg on top.
- *Locro*: A chowder made with potatoes, fresh cheese and avocado.
- *Chugchucaras*: These are pastries, made of pork fat, potatoes, lettuce, tomatoes and avocado. This dish is usually served with a fried egg and originates from Latacunga.
- Meat and fowl: Meat was not a significant part of the indigenous diet before the arrival of the Spanish. Meat is often eaten at weekends and is sold in open-air markets. Much of the beef in Ecuador is raised without hormones and is not aged. Hormones are used in the cultivation of chickens. Pork is the dominant meat used in the Sierra, which is also a corn-growing region.

For large family-gatherings, fattened pigs are sacrificed and most of the parts are consumed. Often a neighbourhood party may share in a pig. While this may be traditionally done in the country, I have also experienced these types of gatherings in the suburbs of Guayaquil. The pig is actually killed in front of onlookers and the party begins.

- *Morocho*: This is made from cracked kernels of white corn cooked in water with cinnamon and milk. It is similar to a hot cereal and is delicious.
- *Patacones*: This is plantain which has been cut up and fried in lard. It is then smashed and refried and is often served with *fritada*, looking like a pancake and cut into one-inch slices.
- *Plátanos*: These are plantains and look like bananas. They may be fried or broiled. Wonderful, especially when served with cream on top. They play a big role in the culture along the coast and are seen by many as a staple.
- Potatoes: Without a doubt, potatoes are a mainstay in the Ecuadorian diet. They are indigenous to the highlands and come in numerous sizes and colours. In the highlands, potatoes may be eaten several times a day and are a central source of vitamin C. Potatoes are boiled and served with a chilli sauce, cheese, peanuts or pumpkin seeds. (The pre-colonial inhabitants prepared potatoes in much the same way.)

  You will find no end to the varieties of potatoes. *Molo* is a style of mashed potato that is served with ground peanuts. The *oca* potato has an unpleasant bitter taste. It becomes

Sandwich stall on 9 de Octubre in Guayaquil.

sweet after it has been exposed to the sun. The pale *oca*, which is similar to a bent icicle, is often used as a dessert, cooked with raw cane sugar. It is also used for making pastry and jelly. The stems are good fodder for cattle and horses. *Mellocos* or butter potatoes don't require sunning. They have a crisp texture and are often consumed after harvesting. *Camote* or sweet potatoes are harvested at lower altitudes. This is a true delicacy.

- Onions: Red onions are the predominant onions in Ecuadorian fare. They may be prepared by soaking them in sugar water along with lemon and salt.
- *Quinua*: This is a unique high-protein grain, indigenous to the Andes. Early indigenous groups found that the *quinua* whole grain could replace a lack of milk or meat in the diet. It has a sweet nutty taste and is high in fibre.
- *Refrito*: This is a combination of ingredients placed into all soups and stews. It is often a mix of red onion, green pepper, tomato, *achiote* and salt. Garlic may also be included. These items are often chopped up.
- *Sanduche Mixto* (sandwich): When I feel like a fairly light lunch, I go for the *sanduche mixto* comprising white cheese (melted) with ham on toasted bread.
- *Tamales*: There are numerous types of *tamales* in Ecuador. They are often made of dough and wrapped in a leaf and then steamed. They are usually stuffed with beef, chicken or pork.

Food Preparation Words

a la brasa	grilled
a la plancha	from the griddle with oil or butter
al vapor	steamed
apanado	batter-fried/breaded
brosterizado	deep-fried
encocado	stewed in coconut milk
frito	pan-fried
hornado	roasted
reventado	deep-fried

REGIONAL SPECIALITIES

Many of the regions of Ecuador are known for specific foods. An entire book could be written on the specialities of each province. The Manabí province is known by many Ecuadorians to have the best food. You will see numerous restaurants throughout Ecuador using the name Manabí in the hope of attracting customers. Not to steal the thunder from professional cookbooks on local cuisine, here is a humble sampling of certain specialities along the coast near Guayaquil.

Pascuales

Many of the working-class inhabitants of Guayaquil would travel here at weekends to eat and party. It is known for *fritada,* pig's intestines, beer and dancing. (Saturdays and Sundays are often referred to *dias feriados* or 'holiday days'.)

Juan Gomez Rendon (Progreso)

This tiny village outside of Guayaquil is a famous stopover for tourists from Guayaquil on their way to or from Salinas and Playas, where there are famous beaches. Many of the people there make their living from the tourist trade. There are numerous stalls or vendors called *ambulantes* who specialise in meat served on a stick, corn-on-the-cob with white cheese (wrapped in paper) and *rellenas* (small potato pies). *Fritadas* are also very popular along with *bebidas gaseosas*.

Zapotal

This is another small village on the way to Salinas which has a number of small restaurants along the highway that specialise in lamb or *seco de chivo*. My favourite place in Zapotal is the Chivo Erotico. *Chivo* means goat and, when I order, I like to jokingly ask to meet the erotic goat but the waitress will always just give me a dirty look.

Water

For the wellbeing of your intestines, drink only bottled or boiled water. These are easily available throughout the country, are of good quality (some are tapped from Ecuadorian springs) and can come distilled or sparkling. Remember that tap water is used in ice, so, in restaurants, request your beverages '*sin hielo*' ('without ice').

Alcohol

Alcoholic beverages have a long history in Ecuador. I find Ecuadorian beer among the finest in the world. I was not a big fan of beer but this changed when I consumed my first Pilsener. It is excellent. Several years ago Budweiser made a campaign into Ecuador but on my last trip, I saw very little Budweiser being served. Instead, the Ecuadorian beers remain more popular, with the favourite brands being Club and Pilsener. There are a number of other local beers such as Chop, Club Café, Club Verde and Biela, but they are not as widely consumed. (Biela is not popular because it is regarded by many as contributing to the downfall of a major bank in Ecuador, its owner accused of using funds from the bank to finance the beer manufacturing.)

Brandies in Ecuador are derived from fruit flavours and not grapes. They are about 30 per cent in alcoholic content.

Some people combine them with fruit juices. One of the local brands is Brandy Naranja.

Chicha was the first alcoholic beverage in Ecuador and used by the Indians. It is made from fermented *cassava* (yuca) in the Oriente, corn in the Sierra and sometimes rice in the Costa. When sugar is introduced, *aguardiente* ('fire-water'), also known as *puro* or *caña*, is produced. This is quite potent, with most Ecuadorian brands containing about 50 per cent alcoholic content. There are a number of Ecuadorian brands of *aguardiente* including Caña Manabita, Cristal, Frontera, Licor del Mono o Guagua Montado and Zhumir.

A few tribes in the Oriente sometimes aid the fermentation process with human saliva, *chicha*-makers chewing the ingredients and spitting them back into the pot to brew. *Chicha* made this way may give you Hepatitis B!

Anisados are alcoholic beverages flavoured with aniseed. Their alcoholic content is about 35 per cent and they have a sweet flavour. At first, it may not seem like a powerful drink but it sneaks up on you. National brands include Anisado Patito and Tropico. *Seco* almost tastes like vodka. It is very inexpensive. The best known brands are Patito Seco and Seco Montero.

SUPERMARKETS AND SHOPPING

One area of retailing which has greatly improved in the last several years is shopping at supermarkets. There are basically two chains in Ecuador—Mi Comisariato and Supermaxi. They each have more than 20 outlets locally and own warehouses in Miami. With nearly 100 supermarkets in Ecuador, there are also a number of hypermarkets which have opened and are similar to Wal-Mart type shops. The availability of US products in these supermarkets, popular a few years ago, has diminished, due, in part, to Ecuador's financial difficulties in the late 1990s. However, there has been a slight rebound and about US$ 29 million-worth of ready-made foods are currently exported to Ecuador from the United States. Pharmacy chains have also played a role in food distribution in terms of snacks, beverages and other supplies for the home.

Megamaxi is part of the Supermaxi chain, both owned by the Wright family.

In my opinion, Supermaxi is as well-run and clean as any large food chain in the United States. The quality of many local products has also improved. Supermaxi offers a discount card. One area that could be improved are the bakeries where the bread sits out and gets hard very fast. Most of the supermarkets are usually open until 8:00 pm.

Much of the shopping in Ecuador is still conducted in open-air markets where many go daily to get the freshest food. However, more and more shopping is done on a once-a-week basis. Two unique products are organic lettuce under the name Andean Organics and a purifier for fruits, vegetables and lettuce called Vitalin. There are several other brands of purifiers but Vitalin doesn't leave an aftertaste. On a trip back from Ecuador, I met a Mormon missionary who was a health official in his local department of health. He indicated he did not feel commercial products were sufficient to clean food products completely and he uses a mixture of Clorox bleach to rid his food of contaminates.

Here is a short primer: To clean food, he used 1 tsp of Clorox to 2 gallons of water. (You may also use ½ teaspoon to 1 gallon of water.) Into the bucket of mixture, place your fresh fruits and vegetables. Thin-skinned fruits and leafy vegetables require soaking for 15 minutes. Thick-skinned vegetables require 25 minutes.

- Then, remove your vegetables and fruit from the Clorox and bathe them in purified water for another 15 minutes. Your food then should be clean for storage and consumption.

BAKERIES

Panaderias (bakeries) are great here! You can get hot, freshly baked rolls for US$ 0.10–US$ 0.25 and a tasty *empanada* (pastry) for $1. Bakeries often have fresh products. Many families will purchase their bread on a daily basis from a local bakery. A number of bakeries will be owned by or have employees from Ambato, which is known to have the best bakers in the country.

Street Stands

The meat from street stands may not be thoroughly cooked, so be careful. Even if there is a respectable crowd around the stand, I have learned from bitter experience that the food may still be contaminated.

FOOD ETIQUETTE

Here are a few tips:

- Smoking is allowed in most restaurants. Someone might ask before they light up but it would be rude to say 'No' or to ask someone not to smoke. Some hotels have adopted a policy of non-smoking rooms.
- Ecuadorians dine out later than is customary in the United States but earlier than other places in Latin America, such as Argentina. A dinner time of between 7:00 pm and 9:00 pm is quite common in most parts of Ecuador. Some people complete a long evening out by going to a hotel coffee shop.
- In most cases, there is a service charge on the bill. However, it is common to give a tip of between 5 per cent and 10 per cent, especially if the service was good.
- In Quito, it is appropriate to dress up when dining in a 'nice' restaurant.
- If you are driving to a restaurant, you should park in front of the eatery so that someone can watch your vehicle.

When you leave, you should pay these 'car guardians' a small amount (usually under a dollar). Valet parking is not common here. Make sure the person watching your car looks as if he regularly works the area.

If you are residing in one area of Ecuador for an extended period of time, it is a good idea to find a restaurant you like and frequent on a regular basis. You will find that, by being a good customer and tipper, the level of service you receive will be greatly increased.

HEALTH TIPS

- Allow yourself a bit of time to adjust to the local cuisine. It would be wise to consume small amounts of food at the beginning and make sure it is well cooked. Always be cautious with uncooked vegetables and lettuce.
- Do not assume that water is safe to consume unless it is bottled. Ask for bottled water, either *agua pura* or *agua con gas*. Make sure you see the bottle opened in front of you if you are in a restaurant. Many Ecuadorians will often clean the top of the bottle with a napkin. Waters and colas are often consumed with straws. The safest way is to boil the water yourself. Once the water cools, it can be recontaminated, so keep purified water in a covered container. Iodine tablets are an alternative when boiling is impractical.
- The classic food-poisoning culprits are salads and fruit. Fruit that must be peeled first, such as bananas, pineapples and oranges, are usually safer. Organic lettuce should still be purified and this is more popular now in many foreigner or gringo-orientated restaurants.

RESTAURANT GUIDE

Ecuador's restaurants range from the very basic to some of the most elegant in Latin America. In the province of Pichincha (where Quito is), there are more than 1,800 restaurants. Guayas province (where Guayaquil is) has more than 1,500. Here is a guide to some of my favourite restaurants in Ecuador, with an emphasis on Quito. One of my favourite delicatessens is El Español, which can be found in several of the shopping centres both in Guayaquil and Quito. One of these branches in Quito is in the tourist area at Juan León Mera 863. This is also one of the few restaurants in Ecuador where the employees wear gloves whilst handling the food.

Cuenca

- La Herradura. Avenida Remigio Crespo in the Zona Rosa. This restaurant specialises in Argentinean dishes and sausages. A full dinner costs about US$ 7.50 and US$ 10 without alcohol. It is decorated in a traditional Argentinean motif.
- Rancho Chileno is located at Avenida España near the airport. It has been operating for 30 years and specialises in unique meat dishes from Chile. Meals go for between US$ 3 and US$ 5.
- Tuto Tutto L' Originale. Remigio Crespo 453 y Miguel Díaz. A small, casual Italian restaurant. Meals average US$ 6.

Guayaquil

- Cielito Lindo. Jorge Pérez Concha 623 between Ficus and Monjas. Located in the Urdesa neighbourhood. Excellent traditional Mexican dishes combined with a good family atmosphere.
- Hotel Continental Coffee Shop. Chile y 10 de Agosto. This is a great place to eat at any hour of the day and is one of my favourites after a long night of dancing. It is still very popular and has been around for years. Can be very crowded.
- La Fontenella. P Icaza y Pedro Carbo. An excellent choice for lunch when downtown and not visited by many foreigners (currently being remodelled)
- La Parrillada del ñato. Avenida Victor Emilio Estrada 1219 y Laureles in Urdesa. This has been one of the best steak houses in Guayaquil for a number of years. The main dining rooms are not air-conditioned but there is always a breeze floating through this establishment. I have eaten here a number of times year after year. It should not be missed.

- Red Crab. Victor Emilio Estrada y Laureles 1208 in Urdesa. A casual and excellent source for all types of seafood dishes.
- Morocho. Portete y 39. This is a small stand in Guayaquil. When I used to live near Portete Street, I loved to go down on a Sunday night to get a small bowl of *morocho*. There are many such stands along Portete.
- Hotel Oro Verde. 9 de Octubre y García Moreno. 'El Patio' coffee shop has been vastly improved. The Oro Verde is now under the management of Argentineans. They have Argentinean beef shipped in just for the hotel.
- Gran Hotel Guayaquil. Boyaca entre Clemente Ballen y 10 de Agosto. For 25 years, I have eaten in the coffee shop and always found it to be reliable with both Ecuadorian and American dishes. A number of the employees have worked there for 20 years or more.

Quito
Ecuadorian
- La Querencia. Eloy Alfaro 2530 y Catalina Aldaz
- La Choza. Av. 12 de Octubre 24-551 y Cordero
- Las Menestras. This restaurant had no address when I last ate there. It is about three doors down from the hotel Mansion de Angel, which is located at Wilson E5-29 y Juan León Mera. It serves excellent Ecuadorian cuisine and seats 25 people at the most. On paydays, which are the 1st and about the 15th of the month, this place is packed at lunchtime.

International
- La Viña. Isabel La Catolica y Cordero
- Avalon. Orellana 155 y 12 de Octubre. Expensive by Ecuadorian standards.
- La Terraza del Tartaro. Veintimilla 1106 y Amazons. Great view with good quality meat and fish.
- Pims. Isabel la Catolica y Cordero. Has a great atmosphere and is very popular.
- Clancy's. Salazar y Valldolid. Great food and is very cosy.
- La Escondida. General Roca N33-29 y Bosmediano. It features Californian cusine.

Café

- La Boca del Lobo. Calama 284 y Reina Victoria. It is very good but only open at night.
- Le Grain Café. Baquedano y Juan León Mera. It is rated well and has a very inexpensive lunch.
- El Cafecito. Cordero y Reina Victoria.

Italian

- Il Risotto Pinto 209 y Diego de Almagro. It is closed on Mondays.
- Pavorotii. Av 12 de Octubre 1955 y Cordero. This is a high-end restaurant.
- El Arcate. Baquedano 358 y Juan León Mera. It serves excellent pizza and great pasta. It is closed on Mondays.
- La Briciola. 1255 y Luis Cordero.

Sushi

- Sake. Paul River N30-166. This is an upscale sushi establishment.

Mexican

Mero Mero. Suiza 343 y República de El Salvador. This is not Tex Mex or Sonoran-style.

French

- El Rincon de Francia. Roca 779 y 9 de Octubre. This establishment was founded nearly 25 years ago and is still excellent. It has a very elegant setting but is not extravagant. It is clearly upscale as many businessmen and famous personalities dine here. The service is exceptional.

Fish and Seafood

- Mare Nostrum. Foch y Tamayo.
- Las Redes. Amazonas y Veintimilla.

Meat

- San Telmo. Portugal 570 y 6 de Diciembre.

ENTERTAINING

'Dutch Treat' ('Going Dutch') or 'plan americano' is not often practised in Ecuador. The general rule is that, if you invite, you pay. This is especially true if you're inviting a woman somewhere. If someone invites you to a dinner or meal, the custom is that you should invite and host that person in the future. Invitations are expected to be reciprocated. One social event in which Ecuadorians use 'Dutch Treat' is called *hacer una baca* or literally to 'make a cow'. This is often a group event when friends or acquaintances decide to go out to eat as a group and each person pays for his own meal.

TABLE MANNERS

Good table manners involve keeping your hands above the table. This is difficult for many people from the United States since we have been taught to keep our hands below the table. Many locals will eat with their arms lightly resting on the table and use the right hand to eat. European norms apply here.

When eating as a guest, you should leave a little on your plate at the end of the meal. If you finish everything, the host will assume you didn't have enough to eat and will offer you more. This is also true with drinking. I once visited a local's home and the hostess was serving beer in her finest glassware. It was a hot afternoon and I had no trouble drinking a full glass. I noticed as soon as it was emptied she would fill it back up, and I thought that, as a good guest, I should finish that as well. I soon found myself slightly intoxicated and realised that it is good manners for locals to fill up their guest's empty glass. So, if you've quenched your thirst, leave some of the beverage in the glass or announce politely that you've had enough.

A drinking tradition among the different classes is that, at informal parties, people will often break into small groups. There will usually be a bottle of beer or another beverage and one glass. People will take turns filling up that glass for each other. The person offered the glass will consume the whole glass. While not very hygienic, this is a very strong bonding practice among many Ecuadorians.

When it comes to food, another aspect concerning manners among many Ecuadorians is when one of the family members goes out to eat. He or she will usually bring something back for the people in the house. This is a practice I still find hard to understand. If my Ecuadorian wife and I go out for a meal, she insists that we get something for the kids, even if they are out somewhere else or have eaten at home. When I am in Ecuador and staying with my mother-in-law, I will bring something back, even if it isn't very much. I usually receive a nice smile, especially if it is pizza from an American fast-food restaurant, which she doesn't eat at very often.

ENJOYING ECUADOR

CHAPTER 7

'The ancient churches and monasteries,
around which the people of Quito have grouped
their lives in village-like cells, are treasure houses
of the greatest collection of Spanish colonial sculpture,
painting, and architecture in all the world.'
—Albert B Franklin

CULTURE

Although yet to be recognised on an international stage, Ecuador has a deep, varied and unique culture.

Regional expression has also been a key factor in the arts since pre-Colombian times. Most arts prior to the Incan conquest developed along the coast. When the Spaniards entered the picture, there was significant and long-lasting change, revolving primarily around Quito. There have also been significant contributions from all parts of Ecuador, with

the materials available in particular areas influencing the development of the arts regionally.

Literature

Ecuador is not generally thought of as a country of readers, in comparison with Argentina or Colombia. When asked why Ecuadorians don't appear to read very much, an employee of a large bookshop in Quito once exclaimed, "*Todos son brutos.*" ("They are all ignorant.") He went on to explain that a significant reason was that books, especially imported ones, were expensive in Ecuador and that few people had the financial means to buy them. In my experience, Ecuador has a very small publishing infrastructure and market for books. Many writers here self-publish or try to sell books on consignment through bookshops, of which there are only a few.

There are a number of bookshops that use different marketing approaches to develop readers, such as small reading groups for children. I once published a small journal on Latin America and presented my journal to an agent to seek advertisers. She told me that many of the advertisers were not interested in the journal because it had too few pictures. Ecuadorians seem to be more attracted to publications that are filled with graphics and pictures. Another disincentive to read is the increasing popularity of television and video games.

The public also does not seem to hold much regard for writers. Most professional writers in Ecuador have to work other jobs to make a living. Despite the tremendous financial pressure, there are a significant number of books published in Ecuador in small press runs with modest sales.

If you read Spanish, you will have a much wider range of books to choose from. My favourite bookshop in Guayaquil has several tables and shelves of books on Ecuador but this stack doesn't appear to grow very often. Books published in Ecuador are mostly paperbacks, and the hardbacks don't appear to be of good quality. There don't appear to be many second-hand bookshops here. However, there is one dealer in Quito who stocks about 8,000 volumes (of mostly paperbacks) in English and a smattering of other languages. This is Confederate Books, located at Calama 410 y Juan León Mera; Tel: (02) 2527-890.

Juan Montalvo (1832–1889)

Juan Montalvo was one of the greatest liberal thinkers in Ecuador's history. He was one of the biggest enemies of Gabríel García Moreno and after García Moreno was assassinated, Montálvo claimed that it was his pen that killed him. He wrote a number of anti-dictatorship essays and published an anti-establishment newspaper called 'El Cosmopolita' in 1866. He believed that metaphors describing beauty would influence one to live a more virtuous life. Many of his works were written in exile, such as *Siete Tratados* (*Seven Treatises*, 1882) and *Capítulos Que se le Olvidaron a Cervantes* ('Chapters that were Omitted by Cervantes', 1895).

Juan León Mera (1832–1894)

Juan León Mera wrote the national anthem and was a large collector of many Ecuadorian legends. He wrote a Romantic novel, *Cumandá, o, un drama entre salvajes* (*Cumandá, or, 'A Drama Among Savages'*) set in the Ecuadorian jungle. Based on the oppression of Ecuadorian Indians and published in 1871, it has been called the first major Ecuadorian novel.

Another famous work of his was *Ojeada Histórico-Crítica sobre la Poesía Ecuatoriana* ('A Critical History of Ecuadorian Poetry'), published in 1868. Ecuador, to him, was divided along Catholic, mestizo and Hispanic lines. He was politically conservative but believed that the country should be united by one language and one religion. Some have said, however, that he didn't regard Indians as equals. In fact, *Cumandá* is about the doomed relationship between the son of a wealthy landowner and a young Indian woman. My personal view is that it actually demonstrates his allegiance with the upper classes and the Catholic Church, rather than the Indians.

Jorge Carrera Andrade (1903–1978)

Born in Quito and a diplomat for Ecuador, Carrera Andrade also wrote much about the Indians. His first book of poems,

Estanque Inefable ('Indescribable Pond'), was published before he left university and was a voice for the destitute Indians, calling for social change. A number of his works have been translated into English including *Secret Country* (1946) and *Selected Poems* (1972). One of his earliest works, *The Perfect Life* was written when he was 18 years old and translated into French, German, Russian and English. This was about a return to the common speech, favouring simplicity over ornamentation.

Jorge Icaza Coronel (1906–1978)

Jorge Icaza Coronel, also from Quito, was a civil servant and the director of the national library. A novelist and playwright, he has been called the father of indigenous literature in Ecuador. Icaza received international recognition for *Huasipungo: The Villagers* (1934), which has been translated into many languages. This book depicts, with brutal realism, the exploitation of the Indians at the hands of their estate landowner masters.

Demetrio Aguilera Malta (1909–1981)

Demetrio Aguilera Malta was one of Ecuador's most prolific and talented novelists. He was a self-educated writer, film director and painter. His first novel, *Don Goyo*, was originally published in 1933 and translated into English in 1980. It is about a patriarch living along the mangrove forests of the Pacific coast near Guayaquil. *Don Goyo* is a social protest against the whites who were attempting to cut down the mangrove forests. In reality, that has sadly already happened along most of the coast. A number of his other novels have also been translated into English, such as *Seven Serpents and Seven Moons* (1979) and *Manuela, La Caballeresa del Sol: A Novel* (1967), bringing Ecuadorian literature to outside markets.

José Joaquín Olmedo (1780–1847)

A poet, statesman and spokesman for the liberation movement, Olmedo's odes commemorating South America's independence from Spain inspired a generation of Romantic poets and patriots. His most famous ode, *La victoria de Junín: Canto a Bolívar* ('The Victory at Junín: Song to Bolívar'), was dedicated to Bolívar's military successes. Romantic in imagery and Neoclassical in form, it is considered by many the finest heroic poem to come out of Spanish America.

Luis Alfredo Martinez (1869–1909)

Writer, painter and politician, Luis Alfredo Martinez's best work is a novel named *A La Costa* ('To the Coast'), written in 1904. This Realist novel portrays a man moving to the Costa from the Sierra for a new life. It is probably one of the best works that objectively describes the regional differences between the Costa and Sierra. An experiment with the Ecuadorian novel, it is also subtitled *Costumbres Ecuatorianas* ('Ecuador Customs'). Luis Martinez's paintings are prized possessions of some of the most important museums in Ecuador.

Gonzalo Zaldumbide (1883–1965)

Writing in the early part of the 20th century, Zaldumbide exuded a spirit of optimism in his writings. He was heavily influenced by Uruguayan Jose Enrique Rodó. One of his best known works was an essay entitled 'De Ariel'. Zaldumbide also published a Realist book entitled *Egloga Trágica* ('Tragic Eclogue'), in which he describes the emotion felt upon returning home after a long time abroad.

Jenny Estrada

Jenny Estrada began her career as a reporter in 1968, opening the way for feminine participation in the newspaper *El Universo*. Here, she consolidated her career through political editorials, interviews with a human perspective and analytical articles. She has built a multifaceted career in public service and as a writer-historian. Her book, *Del Tiempo de la Yapa*, a chronicle first published in 1994, is about life and customs in Guayaquil, where she was born. She has penned over 10 books and written a remarkable history of the coastal cowboys called *El Montubio*. She continues her writings and is completing a broad study of the oil industry in Ecuador. She

Jenny Estrada, renowned historian and author of numerous books about Ecuador.

believes that Ecuador still lacks well-defined objectives, which hinders its progress. She feels that Ecuador would return to economic prosperity if it returned to its agricultural roots. In 1998, she won first prize in the Concurso de Reportajes (News Articles Competition) sponsored by Oderbrecht, a construction firm.

Michelle O Fried

Michelle O Fried is a good example of a self-published author in Ecuador who has supported herself from consulting and through her writing. Coming to Ecuador as an outsider when she was a young adult, Ms Fried has a Masters degree in nutrition from Teachers College, Columbia University. She has an intense desire to learn about Ecuador's culture and is very active in the development of both health and food studies. She has been associated for many years with the Centro Ecuatoriano para la Promoción y Acción de la Mujer (CEPAM) in developing numerous food and health programmes throughout the country. She self-published *Comidas del Ecuador: Recetas Tradicionales para Gente de Hoy* ('Foods of Ecuador: Traditional Recipes for Today') in Spanish in 1986. This remains a bestseller in Ecuador. Available only in Spanish, it can be purchased in the United States through Kitchen Arts Center (http://www.kitchenartscenter.com) or the South American Explorers' Club. Look out for her latest book, *Food of the Andes*!

Rodolfo Perez Pimentel

The leading biographer in Ecuador is undoubtedly Rodolfo Perez Pimentel. He is a trained attorney and practises as a notary. He has published several books about Ecuador including *El Ecuador Profundo—mito, Historica, Leyenda, Recuerdos, Anecdotas, y tradiciones del país* ('Deep Ecuador— Myths, Histories, Legends, Memories, Anecdotes, and Traditions of the Country') in several volumes in 1988. His largest work is a seventeen-volume series (*Diccionario Biographia Del Ecuador*) featuring over 1,600 biographies on Ecuadorians and people who have influenced Ecuador. He is planning to complete up to 22 volumes. He loves his country deeply and the goal of this immense work is to 'inform

Rodolfo Perez Pimentel, author of numerous books on the history of Ecuador. He has published nearly 20 volumes of biographical information about Ecuadorians and foreigners who have had an impact on Ecuador.

and develop a national identity'. To attain this goal, he has now published all his works online for free at http://www.ecuadorprofundo.com.

Modern Poets

Ecuador has a number of fine poets who sensitively depict the soul of Ecuadorians. A very good anthology was published in 1997 called *Between the Silence of Voices—An Anthology of Contemporary Ecuadorian Women Poets*. Editors Alicia Cabiedes-Fink and Ted Maier did a fine job of editing and translating poems from nine women from different levels of Ecuadorian society and different geographical regions.

A prime example of such artistry is Ruth Bazante Chiriboga, born in 1942, who is one of Ecuador's preeminent poets. Editors Alicia Cabiedes-Fink and Ted Maier describe Ruth Bazante as 'a poet of immense power and depth'. They make note of her explorations into the soul and the eroticism in relationships. Bazante has published two major collections of her work in *Frito dentro, gritofuera* (1987) and *Manual de las cicatrices* (1988).

I Am (Estoy) is one of my favourite poems by Bazante:
Estoy inundada de usted
hojarasca de sol,
humus febril.

Estoy con usted
en mis irrealidades
taladrándome;
con usted sobre mi piel
susurrándome
Sueño armonioso
sol adentro en mis ríos.

I am flooded by you
dead leaves of sun,
feverish humus.

I am with you
in my unreality

boring into me;
with you
on top of me whispering.

Perfect dreams in chords
sun inside of rivers.

Painting

Painting runs deep in the soul of Ecuadorians. It is an expression of their spirit.

Quito School of Art

Ecuador's greatest gifts to the world in the realm of architecture, sculpture and painting can be found in Quito. Quito is probably the only place in the world where you can find 30 churches within an area of eight blocks. With the conquistadors came Dominicans, Franciscans, Augustinians and priests from other orders. Perhaps it became some sort of competition between the orders to venerate their respective saints with yet another church, cloister or religious monument! You will be mesmerised by the colonial ambience of the Old Town area. For a nearly 300-year period, Quito was the centre of art production in Latin America. In the mid-1550s, Friar Ricke, a Franciscan, began the seedlings of what would become known as the Quito School of Art. Approximately 100 churches, monasteries, convents and plazas were built during the colonial period in Quito.

The Catholic Church required a consistent supply of sculptures and paintings for its aggressive campaign of building churches. Ricke began the Colegio San Andrés in 1553 with limited materials. The indigenous population was taught numerous skills. When you explore the ancient streets of Quito, you will notice that much of the architecture and adornments were constructed by Indians. The Catholic Church also used the arts as a form of assimilating the Indians into the Catholic religion.

Magnificent wood carvings and sculptures were produced during this period. The great Quito sculptors were, in chronological order, Bernardo de Legarda, with his winged virgins; Pampite, whose crucified Christs invite meditation; and Manuel Chili 'Caspicara', the artistic innovator. Many of Caspicara's sculptures can be found in The Cathedral and the Monastery of San Francisco. The movement and realism of Caspicara's paintings and sculptures reveal much technical and aesthetic quality, attention to detail and anatomical study.

The great Quito artists were Dominican Friar Pedro Bedon, who painted in the last quarter of the 16th century; Miguel de Santiago with his series of paintings dedicated to the lives of the saints; and Nicolas de Goribar, Miguel de Santiago's disciple.

20th Century Art

Contemporary Ecuadorian artists include Manuel Rendon, considered one of the best Expressionists in the world; Enrique Tabara, famous for pioneering the use of pre-Colombian motifs and images; and the Indigenous Expressionists Oswaldo Guayasamín, Eduardo Kingman, Guerrero and Paredes.

Eduardo Kingman

Eduardo Kingman was the other major social Realism painter in the 20th century. Indian and Andean environments dominated his work. He was born in 1913 to an Ecuadorian mother and an American medical doctor from Connecticut. Ecuador's best known muralist, he was heavily influenced by the Mexican muralist Diego Rivera.

Much of his work depicts the forced labour of the Indians and their suffering. With heart-rending and realistic scenes, this figurative artist revealed an interest in the human being and his internal drama. Dynamic forces are created with strong, sharp and heavy lines used to draw the human figures. You will also notice a great deal of emphasis on the hands of the subjects. Kingman spent much of his career in the promotion and education of art both in Ecuador and in the United States.

Oswaldo Guayasamín

Guayasamín was born in 1919, the eldest in a family of 10 children, to an Indian father and a mestizo mother. Born to create, he began selling his sketches to tourists at the age of 10. His social Realist work revolves around indigenous themes as well as mestizo and black issues.

Guayasamín's first major exhibition was in 1942, after which he studied under the master muralist Orozco from Mexico. Oswaldo Guayasamín has exhibited his work internationally, including at the Museum of Modern Art in Paris. The Age of Ire, a series of 250 paintings, deserves special mention. He was also an active social protester and supporter of the Cuban revolution. Oswaldo Guayasamín passed away in 1999. You may obtain more information about this outstanding artist at http://www.guayasmin.com

Tigua Paintings

As if landing in Brigadoon (you know, that small misty town that only awakens one day in a hundred years), there is a small village of Quichua-speaking Indians, called Tigua–Chimbacucho. The village is located some 54 km (33.5 miles) west of Latacunga on the Latacunga–Quevedo road. The Tigua are gaining recognition for their charming paintings.

In the 1970s, Julio Toaquiza, a poor farmer in Tigua, was encouraged by a dealer of art in Quito to apply his talents to a sheepskin canvas, rather than on drums and masks, as his ancestors used to do. Painted with chicken feathers on sheephide stretched on decorated wooden frames, his paintings depict daily rural life in the Andean mountains. These colourful paintings were originally done with enamel paints but increasingly with oils and acrylics. They depict many facets of festivals such as Corpus Christi and numerous indigenous rituals. Tigua paintings have been showcased around the world and have produced significant income for many residents of this small hamlet. Toaquiza now trains his children and others in his village to carry on his art.

Crafts

Ecuador possesses some of the most talented craftsmen in the world. I first realised this when I observed the number of seamstresses in Guayaquil and the immense patience they had with their work. When you see the beautiful colours

Tigua artist and his wife selling their paintings in the Sierra.

of the clothes that are worn by many of the indigenous population, you will appreciate the tremendous creativity of Ecuadorians.

Andean cultures boast a long tradition of weaving abilities, far surpassing those of Europe in the same era. The best Andean weavers could produce material with as many as 500 two-ply woollen wefts per inch, compared to just 100 in Europe before the Industrial Revolution. Weaving is a speciality for Ecuador and it is basically a family affair where weaving can vary dramatically from one township to another. The initiated can distinguish which region the weavers are from by the colours of the weave.

Materials such as cotton, llama and alpaca wool were traditionally used to create complicated brocades, tapestries, double cloth and gauze. With the arrival of the Spanish in the mid-1500s, new resources were introduced, such as silk embroidery yarns.

The Otavalo Indians north of Quito have successfully taken Ecuador's weavings to the world. While many indigenous groups in Ecuador remain in poverty, the Otavalos have been very successful in business and done much to keep their culture intact. There are certain areas of Ecuador where men predominantly do the weaving. Many of the woven products have become highly specialised. For example, *alpargatas* is a specialised shoe (which looks like a tennis shoe) that was introduced by the Spanish and is widely made in Imbabura.

Zuleta Embroidery

Ecuadorians seem to enjoy working with their hands and are good at intricate, detailed and tedious work.

The women from the Zuleta area have long been known for their embroidery, even before the Spanish arrived. Their original work showed a fondness for vibrant colours and was used mainly to decorate women's clothing. The Zuleta designs have not changed much over time and have become cultural icons, treasured as part of their unique heritage.

In the 1940s, Zuleta embroidery would have its big international break. It was then that former president, Galo

Plaza Lasso, and his wife, Doña Rosario, were inspired to start a workshop for women in Zuleta. This was the beginning of the Zuleta Embroidery Workshop. This workshop produced items for sale, promoting this craft further afield, giving the women an opportunity to supplement their income. The workshop in Zuleta proved a huge success, producing numerous articles such as exquisitely embroidered tablecloths, blouses, placemats and towels, whilst significantly increasing family incomes. Some women have actually started their own independent workshops.

The Zuleta Embroidery Workshop is now managed by the Galo Plaza Lasso Foundation, benefitting over a hundred families in the Zuleta region. Their items are sold all over Ecuador. They have a small shop in Quito at Veintemilla y 6 de Diciembre named Bordados Zuleta. You will be amazed at the attention to detail and the wonderful colours on show. You can find out more about the Zuleta Embroidery Workshop at http://www.ecuadorexplorer.com.

Panama Hats

What did Teddy Theodore Roosevelt, Al Capone and Winston Churchill have in common? The answer: the Panama hat.

Before I first visited Ecuador, I knew that Panama hats were really from Ecuador and not Panama. But when I asked locals where I could purchase a Panama hat, they looked confused. That was because the Panama hat here is called *sombrero de paja toquilla* (which means 'hat of *toquilla* straw') or *jipijapa* (named after the town in the Manabí province where this hat was said to be have been first produced). So how did the name Panama hat come about? One story goes that US President Teddy Roosevelt visited the Panama Canal, and saw and liked the hat, a favourite amongst the canal workers. He returned to the States wearing one and the newspapers coined the name, which has stuck ever since. Other people say that it was at Panama that these hats were first shipped to every corner of the world, hence the name. No one knows for sure. What we do know is that they were originally manufactured in Jipijapa and Montecristi, both villages in the Manabí province on the coast of Ecuador. The Panama hat industry has now spread to Cuenca, Azuay and Cañar, and each hat can sell for US$ 400, US$ 2,000 or even US$ 3,000!

In the early 1900s, the hat became a fashion statement around the world. Ironically, it was viewed as a lower-class accessory at home. During the 1940s, these hats were a significant income-producer for Ecuador but this is less so over the last few decades.

The craft was passed down from family to family, but there are fewer craftsmen weaving the hats now. They make other products which sell better, such as baskets. One of the features I like about the hats sold here are the balsa wood boxes that come with them, marked 'Ecuador' on the outside. The family that manufactures these handsome boxes has been doing so for over 50 years and work out of their home in Montecristi. There seems to be a drop in the general quality and price of the Panama hats manufactured nowadays, and they are mainly sold to visiting tourists.

Tagua Ivory
Small coastal villages such as Curía San José, La Entrada and El Saldo cultivate palm trees that yield the *tagua* nut. Growing

Panama hat-making—meticulous work, but in good company.

from the seed *Phytelephas*, these trees can grow up to 20–30 ft (6–9 m). Needing about 10 years to reach full maturity, the nut is cut and polished and is remarkably similar to the ivory of animals, such as elephants, whales and walruses, which are hunted and killed in different parts of the world. Ecuador is the world's largest producers of this nut, used to make some of the finest buttons in the clothing industry from the late 1800s until World War II. Some of these buttons were even used on United States Army uniforms. The synthetics industry hurt this demand, however, and *tagua* ivory is now mainly used to make dice, dominoes, chess pieces, religious figurines, miniatures and jewellery for tourists.

Masapan

I will never forget the first time I saw *masapan* ornaments, better known as bread dough dolls. It is a craft unique to Ecuador whereby bread dough figures are painted to produce fabulously beautiful and decorative dolls. They are very popular at Christmas and are said to have originated from a small suburb north of Quito called Calderón. Regardless of their origin, they make lovely decorations and excellent

Masapan ornament maker at work in Calderón.

gifts. I've noticed that the quality of the craftsmanship has improved dramatically over the last 25 years and *masapan* ornaments are now exported all over the world.

Music

It has been said that the haunting melodies from the Andes can make an Irishman cry, given the latter's love for moving melancholic songs. When you hear the unique instruments and mournful vocals of Andean music, I think you might agree that it is difficult to remain unmoved. Quechuan poet June Ireland describes it better:

Andean Music
Andean music
is a waterfall
encountered in a quiet forest:
playful and powerful at the same time.
Andean music
is the voice of the wind
that howls among the high rocks:
nothing but air, but nevertheless very strong.
Andean music
is the flight of the condor
making a design against the sky:
it appears to be art, but gives sustenance.

Antikuna ñauraytaki (Quechuan version)
Antikuna ñauraytaki
Chay paqcha tarikun
juk sunqoyakusqa sacha sachapi:
puqllayqachaq ye atipaq chay kikinmantapacha.
Antikuna ñauraytaki
wairaqpa kunkanmi
pura sayaq qaqakunapi autiq:
wairallamanta paqarisqa zhaqa ancha kallpayuq.
Antikuna ñauraytaki
kunturpa phawayninmi
janaqpachapi qellqayta ruwan:
ricukun allin ruwasqa, zhaqa kausaytataq qon.

The roots of Ecuadorian music have been traced back to pre-Colombian times. The earliest music was said to have been influenced by the 'whistling echo' or 'singing' of water vapour from heated water, and by the sounds made by animals such as the toad and ape! The earliest musical instruments are believed to have been conches and flutes. Different types of flutes were commonly used, such as *quenas, samponas* and *chirimías* (large, transverse flutes made of bamboo).

Indigenous music was traditionally played during religious rituals, courting activities and life cycle ceremonies, to alleviate the tedium of work, and for recreational purposes. A group of African people inhabit the Chota Valley of the northern plains. The combination of African, Andean and European cultures produced a very particular kind of music, that has become popular even outside the region. It is called *bomba*, after the drum that creates the rhythmic base for this music and its dances.

The blacks living in the province of Esmeraldas, located on the northern coast of the Pacific Ocean, have retained much of their African cultural heritage. The *marimba*, also an essential part of the old traditions, was imported directly from Africa. Their vocal music includes a large repertory of music for funerals and celebrations of life that are sung with a heavy percussion accompaniment. Petita Palma considered a national treasure of culture in Ecuador is the grand heiress of *marimba* in Ecuador. She continues the tradition of the *marimba* through her group, Grupo Folclório de Petita Palma.

When the Spaniards arrived, the Catholic Church forbade the playing of native music and many of the traditional instruments were destroyed. The Church dominated the music scene during colonial times and ordained Spanish priests were appointed as choir directors. The harp was introduced.

However, by the end of the 16th century, professional musicians began to take the place of priests. Many of these musicians were creoles or mestizos who introduced new traditions or fused old and new ones. The three most distinctive styles of music to develop in Ecuador are the *sanjuanito*, the *pasillo* and the *pasacalle*. Catholic and indigenous religious traditions influenced the hypnotic, trance-like and melancholic rhythms of the *sanjuanito*, played during the Festival of San Juan in the Otavalo region every June, to coincide with the summer solstice. The *pasillo* is slower in rhythm and originates from the classic Viennese waltz. It originates from folk culture and has a slow rhythm, poetic and sentimental texts and melancholic melodies. The *pasacalle* has its roots in the Spanish *pasodoble* and is written in 2/4 time. Other popular rhythms in Ecuadorian music are the *albazos, tonadas, danzantes* and *carnavales*. Many originate from the music of the indigenous population. Another popular Andean rhythm and dance is the *huayno*, which sounds very happy and originates from Andean rural villages. A sadder tune is the *yaraví*, which became popular during the 18th century and is accompanied by guitars.

Ecuador boasts thousands of professional musicians who are, sadly, unheard of outside the country. In the 1960s, the wonderful musician Guido Garay brought the folk music of the *montubio* (slang for 'ignorant farm worker') to the rest of the country. Mr Garay, now in his 80s, was a trained accountant but gave that up in 1940 to become an opera singer. In 1965, a friend of his found an old book written in 1929 about the folklore and music of the Montubios. He was encouraged to put on a show, although he thought that no one would like the music, especially the upper classes. Mr Garay was pleasantly surprised by the warm reception, and for 10 years performed more than 300 shows with his troupe all over Ecuador to standing-room-only crowds. But when one of the founding members died, Mr Garay stopped the shows. He sold his rights to the recording studios and now lives quietly in a second-floor apartment in Guayaquil. Much of his music is performed by school children during festivals along the coast and used in folklore celebrations.

There are some current success stories with musicians who ply their trade. Jazmin is a sensual and attractive singer under the direction of her husband and manager who has carved out a niche in the music industry. Affectionately known as

The talented but humble Guido Garay.

'The Queen of Tecnocumbia', she has released a number of CDs over the last 10 years. However, she is clear to point out that, in Ecuador, it is very difficult to survive off CD sales because of the amount of piracy. Fortunately, she is in large demand in Ecuador, playing live at a number of fiestas. She has broadened her career now as the host of her own late afternoon television show on Ecuavisa Internacional which broadcasts all over the world.

Segundo Rosero was born in the small hamlet of Pimampiro. At a very young age, he started to play the guitar and played throughout the Sierra. The most famous singer from Ecuador, Julio Jarmaillo, heavily influenced his style. While he is best known for performing the *pasillo*, he adjusted to market demands and was instrumental in the *rockola* style of music in the 1980s. He has attained international success and is better known in markets such as Peru than in Ecuador. In 2004, he made his acting debut in the Ecuadorian-directed and produced film *Cómo Voy A Olvidarte* ('How Will I Forget You'). While a love story, this is an excellent depiction of the struggle between social classes in Ecuador and the racism which pervades much of society. (For more information, visit http://www.segundorosero.com.)

Land Of Lore

What is a chapter on culture without a taste of the folklore of the land? Ecuador has thousands of myths and stories depicting numerous aspects of its intricate cultural influences from Spain, Arabia and Africa. One way to understand a country better is to visit different regions and ask residents for interesting stories from their region. Here is a small sampling of local folk stories:

Beautiful Women of Chone

The most beautiful women in Ecuador are believed to come from a small town named Chone in the Manabí province. (Although most Ecuadorian men will say most women from the Costa are good-looking, with their big hips, small waists, nice legs and pretty features.) Chone women are regarded as particularly feminine and sexy with their cinnamon-coloured skin, curly hair and brown eyes. After many years of visiting and living in Ecuador, I occasionally come across a woman from Chone. When I ask her if she is from Chone, she is usually flattered.

I have heard varying stories explaining why the women are so beautiful. Some say that it is due to the intermarriage of the Spaniards and Indians from hundreds of years ago. Chone's own legend goes like this: When the Indians inhabited the area, there were no doctors to deliver babies. Witches, thus, stood in as midwives and instructed the mothers to drink a special elixir, called 'filter of love', at the time of birth. This elixir, made from special ingredients including roses, gave little girls cinnamon-coloured skin and an unearthly beauty.

The Veiled Woman

In the city of Guayaquil, there is an old tale about a mysterious woman dressed in black. She would walk the streets in the middle of the night and flirt with the men who approached her. No one could see her face because it was covered with a black veil. When men approached her, she disappeared into the shadows. One night, an admirer decided to follow her. He was later found unconscious. Many believe that when she removed her veil, he had seen that she had the face of a skeleton.

The Rich Man and the Poor Man

Many years ago, in the small village of Zaruma in the province of El Oro, there was a very rich man. One day, he was walking and came across a poor man. The rich man acted as if the poor man was beneath him and told him he smelt bad.

Later, the rich man visited a witch on some business. To his horror, the witch foretold that he would lose all his fortune to the poor man. The rich man anxiously sold all his belongings and bought a large diamond, which he hid in a turban on his head. One day, when he was walking by the beach, a large wind suddenly whipped up, knocking the turban off his head and the diamond into the sea. He jumped into the sea after his diamond and dived again and again into the waters but couldn't find it.

The next day, the poor man was at the market and bought a fish for a few cents. When he got home, he sliced the belly of the fish open and was amazed to find a large diamond sparkling at him. Overnight, he had become the richest man in his village. The moral of this story is: don't feel hatred or disdain for the poor because one day you could be poor yourself.

PILGRIMAGES

For many Ecuadorians, Catholicism is part of their national identity. And for many Ecuadorian Catholics, religious festivals and pilgrimages are an intrinsic part of their faith. Each festival has a patron or *alcade* (mayor) who serves as the leader of the festival. He must organise and personally finance the festival. Refusal to do so is seen as resulting in bad luck for the town but adherence is seen as bringing good luck and a position of leadership in the community.

Thousands of worshippers, seeking guidance and miracles, attend a number of pilgrimages throughout the country. This is one occasion when the upper and lower classes mingle and these events became increasingly popular in the late 1990s, when Ecuador reeled with social and economic problems.

Here are some of the more popular pilgrimages:

- La Virgen de el Cisne (17–20 August) is one of the most popular in Ecuador where some people walk for as long as three days. The site is located outside of Loja in a beautiful cathedral in a sparsely populated area. A number of the visitors come from Peru. (For more information, visit http://www.lojanos.com/virgindelcisne.htm)

- Virgen de Agua Santa de Baños, Tungurahua province. Easter week.
- Cristo del Consuelo Guayaquil, Guayas province. Easter week
- Jesús del Gran Poder, Quito. Easter week
- San Jacinto, Yaguachi. 16 August.
- 8 Virgen de la Natividad de Huayco, Bolívar province. 8 September.
- Virgen del Quinche, Pichincha, 21 November.

Be Prepared

Remember that hotel accommodation in these areas at these times can be booked months in advance and that facilities may be limited. Many visitors will opt to camp out. Transportation facilities are usually also stretched to the limit during these periods.

HOLIDAYS
Christmas

Christmas, as in other parts of the world, is a very important celebration here. This being winter time in Ecuador, much of the country is on holiday. For schoolchildren on the coast, the winter break follows the South American system and is from December to April. Schools in the Sierra are like schools in the United States, holidaying from August to September. Christmas decorations, especially in commercial areas, start to appear by early November.

Christmas Eve

Christmas Eve is referred to as Noche Buena here. The typical celebration includes the preparation of a turkey, starting at midday. After the financial crisis in the late 1990s, ham or chicken became the primary dish served during the Christmas celebrations. The whole family takes part and the mood is quite festive. People also do a lot of shopping at this time and many will purchase a new set of clothes for Christmas. Children often write letters to baby Jesus and place these requests in their shoes by their bed.

Large nativity scenes are also very popular and there are contests for the most beautiful. Nativity scenes can occupy an entire corner of a home and can be quite extravagant. Christmas trees were first used in Ecuador in 1945 but now plastic trees made of cellophane are more common. At about 10:00 pm, family members may eat *pan de yuca* (tapioca bread), *pan de pascua* (Christmas bread, a sort of fruit cake), white cheese cut in cubes and drink hot chocolate. Dinner usually begins at midnight, as many families will stay up all night.

New Year's Eve

New Year's Eve is one of the most exciting holidays in Ecuador. Just before Christmas, you will see *papier-mâché* faces for sale all over Quito and Guayaquil. The traditional celebration of Año Viejo (Old Year) is still observed. This

Preparing effigies for Año Viejo.

An effigy of the film character ET, made for Año Viejo.

holiday is about getting rid of the old and celebrating the hope of a new year. Much of the partying began at the time of the conquistadors, when they would stuff dolls full of straw during religious fiestas and set them on fire. Explosives would also be stuffed inside the dolls, which would often be waved and twirled around. In 1842, there was a severe yellow fever epidemic and on the last day of the year, thousands of clothes belonging to people who had yellow fever were burned in the hope of wiping out the illness. These clothes were even put on dolls designed to look like the people who had passed away.

This tradition has continued throughout the years and is spectacular. While the extravaganza is countrywide, Quito and Guayaquil have the best celebrations. Guayaquil comes ablaze with an orange glow over the entire city. These Año Viejo dolls, often life-sized, are set on fire after being doused in petrol at midnight, along with fireworks (often imported from Colombia). Many people will dress up as old widows and stand on the streets with the stuffed dolls crying and singing: '*Se va a morir mi viejo*' (literally translated 'My old man is going to die'). Many participate in this tradition of dressing up as old women, and children ask for money in the streets. Families gather and will often dance through the night until dawn. If you are faint of heart, the celebration can be a little intimidating.

The making of the Viejo dolls is a cottage industry.

The fires outside my house windows once got so close that I was afraid that my house would go up in flames. The neighbours thought I was crazy when I became concerned. On the other hand, my kids loved the Colombian rockets we bought for that evening and Ecuadorians tend to take the celebration in their stride. It has become more dangerous over the years with heavy explosives being used and sometimes even nails. Numerous fires are lit in the streets of Guayaquil and injuries have been reported.

Other New Year's Eve traditions include eating 12 grapes at midnight and setting luggage outside the house to bring good luck and much travelling in the forthcoming year.

Calendar of Festivals and Holidays
Public Holidays

1 January	New Year's Day
1 May	Labour Day
24 May	Anniversary of the Battle of Pichincha
24 July	Simón Bolívar Day
10 August	Independence Day
9 October	Foundation of Guayaquil (Guayaquil only)
12 October	Dia de la Raza
2 November	Memorial Day/Dia de Difuntos (All Souls Day)
3 November	Foundation of Cuenca
6 November	Foundation of Quito
25 December	Christmas Day

Holidays With Variable Dates

Carnaval	February or March
Holy Thursday	March or April
Good Friday	March or April
Easter	March or April

ENTERTAINMENT

> 'No one with the spirit of roaming within him
> can live long in Ecuador without cherishing
> a growing desire to explore its unknown parts.'
> —Alfred Simson, *Travels in the Wilds of Ecuador.*

You will never lack entertainment while in Ecuador. From ancient Indian markets to amazing national parks, Ecuador offers a diverse number of attractions for the visitor or resident. The country is still surprisingly untouched by tourism and that adds to its charm.

This brief section will introduce you to three of Ecuador's cities (Quito, Guayaquil and Cuenca), Ecuador's Indian markets, national parks and a few other things to do in this land of unsurpassed beauty.

QUITO

> 'Every street of Quito has its story; every stone its history.'
> —Victor Wolfgang von Hagen.

The cultural centre of Spanish America, Quito was declared a World Heritage Site by UNESCO in 1978. It is also the world's second highest capital city after Bolivia's La Paz and the main gateway for most foreigners to Ecuador. Many flights land in Quito at night. If you have an opportunity, choose a daytime flight so as not to miss out on the spectacular view.

Quito sits at over 2,743 m (9,000 ft) above sea level, nestled in the Andean mountains. The city extends through a narrow valley and is shaped like a forefinger. It rests on the ledge of a canyon with the volcano Pichincha to the west. The city grew most considerably in the 1960s and 1970s when oil exports took off. It now has about 1.6 million inhabitants. The weather is spring-like year round, with temperatures ranging from 22°C (72°F) to 8°C (45°F). Its rainy season is from October to May.

Quito is a fascinating blend of the ancient and the modern. The Old Town area is very well preserved and maintains much of its colonial charm. I have never tired, in 20 years of visiting Quito, of walking its narrow cobblestone streets and smelling *fritada* and *choclo* on the breeze. There is so much history in Quito that the ghosts almost reach out and touch you. Probably the best preserved historic centre in Latin America, the Monastery of San Francisco, the Church of Santo Domingo and Jesuit Church of La Compañia are all well worth a visit. Their rich interior decorations are pure examples of the Baroque School of Quito: a fusion of Spanish, Italian, Moorish, Flemish and indigenous art. Quito's museums are filled with pre-Colombian art and the city is full of ornate churches built during the times of the Spanish conquest. The Indians were largely responsible for constructing much of the architecture of this enchanting city.

Quito is also a delightful place to watch the world go by. My favourite spots are in the popular parks and along the Avenida Amazonas.

Getting around Quito is fairly easy. Despite a new address system, most residents still use the old method of locating addresses. Cabs are a common mode of transportation. *(For more information, refer to* Chapter Five, Settling In.*)* One of the newest transportation developments has been the electric trolley. It is inexpensive and traverses the north and south of Quito. It follows Avenida 10 de Agosto to the shopping centre

Quito's picturesque colonial streets.

Recreo on Avenida Maldonado in the old city. Pickpockets do a brisk business, especially during rush hour, so do be careful.

Sightseeing

I highly recommend the book *Walks Through Colonial Quito* by Oscar Valenzuela-Morales. He is a transplant from Chile and has lived in Quito for 20 years. Some of his walks can be accessed at

http://www.quitoforum.com/paseo/eng/historia.htm. This book, both in Spanish and English, offers seven different walks which give a good grounding on the history of Quito. It is available at most bookshops in Quito. Quito does not seem to have changed much from the 1860s when Friedrich Hassurek described it as a 'spellbound town from Arabian Nights.'

Interesting Sites

- **Palacio de Gobierno**
  Garcia Moreno y Chile
  This Neoclassic Presidential Palace of pink quarry is open Tuesdays to Thursdays from 9:30 am until 12:30 pm. Admission is free. It was on these steps that Gabriel García Moreno was shot and then hacked to death in 1875.
- **Plaza de Santo Domingo**
  Bolivar y Guayaquil
  This is the site of a popular artists' market at weekends. The Church of Santo Domingo is found here.
- **The Church of Santo Domingo**
  This church and convent date from the 17th century. Its façade is Neoclassical, its decorations Moorish and its altar Baroque.
- **Church of La Merced**
  Cuenca y Chile
  Began in 1700 and completed in 1742, this cloister contains a lot of fine art, including works by Francisco Albán. It also has the tallest church tower and largest bell in Quito.
- **Plaza de la Independencia**
  Venezuela y Espejo

At the centre of the Old Town, the city was basically planned from this site. The Cathedral is a stone's throw away, and this church contains the tomb of the Independence hero General Antonio José de Sucre. Visiting hours are 8:00 am–10:00 am and 2:00 pm–4:00 pm daily, except Sunday. Admission is free.

- **Church of La Compañia de Jesús**
García Moreno y Sucre
The Company of Jesus Church is one of the most ornate buildings in all of Latin America. Built in the Baroque style by the Jesuits between 1605 and 1763, it is adorned with more than seven tons of gold in its gilded walls, balconies and its elaborate, ten-sided altar.

- **Monastery of San Francisco**
Mideros y Imbabura
It is believed to be the first religious building constructed by the Spanish in South America, and work on this Early Renaissance-styled church began in 1534, just weeks after Quito was founded. It boasts a gold altar, ornate woodcarvings and intricate designs. San Francisco comprises an area of some 30,000 sq m (322,917 sq ft), including a plaza, the Iglesia Mayor, the chapels of Cantuna and Villacis and a large convent with magnificent cloisters. It is open 9:00 am–12:00 pm and 3:00 pm–6:00 pm.

- **Museo del Banco Central**
6 de Diciembre y Patria Avenues
The Central Bank Museum contains one of the finest archaeological and gold collections in the Americas. Some of its 1,800 items date as far back as 1,200 years and include pre-colonial, colonial and contemporary works. It is open everyday except Monday.

- **Museo Guayasamín**
Bellavista
The Guayasamín Museum houses the beautiful personal collection and workshop of Oswaldo Guayasamín, Ecuador's world-famous artist. Admission is free. Opening hours: Monday to Friday, 9:30 am–1:00 pm and 3:00 pm–6:30 pm; Saturday, 9:30 am–1:00 pm.

- **Casa Museo María Augusta Urrutía**
  García Moreno 760 y Sucre
  María Augusta Urrutía was a philanthropist and this was her home, left much as it was in the late 19th century, and complete with period furnishings. Opening hours: Tuesdays to Saturdays, 9:00 am–5:00 pm.
- **Biblioteca Ecuatorina Aurelio Espinosa Pólit**
  Jose Nogales N69-22 y Francisco Arcos
  Located in the Cotocallao area on the outskirts of Quito, this is the largest library in Ecuador, with more than 300,000 volumes. It is an excellent facility for resources for research on Ecuador. Closed on Mondays only. Alas, books here are not allowed to be checked out. There is also a very interesting museum connected to the library, which contains the clothes García Moreno was wearing when he was assassinated.
- **Train to Cotopaxi**
  At weekends, a train runs from Quito to Cotopaxi Volcano Park. It usually leaves Quito at 8:00 am and Cotopaxi at 2:30 pm, returning to Quito by 5:30 pm. It is a three-hour trip each way. The train station is located at 315 Maldonado Street. Be sure to get your tickets the day before departure. The price for foreigners is US$ 25.

Shopping

Quito abounds with numerous shops for both the tourists and locals. Here are some of my favourites in Quito:

Gift Shops

- Ahuacuna: Avenida Amazonas 1036 y Pinto, Galeria Latina, J.L. Mera N23–69; tel: (02) 221-098
- Mundo Arte: Avenida Amazonas 2019 y 18 de Septiembre
  Just across from the Hilton, this is an established shop with numerous high quality gifts from all over Ecuador.

Shopping Centres

Quito has a number of upscale shopping centres where Ecuadorians love to congregate. The food courts have a number of Ecuadorian-style restaurants as well as North American franchise units. Most shopping centres close at 8:00 pm. Here are a few:

- Centro Comercial Iñaquito, better known as CCI. Located on Amazonas y Naciones Unidas.
- Centro Comercial El Jardín on República esquina Amazonas
- Quicentro on Naciones Unidas y Av 6 de Diciembre. This is my favourite shopping centre in Quito. It has almost everything you need.

Traditional Markets

Many Ecuadorians go to the traditional markets in Quito. These give visitors a real insight into Ecuadorian culture but be sure to watch out for pickpockets. *(There is a more comprehensive write-up on markets toward the end of this chapter.)* No matter which market you decide to go to, you are guaranteed to be in awe of the life that fills the air there and by the things you'll see.

One of the most famous markets is a couple of hours north of Quito called Otavalo (open every day except Mondays and Fridays). This market is best known for clothing and gifts, such as ponchos, pipes and many other bags and clothes that are beautifully coloured and traditionally made by the same the hands that sell them. When you go to an open-air market, you'll get your chance to try out your bargaining skills. Here are some rough estimates of some prices in US dollars:

Hammock	US$ 12
Knit Hat	US$ 3
Pants/trousers	US$ 7
Pipe	US$ 2–30
Poncho	US$ 16–20
Shirt	US$ 6
Shoulder Bag	US$ 2–6
Sweater	US$ 10
Tapestries	US$ 5–25

Here are some of my favourite markets inside Quito, some of which you won't find in many tourist guides: Mercado Central, Pichincha y Esmeraldas, Mercado Santa Clara, Versalles y Marchena and Mercado Ipiales. If you don't mind stolen or counterfeit goods, you will be able to find almost anything under the sun at Mercado Ipiales.

Nightlife

Quito has a very enticing nightlife. It is not as large as in other South American cities but you will definitely feel at home here if you're a nocturnal animal. Quito's nightlife ranges from salsa to raves, from English-style pubs to karaoke beer lounges. The bars generally close at 2:00 am or 3:00 am. Discos are another story. There are several *discotecas* (discotheques) that stay open until dawn.

Cover charges usually range from US$ 1 to US$ 3.50 and are on the rise. The entrance fee system in Ecuador works like this:

- Cover charge: You pay a certain amount to get in the door but that won't cover the cost of your drinks; or
- *Consumo minimo*: there is no cover charge, but you have to spend a minimum amount or you pay the difference when you leave; or
- *Entrada con derecho*: by far the most popular in Quito. You pay a cover charge and they give you a ticket or token for a free drink.

Here are a few of my personal favourite places:

- **Ñucanchi Peña**
  Avenida Universitaria 496 y Armero
  Peñas are folklore clubs or bars that have traditional music performances that are often quite expensive. This club is fairly inexpensive (about US$ 4 cover charge) and presents some of the best talent there is in Ecuador. I highly recommend it! The crowd is largely Ecuadorian.
- **Seseribó**
  Veintimilla y 12 de Octubre
  Salsa music is the speciality here, and this is, allegedly, the best place for salsa in the whole of Ecuador.

- **Veradero**
  Reina Victoria 17-51 y La Pinta
  Good Cuban music and food.

Hotels

There are literally hundreds of hotel options in Quito. Here are some of my favourites. Don't be afraid to ask for discounted rates, especially if you're going to stay for a number of days. The longer you stay, the more discount you should receive. This is even possible at the larger 'luxury' hotels. Some major hotels offer special prices for Ecuadorian citizens and residents.

- **La Mansión de Angel Hotel**
  Wilson E5–29 y Juan León Mera
  Website: http://www.larc1.com/ecuador/angel/angel.html
  The US representative is LARC.
  Website: http://www.larc1.com
  Tel: 1-800-327-3573 for calls from US and Canada.
  This is a charming boutique hotel with beautifully decorated rooms. Located in the Mariscal Sucre neighbourhood, called the cultural and gastronomical centre of Quito, it is a 20-minute drive away from the international airport in the north of the city.

- **Hotel Sierra Madre**
  Veintimilla 464 y Luis Tamayo
  Website: http://www.hotelsierramadre.com
  The US representative is LARC.
  Website: http://www.larc1.com
  Tel: 1-800-327-3573 for calls from US and Canada.
  This is an excellent mid-priced hotel, styled after a Spanish villa. The rooms are clean and the staff helpful.

- **Hotel Majestic**
  Mercadillo 366 y Versalles
  Website: http://www.majesticquito.com
  Very well-run hotel in the budget category.

- **Hotel Santa Maria**
  Inglaterra 933 y Mariana de Jesus
  Website: http://interhotel.com/ecuador/en/hoteles/32200.html

The lobby of La Mirage Garden Hotel and Spa, heaven on Earth in Cotacachi.

A good value-for-money hotel with a great restaurant serving traditional Ecuadorian cuisine.

Cotacachi

- **La Mirage Garden Hotel and Spa**
  Website: http://www.mirage.com.ec
  This is one of the finest and most expensive hotels in Ecuador. Spread over 13 acres in this lovely village, its owners have constructed a remarkable oasis of a hotel/spa. La Mirage can compete with the best spas in San Francisco or Paris. The service is among the best that I have ever experienced anywhere on earth. The employees should be very proud of their accomplishments in a country where good service is not the norm. The food is excellent and formally presented. The hotel's spa is spectacular and offers a variety of services. I would highly recommend it for a romantic honeymoon, seeing that it even has a wedding chapel! Otavalo is only 15 minutes away.

CUENCA

'Two things impressed Alsedo: the ordered loveliness of Cuenca and its magnificence.'
—Albert B Franklin

Cuenca is well worth a visit. Cut off from the rest of Ecuador for hundreds of years because of its rugged topography and its undeveloped communications and road systems, this city has remained resolutely colonial in character. Cuenca rests at 2,596 m (8,517 ft) in the southern Sierra. Despite being the third largest city in Ecuador and a major producer of Panama hats, jewellery, textiles, lace and leather goods, Cuenca has managed to retain a provincial air. Its whitewashed buildings, interior patios, ironwork balconies and flowery public plazas give it an Old World charm.

Sightseeing

- **El Sagrario Church (Old Cathedral)**
  Mariscal Sucre y Luis Cordero
  This church was constructed in 1557 at the time Cuenca was founded. Some of its foundations are stones from the old Inca city of Tomebamba, present-day Cuenca (which means 'basin' in Spanish). It was the Inca Túpac Yupanqui who founded Tomebamba, giving it the name which means 'space like the sky'.
- **Todos Los Santos Church**
  Calle Larga y Bajada de Todo Los Santos
  The first Catholic mass held in Cuenca was on this site. A newer church replaced it during the 19th century.
- **Museo del Banco Central**
  Avenida Huayna Capac in front of Calle Larga
  Cuenca's best museum, the Central Bank Museum, contains a major display of Inca and Cañari archaeological items and religious art. It also hosts ever-changing art exhibitions and a permanent collection of old black-and-white photographs of Cuenca.
  This museum also owns an Incan archaeological site, the Archaeological Park of Pumapungo, which contains tens of thousands of important archaeological objects.
- **Museo de Arte Moderno**
  Marisal Sucre y Talbot
  The Modern Art Museum has both permanent and changing collections that show off the wide diversity of Ecuadorian art.

Ingapirca is the largest surviving Incan structure in Ecuador.

- **Ingapirca**
  Ingapirca (which means 'Wall of the Inca') is located just two hours or 70 km (43 miles) north of Cuenca. It is the largest and best example of Incan architecture in Ecuador. There is a small museum at the site, which includes a fascinating temple of intricate stonework and is thought to have been a Cañari observatory which was later converted into an Incan temple to the Sun God. The long axis of its elliptical shape lies precisely along the east-west line, and its structure is said to look like a puma, a sacred animal to the Inca, from the sky.
- **Chordeleg**
  A very short drive from Cuenca, this small village features a weekly market which sells numerous arts and crafts including unique ceramics, jewellery and embroidery work on shawls.
- **Gualaceo**
  Another short drive from Cuenca, this town is full of artisans. It has a very good traditional market on Sundays. Another good local Sunday market, located 26 km (16 miles) south of Gualaceo, is at Sigsig.

Hotels

- **Hotel Crespo**
  Calle Larga 793
  Website: http://interhotel.com/ecuador/es/hoteles.html
- **Hosteria Uzhupud**
  Via Paute Km 32, Chican-paute
  Website: http://interhotel.com/ecuador/en/hoteles.html
  Located a half-hour from Cuenca in Paute, this is in an absolutely gorgeous location; a very peaceful environment full of flowers and birds.

GUAYAQUIL

> 'Guayaquil is like a threshold between the world of today and the world of pre-history.'
> —Albert B Franklin.

In my first edition of this book, I wrote, 'Guayaquil is a tropical paradise that few foreigners like at first glance. There is no middle ground with Guayaquil. You will either love it or hate it.' As for me, it captivated me on my first visit, some 26 years ago. Ecuador's main port town, a sensual place where fortunes are made and lost, resembles a Middle Eastern city with large cement buildings and crowded streets filled with people of all social classes. I think Guayaquil would have made the perfect set for a Clark Gable, Humphrey Bogart or Indiana Jones film. However, not many foreigners visited except on the way to the Galápagos. Guayaquil was often described by visitors as the armpit of Ecuador. A visit to Guayaquil today would leave few referring to it as the armpit of Ecuador. After a major government change in Quito, a number of representatives from Guayaquil were able to pass legislation, which guaranteed that a certain percentage of personal tax revenue from Guayaquil residents would be used exclusively for the reconstruction and modernisation of Guayquil. Locals were elated that they would be assured that a portion of their income was not going to be funneled to Quito. A miraculous change has occurred over the last six years. I can confidently say that Guayaquil should be visited and enjoyed. It is becoming a world class city.

Many of the street vendors are gone and have been moved to specialised market areas and the beginning of the reformation has taken place in the Malecón, which prior to 2000 had become very rundown and dangerous. However, there was a certain charm of the street life which is now gone.

Guayaquil doesn't offer the visitor or resident the colonial environment the Sierra does and the weather can be quite daunting between January and May. However, Guayaquil has a certain magic that bites like a mosquito, leaving you with a fever for living. I think Guayaquil offers all that is good and bad about Ecuador; its slums, muggers, beggars and squashed rats are the perfect foil to its posh suburbs and shopping centres, riverfront walks and frolicking iguanas.

Weather-wise, June and December are quite pleasant and can get cool in the evenings. It is advisable to take a light jacket with you.

Prior to the Spanish settling in Guayaquil in 1537, Guayaquil was populated by Indians. The natural port was developed into one of the largest on the Pacific coast and it became a large shipbuilding region because of the tremendous amount of timber in the area.

Interesting Sites

- **La Catedral or The Cathedral**
  Chimborazo y Clemente Ballén
  This double-belfried cathedral sits smack in the middle of Guayaquil. It has been destroyed by fire several times, the latest in 1902.

- **Botanical Garden**
  This is located in the Las Orquideas neighbourhood and is open almost every day. It has over 320 plant species, 70 species of birds and 60 species of butterflies. If you ove orchids, you will find one of the best exhibitions in the country here, with more then 50 specimens on show. There is an admission fee of US$ 5. Be sure to take a taxi and have it wait for you, otherwise you will have to walk a long way through unsafe neighbourhoods to flag one.

- **9 de Octubre**
  This is the large avenue that runs down the middle of Guayaquil. Start your walk from the Malecón Simón Bolívar and head straight down 9 de Octubre to the US Consulate. This is a marvellous street that people from Guayaquil love. It is bustling with life; banks, large shops, restaurants, beggars and street vendors.

- **Malecón 2000**
  The Malecón 2000 is a reconstruction project along the riverfront walkway and street facing the Río Guayas (Guayas River). Its objective is to transform the pier into one of the most important civic-tourist-commercial sites from South America. This was where most of the early trade in Guayaquil took place. Nowadays, it is the site of numerous fiestas and art exhibits. There is a wonderful IMAX theatre here and boat excursions run with food and drink. (Visit http://www.malecon2000.com.)

- **Museo Antropológico y de Arte Contemporáneo (MAAC)**
  Malecón 2000.
  Tel: (04) 256-6333

- **Cerro Blanco**
  This is an ecological reserve located just outside of Guayaquil at Kilometer 16.5 Via a la Costa. It is a protected coastal tropical forest with an estimated 600 plant species, 33 mammal species (including monkeys, white-tailed deer, jaguar and puma), and 211 bird species (eight of which are endangered). The Fundacion Pro-Bosque (Pro-Forest Foundation) protects this 5,000-hectare forest. Tourists can visit the nature trails and organic farms here, but reservations are required, except on Sundays.
  Details can be obtained from the office at Edificio Promocentro. Tel: (04) 416-975
  Email: vanhorst@ecua.net.ec

- **Monument to Simón Bolívar**
  Chimborazo y Ballén
  Simón Bolívar was the force behind the fight for Latin America's liberation from Spain. This monument to him stands in the middle of a small park called Parque Bolívar,

A navy band performing at the Malecón, circa prior to redevelopment.

which is famous for its friendly resident iguanas. The park is very well maintained and offers substantial shade from the strong sun.

- **Las Peñas**
  This small neighbourhood was part of the original city that dates back to the 16th century. Colonial architecture, art galleries and the oldest church in Guayaquil (the Church of Santo Domingo) can be found here. While once considered a dangerous neighbourhood, the area has been extensively developed with private security. Not to be missed.
- **Nobol**
  This is a small village just 30 minutes outside of Guayaquil and is rarely visited by foreigners. The body of the patron saint Narcisa de Jesús Martillo Morán lies here in a transparent casket. Many of the food vendors here dress in white.
- **Puerto Hondo Mangrove Ecotourism Project**
  Just outside Guayaquil, near Cerro Blanco, 1 km (0.6 miles) along the Via a la Costa is the Puerto Hondo Mangrove Ecotourism Project. Here, you can take canoe rides through the mangroves and more than 40 bird species call it home, including the white ibis, yellow-crowned night heron and rufous-necked wood rail.

Barrio Las Peñas, Guayaquil.

Contact: Eric Horstman, Fundacion Pro-Bosque, Casilla 09 01 04243, Km.16 Via a la Costa, Guayaquil.
Tel: (04) 872-236/871-900 ext 32-280
Email: vanhorst@ecua.net.ec

Shopping Centres

I recommend the following shopping centres:

- Mall de Sol: new, big and near the airport. Relatively expensive, it has American fast-food restaurants and a comfortable cinema.
- Policentro: nice and more affordable with restful water fountains.
- Entre-Rios
- Riocentro
- Plaza Quil
- Albán Borja
- Unicentro: downtown by Parque Bolívar.

Markets
- **La Bahía**

  This is an open-air market located just outside downtown on Carbo and Villamil between Olmedo and Colón that looks like a bazaar. There is a lot of activity with people looking for bargains. I used to come here in the early 1980s to buy such things as peanut butter and other items from the United States. This market has developed into a place which sells surplus goods from ships visiting the port. Watch out for pickpockets. The vendors are no longer selling in the street as before and now are required to be in stalls.

- **El Mercado de Artesanía**

  Loja y Córdova, edge of Las Peñas

  The Artisans' Market is held inside a huge warehouse-type structure that spans a whole block. Many handicrafts and jewellery are sold from small stands. Lots of bargains. You can easily spend several hours here. It is just as popular with Ecuadorians.

Nightlife
Residents from Guayaquil love to party. There is no shortage of nightlife from discos to gambling halls on 9 de Octubre. In fact, Guayaquil is notorious for providing its visitors with more action after dark than during the day. The scene varies from discos that rock until dawn to beer-guzzling pubs, but they all have an exotic tropical vibe.

- **Alto Nivel Discoteca**

  Av. Jun Tanca Marengo

  The cover charge is US$ 10–US$ 14. Thursday nights is 'Ladies Night' and it's free for females. There are three bars featuring a discotheque, salsa room and a *peña*. The live music presented in the *peña* has some outstanding local talent. The price usually includes all drinks. However, you have to work pretty hard to attract the attention of the waiters.

- **Equs Bar**

  V. And Estrada 819 and Fig Trees

Tel: (04) 382-261/889-807

Good live bands jam here.

- **Café del Sol**
  Vitor Emilio Estrada e llanes in Urdesa.
  This is both a bar and restaurant.
- **Arthur's Café** located at the end of the street in Las Peñas barrio has great nightlife and there are usually live bands. Your author sat in with the local band in October of 2005 and played the piano.

Hotels

- **Hotel Continental**
  Chile y 10 de Agosto on Parque Bolívar
  Website: http://www.hotelbook.com/static/welcome_12600.html
  One of the classiest hotels in the city, its restaurants have won various international gastronomy awards.
- **Hotel Oro Verde**
  9 de Octubre y García Moreno
  Website: http://www.ecuadordiscover.com/hotels/oroverde_Guayaquil.htm. Best downtown venue.
- **Hotel Plaza**
  Chile 414 y C. Ballén
  A mid-priced downtown hotel.
- **Hotel Rizzo**, Ballén 319
  Website:
  http://interhotel.com/ecuador/es/hoteles/64971.html
  Downtown location with a good Ecuadorian restaurant.
- **Hotel Ritz**
  9 de Octubre 709
  Tel: (04) 530-120/324-134; fax 332-151
- **Hotel Castell**
  Av. Miguel H Alcívar y Calle ulloa in Kennedy North
  Website: http://www.hotelcastell.com
  Excellent mid-priced hotel.

INDIGENOUS MARKETS

One of the most unique features of Ecuador is its market tradition, where people gather to buy and sell animals, food and other items. Indian markets can be traced as far back as 4,000 years ago. Many of the markets exist, as they have for centuries, with the purpose of trade, not tourism. However, there are a number of markets that have become more touristy of late, such as the famous Otavalo market.

I've given you my market schedule already but please remember that there are seldom facilities, and that thieves and pickpockets are shopping whilst you are. Do also exercise caution when consuming any food. That said, I promise you will get a real look into indigenous society when you do visit these markets.

I find it amusing to watch business being conducted in dollars but prices quoted in sucres. Bargaining is a very real part of these markets. One clue to successful bargaining is to go early. I often ask for a discount because I am the first customer of the day. You will likely receive one as a good luck measure by the vendor for the rest of the day. Another key to bargaining is to remain emotionless and detached, not showing how much you admire the item you wish to purchase. Also, most vendors will offer discounts for purchases of larger quantities. Most animal trading takes place early in the day.

Market Schedule

Monday

- **Ambato**

  This is a wholesale market for regional products. Traditional items are also on sale. It opens at about 8:00 am and starts to wind down about 3:00 pm. There are numerous markets throughout Ambato but the principal one is at the Mercado Central which is on the outskirts of Parque 12 de Noviembre. The markets here also sell some of the most beautiful flowers on Earth. The time to come for fruits and flowers is February, during the Carnaval festivities.

Tuesday

- **Latacunga**

  This traditional market starts at 8:00 am and finishes about 1:00 pm. There are lots of exotic fruits on sale. It is also open on Saturday.

Wednesday

- **Pujilí**

  Some 90 km (56 miles) south of Quito, this market is dedicated to trading within the indigenous community, i.e. this is the real thing. Open from 8:00 am until 1:00 pm, there are very few foreigners here. You will see llamas loaded with colourful fruits and vegetables and people from some of the smallest hamlets. It also operates on Sundays.

Thursday

- **Plaza Rotary**

  In Cuenca, this is a small-sized market selling numerous handicrafts.

- **Saquisilí**

  Open from 8:00 am until 1:00 pm, this is one of the most traditional and exciting markets in Ecuador. There are five main markets which seem to specialise in one type of merchandise, such as food, tools or weavings. The animal market is amazing and starts fairly early at about 8:00 am. You will see buses coming in with animals on the roof and people with wads of cash bargaining. The bargaining doesn't seem to get too loud or exaggerated. It is a very dusty extravaganza. More and more tourists attend nowadays. In November 2000, I observed about 40 to 60 tourists going picture-crazy seeing guinea pigs and other exotic animals being sold.

- **Tulcán**
  Near the Colombian border, this market begins at about 8:00 am and ends at 3:00 pm.

Friday

- **Cotocachi**
  North on the Pan-American Highway, this is a meeting place for producers, buyers and friends. Open from 8:00 am to 2:00 pm.

Saturday

- **Otavalo**
  Otavalo Indians are the most prosperous craftsmen in Ecuador. It is not surprising, then, that this market is the largest market in Ecuador. Prices, while still negotiable, are generally higher than most other markets. As an indication of how touristy it has become and the predominance of white foreigners, locals refer to Otavalo as Ottawa! Many tour companies leave Quito early in the morning or some visitors even spend Friday night in Otavalo. While Saturday is the big market day, Otavalo has turned into a daily market, except for Mondays and Fridays. You can buy almost anything here from ponchos to wooden goods to Indian jewellery.

- **Zumbahua**
  Drive south on the Pan-American Highway through the Avenue of the Volcanoes to this trading place of llamas, riding horses and Tigua art.

Sunday

- **Santo Domingo de Los Colorados**
  Beginning at 8:00 am, this market lasts until late in the afternoon. This is a unique market as Santo Domingo is situated at the crossroads of the Sierra and the Costa.

Tailors hard at work at Saquisilí market.

The locals here will represent distinct areas of Ecuador. In the city centre, this market is usually jam-packed with people.

NATIONAL PARKS

Ecuador is a very small country and much of the land has been exploited for commercial use. In the 1970s, the government started to set land aside for preservation to protect Ecuador's diverse but fragile ecology. There are more than 20 national parks or protected areas, which include about 17 per cent of Ecuador's terrain. The national parks:

- Andes: Cajas National Recreation Area, Chimborazo Reserve, Cotacachi-Cayapas Ecological Reserve, Cotopaxi National Park, El Angel Ecological Reserve, Ilinizas Reserve, Pululahua Geobotanical Reserve and Podocarpus National Park.
- Amazon: Cuyabeno Reserve, Limoncocha Biological Reserve and Yasuní National Park.
- Andes-Amazon: Antisana Ecological Reserve, Cayambe-Coca Ecological Reserve, Llangantes National Park, Sangay National Park and Sumaco-Galeras National Park.
- Coast & Galápagos Islands: Bosque Protector Cerro Blanco, Machalilla National Park, Mataje-Cayapas Mangrove Reserve, Manglares Churute Mangrove Reserve and Galápagos Islands National Park.

Cajas National Park

This is a beautiful park located just 29 km (18 miles) west of Cuenca with more than 270 Andean lakes. Its high-altitude grasslands are home to lovely birds such as hummingbirds, gray-breasted toucans and giant conebills. You can take a bus from Cuenca to the park information centre where there is a basic refuge with beds and a kitchen. A fee is charged for foreigners.

Cotacachi–Cayapas Ecological Reserve

Along the western cordillera of the Andes, this reserve straddles both Imbabura and Esmeraldas provinces. It covers an impressive range of ecosystems, from coastal tropical forest to pre-montane and montane cloud forest to *paramo*, ranging from 200–4,939 m (656–16,204 ft) above sea level.

Wildlife Galore

Its fascinating wildlife includes spectacled bears, anteaters, jaguars, tapirs, monkeys, caiman, bats and more. The tropical forest section of this reserve is part of an ecosystem that has almost entirely disappeared in other coastal areas of South America. More than 20,000 species of plants have been recorded along with 500 bird types, making it one of the most biologically diverse regions on Earth.

The spectacular area around Cuicocha Lake is wonderful hiking terrain. This collapsed volcanic crater has a lake that is 0.19 km (0.12 miles) deep and 3 km (1.9 miles) in diameter. You can take a boat ride on the lake. You can get there by driving north from Quito towards Otavalo and continuing on to the town of Cotacachi. The more adventurous can enter the reserve from the lowlands by canoe via the San Miguel entrance.

Cotopaxi National Park

The most popular national park in Ecuador, the snowcapped Cotopaxi Volcano is Cotopaxi National Park's main attraction. The park covers 33,393 hectares (82,514 acres) that are primarily *paramo* (high altitude grassland), offering excellent hiking, climbing and mountain biking opportunities at temperatures varying from between 0°C to15°C (32°F to 59°F). I recommend the guidebook *Climbing and Hiking in Ecuador* (4th edition, published by Bradt Travel Guides) by Rob Rachowiecki, Mark Thurber, and Betsy Wagenhauser for some good hikes.

You can also visit the park's museum to view llama herds and Incan ruins. Conveniently located one and a half hours south of Quito in the Pichincha, Cotopaxi and Napo provinces, the park is accessible by car or on foot, but there is no public transportation within the park. There are two entrances, one south of Machachi and another north of Latacunga on the Pan-american Highway.

Your Personal Tour Guide

Numerous tour companies can offer you guided tours of the Cotopaxi area but there is an excellent guide that you will not find in the phonebooks or mainstream guidebooks. Sitting in his ten-seater, four-wheel-drive truck on the road to Cotopaxi Volcano is Luis Medardo Topanta Q. He is waiting to share with you all he knows about this magnificent region. But he can only speak Spanish.

I spent a wonderful day with him visiting several markets in the Latacunga area. His prices are negotiable and he can arrange almost any type of excursion. He even took me to see a shaman which is not any part of any type of tour. He is very well known in the markets and the surrounding area and can provide a tremendous amount of insight into Ecuadorian culture. He lives in Parroquia Guaytacama, about 8 km (5 miles) from Saquisilí, but can be found most mornings at the main entrance to the Cotopaxi National Park.

He can be contacted through the Hacienda San Agustin De Callo at tel: (03) 271-9160.

Cayambe–Coca

This protected area covers extensive Amazon forests, cloud forests and *paramo* ecosystems in the eastern cordillera. There are several volcanoes in the reserve, including the Cayambe (5,790 m or 18,996 ft), Cerro Puntas (4,451 m or 14,602 ft), Saraurco (4,695 m or 15,402 ft) and the Reventador (3,485 m or 11,434 ft). There are 81 lagoons in the reserve, including the San Marcos and Puruanta, and the Papallacta lagoons.

Besides the snowcapped volcanoes, one of the most spectacular places in the reserve is the San Rafael waterfall (130 m or 426 ft) high along the Coca River, the highest in Ecuador. The Cayambe Volcano is one of the hardest climbs in Ecuador. And look out for the young and active Reventador Volcano! The main access is from Olmedo to San Marcos lagoon, where there is a visitor's centre. Another access is trekking from the Papallacta Pass from Quito to Baeza.

Chimborazo Reserve

Chimborazo is the highest summit in Ecuador, standing at 6,310 m (20,702 ft). The Chimborazo and Carihuairazo (5,100 m or 16,732 ft) volcanoes are hot favourites with mountain-climbers, backpackers and trekkers. With a terrain ranging from 3,800 to 6,310 m (12,467 to 20,702 ft), be prepared for cold temperatures and bring your own sleeping bags as the places of refuge here are very basic, although fireplaces and cooking facilities are provided.

There is a Vicuñas Reserve here (with a government-donated stock of some 600 wild *vicuñas*, graceful wild llamas native to the Andes Highlands) on the north-east side of Chimborazo Volcano. This reserve is accessible by road from either Riobamba or Mocha.

OTHER THINGS TO DO

My best sources for unique and fun things to do in Ecuador have been the local papers. Many of the news services do a good job but many of the articles run in the papers require you to read Spanish.

(There are some good books listed in the Resource Guide *at the back of the book which will give you an insight intoto tourist sites.)*

Bike Riding

Thanks to the Inca's extensive network of roads and bridges and its mountainous terrain, Ecuador is gorgeous biking country! Some world-class descents include the slopes of Cotopaxi Volcano, the Pichincha Volcano and trips that take riders from the heights of the Andes to the Amazon Basin. Another magnificent route is a 60-km (37-mile) stretch referred to as La Ruta de las Cascadas near the Tungurahua Volcano, about two hours south of Quito. The route starts at El Pailón de Deablo and runs for about 20 km (12 miles) where buses can be taken back to Baños. For hard-core bikers, the most rigorous part of the course continues on to Puyo.

Bikers will be pleased to know that there are biker-friendly buses and pickup truck taxis, and readily available lodging and food in most rural areas. But bike defensively on public road, as Ecuadorian drivers are not used to seeing bicycles on the road. Quito, I've heard, is one of the worst places to bike. Maps of varying scales can be found at the Instituto Geografico Militar behind the Casa de la Cultura. Don't bet your life on directions given by locals, as they'll send you off on a wild goose-chase rather than admit that they don't know which way to go. Here are a few websites to check out:

- http://www.bikingdutchman.com, and
- http://www.ecuadorexplorer.com/html/biking_tours. html.

Parasailing

There is a beautiful beach for parasailing on the coast in a little hamlet called Crucita in the province of Manabí, about one and a half hours from Manta. You can also do some hang gliding here.

A scenic spot is a hill called Balsamaragua which is about 100 m (328 ft) above sea level. And while you are there, visit the far end of the beach outside of Crucita, called La Boca, where the Portoviejo River empties into the sea. Here, in an area of about 6.7 hectares (20 acres), you can find eight species of birds and the blue crab.

A number of small restaurants are also located in La Boca which serve, amongst other seafood delicacies, fresh sardines—a favourite with Ecuadorians.

Isla Puná

Isla Puná is a little-visited island near Guayaquil which is just opening up to tourists. Isla Puná or Puná Island, boasts the endangered saffron siskin (a small, brown-streaked, yellow-marked bird), priceless Incan relics and much pirate history.

To get there, you can take a boat on the Guayas River on the first Sunday of each month. The boat leaves Guayaquil at Cuenca y la Ría at 8:00 am and arrives back at Guayaquil at 6:00 pm. On other days, there is a transport boat leaving from the same pier. This returns the following day, meaning that you will have to spend the night on the island. I recommend the Hotel Miramar. On 24 September, the island has the celebration of the Virgen de las Mercedes (Our Lady of Mercy.   .

Thermal Baths

One of the most enjoyable experiences I have had in Ecuador was at a little-known thermal bath named Baños de San Vicente, located off the highway past Progreso on the way to Salinas. You take a dirt road from the sign at the highway nearly 16 km (10 miles) through the desert and you arrive at a unique oasis that is enjoyed by very few tourists.

Operated by a private concession, it is owned by the government. Years ago, the baths were basically just an ancient mud hole. Now, food is provided and the baths are housed inside a unique-looking structure. The buildings are set in an oasis in the desert, making you feel like you are on another planet! You are given a mud-massage then moved outside to bake in the sun. Do be careful not to stay outside too long. Ten to 15 minutes is about enough—any longer and you will probably burn. There is a small hotel outside the complex. It is very tranquil here and a wonderful way to de-stress. Admission is just a few dollars and the service is reasonable. (Tel: 282-195. It is open daily.)

The most famous Ecuadorian town for hot baths is Baños (*baños* means bath in Spanish). The thermal baths here are heated by the active Tungurahua Volcano (*tungurahua* means 'little hell' in Quichua) just 10 km (6 miles) away. The best known bath here is La Piscina de La Virgen which has hot showers and concrete pools, some directly under a waterfall. The etiquette here is not to bathe nude but in a swimming costume.

South American Explorers

This is a non-profit entity that is dedicated to the spreading of information about Latin America. The South American Explorers have a clubhouse in Quito where there is at least one expatriate with an intimate knowledge of Ecuador. Their other clubhouses are in Lima and Cuzco in Peru and their US headquarters is in Ithaca, New York. An annual membership entitles you to receive their magazine, free trip reports and

Water

Do avoid drinking the water as it usually has a strong mineral content. The thermal waters can get as hot as 50°C (122°F). Other favourite locations in Ecuador for thermal baths are Oyacachi and Papallacta.

assistance in trip planning. I highly recommend this club if you're just visiting or going to stay in Ecuador for a length of time. It is an excellent place to find information on rentals and information about Quito and Ecuador in general. The privileges of membership include discounts with a number of establishments in Ecuador. You can contact them at explorer@saexplorers.org or find out more at

http://www.saexplorers.org.

Libraries

- **Biblioteca Ecuatoriana Aurelio Espinosa Pólit**
  José Nogales N69-22 y Francisco Arcos Cotocollao, Quito
  Tel: (02) 249-1156
  This is excellent for its research on Ecuador.

Bookshops

- **Abya Yala**
  Avenida 12 de Octubre 1430 y Wilson, Casilla 17-12-719, Quito
  Email: editorial@abyayala.org
  Website: http://www.abyayala.org/
  Tel: (02) 256-2633 / 250-6247
  This is a great shop with thousands of books on almost any subject on Ecuador, with a particular emphasis on ecology and the environment. (
  Interestingly, http://www.abyayala.com/ and http://abyayala.nativeweb.org are also great web resources on Latin America. Funny how the word *abya-yala* caught the fancy of so many! This is a Kuna expression meaning 'ripe earth' and the name the Kuna people gave to the Americas.
- **Confederate Books**
  Calama 410 y Juan León Mera, Quito
  Tel: (02) 252-7890

One of my favourite haunts—Biblioteca Ecuatoriana Aurelio Espinosa Pólit.

This is quite a unique shop that attracts mainly expatriates and foreigners.

- **Libri Mundi**
  Juan León Mera 851 y Wilson, Quito
  Website: http://www.librimundi.com
  It carries a wide range of books on Ecuador in Spanish and English and a number of foreign newspapers. There's another shop at Quicentro.

Gay Life

There is a considerable gay community in Ecuador. The year 1998 was a hallmark year for gays as the Ecuadorian constitution was amended to prevent any discrimination against any person for their sexual orientation. While this was a considerable step for gays, attitudes are still largely anti-gay in Ecuador. In 2001, a number of establishments that catered to gays in Guayaquil were closed down.

Quito has a number of nightclubs and services that cater to gays. In Guayaquil, many gays meet in the area called Primero de Mayo y Esmeraldas. In Quito, the Mariscal and Colon districts house many of the gay bars and meeting places. The best website for information on gay club life in Ecuador is http://gayecuador.com/. A gay-oriented tour company for Ecuador is Zenith Travel, whose website is http://www.zenithecuador.com/.

Films

There are a large number of cinema chains throughout the major cities of Ecuador. Most of the major shopping centres have cinemas. Listings can be found in the newspapers. Most are quite modern and the quality is good. CineMark is one of the largest chains here. Its Ecuadorian web page is http://www.cinemark.com.ec. Most cinemas have snack bars that look just like the ones in the United States.

Television and Radio

Ecuador has a considerable number of radio and television stations. The systems used here are UHF and VHF. There are numerous radio stations in Ecuador. My favourite is

Radio Cristal 860 AM in Guayaquil. Also known as the Voz del Pueblo, it broadcasts many programmes on different topics. My favourite is an announcement programme which allows anyone to place almost any type of announcement. For example, one can announce a lost cat or cow. In my case, my family was once worried about my whereabouts and were going to call Radio Cristal to announce my disappearance. They waited a few more hours before making a call to discover that I had been delayed at a *cantina* (bar) with a few of my friends having a few beers. Time certainly can slip away when you're enjoying yourself in Ecuador.

Now for a real treat. Most travel writers dream of finding that unknown place or experience that has not been revealed to the outside world. Can you imagine having been the first outsider to the 'Running of the Bulls' in Spain? Well, I found an experience in Ecuador that is not well-known outside of Ecuador nor to outsiders and will provide you with an exceptional experience of Ecuadorian culture.

Along the interior of the coast south of Guayaquil up to the Manabi province there exists a very unique group of Ecuadorians. The Montubios are a mixed race of Indian, white and black. They have been instrumental in Ecuador's agricultural development and are very hardworking and

Ecuadorians enjoy a dance at the rodeo in Salitre.

A lovely princess with proud eyes at the Salitre rodeo.

possess their own unique culture. For years I had heard of them and read about their culture. Finally, I had one of the most unique experiences of my life when, on 12 October 2005, I attended one of their rodeos in a small hamlet outside of Guayaquil called Salitre. Rodeos in Montubio land have existed for hundreds of years and have virtually been unnoticed by the outside world except when rodeo stands have collapsed and maimed or killed attendees.

In celebration of 'Día de Raza', the Association of Rice Growers sponsors an all day celebration with a wonderful rodeo. The grandstands seat 4,000 revellers for lots of rodeo events and pomp and circumstance. These cowboys are tough dudes and compete for fame and glory. It also presents women competitors ranging from 13 to 16 years of age. The pounding music, flowing beer and guns blaring every time the crowd is pleased, are not for the faint of heart. The rodeo starts about noon on Ecuador time. You need to arrive early for a seat and remember, once you are seated, there is really no way out. The rodeo lasts until late in the afternoon and partying continues throughout the night. There are thousands of people outside the rodeo who attend an outside dance. It is a wonderful experience if you want to experience something unique. Out of the approximate 10,000 people there, I appeared to be the only foreigner. Many of the people were excited that an outsider was present. At the end of the day of festivities, Montubios will ask others how the fiesta went. They will say "the fiesta was great, someone died" or "the fiesta was not so good, no one died".

LANGUAGE

CHAPTER 8

'Class distinction pervades the language as well.'
—Albert B Franklin, *Ecuador: Portrait of a People*

In Ecuador, there are about 12 million Spanish-speakers; about 3 million speakers of American Indian languages; 65,000 English-speakers; 32,000 German-speakers; 11,000 Bokmål- or Dano–Norwegian-speakers; 7,000 Chinese-speakers; and 1,800 Arabic-speakers. If you're going to live in or visit Ecuador, Spanish is the most useful language to master, although American Indian languages (especially Quichua) may be the first language of many indigenous people.

ECUADORIAN SPANISH

Spanish is the official language, spoken by about 90 per cent of the population. If you're looking for a school to study Spanish, good news, Ecuador is one of the most popular destinations in Latin America for *estudiantes del idioma español* (students of the Spanish language).

The form of Spanish used here is more accurately referred to as *castellano* (Castilian), the basis of modern standard *español* (Spanish). Castilian was commonly spoken in northern and central Spain and became the official language in the 15th century. It came to be spoken in southern and western Spain but with a different accent. (The most obvious difference between northern and central Castilian and southern and western Castilian can be heard in the pronunciation of the letter *c*. In the northern and central region, it is pronounced as an English 'th'; and in the southern and western regions as an English 's'.) It was the southern and western form of *castellano* that became the standard in Latin American Spanish.

Accents

There are three distinct Spanish accents or intonations in Ecuador originating from the Costa, the Sierra and the Oriente regions. After some time here, you will be able to distinguish which part of the country the speaker comes from. Look out also for the regional differences in pronunciation and words. One of the most interesting accents in Ecuador is from the inhabitants of Cuenca. They have a very graceful lilting quality to their speech, as if they are singing when they speak. Ecuadorians outside of Cuenca often describe the Cuencanos language in this way: When one Cuencano is speaking you have a solo, when there are two Cuencanos speaking you have a duo, and when three Cuencanos are speaking you have a trio. However, if there are more than three Cuencanos speaking you have a choir.

Along the coastal region you will find that most inhabitants will drop the *s*, *y* and *z* off the end of a word. This can cause

havoc for a nonnative speaker. For example, if one is to say *los libros*, *los pollos* or *los zapatos,* the listener will hear *lo libro*, *lo pollo* and *lo zapato*. The nonnative speaker will wonder why the *s* has been dropped off plural nouns. An example of the *z* being dropped in coastal speech is with the word *lápiz* (pencil) and *maíz* (maize), pronounced as *lapi* and *mai*.

Many linguists believe that the Spanish spoken in Quito and Loja is the purest form of Spanish spoken in Ecuador. There is a slight difference in the cadence of Spanish spoken in the Sierra as opposed to the Costa or Oriente regions. There is a small stress on the third syllable from the end of the word. When Serranos speak, it almost sounds like music and some people have compared their pronunciation to birds singing. However, many Serranos find this comment derogatory. The Serranos enjoy pronouncing their *r* letters. So much so that the Costeños like to do the same, calling them Serranos! The Serrano would pronounce *carro* (car) as *carro* whereas the Costeño would say *caro*. The regional accents really come into play with words like *caballo* (horse), which sounds like *cabasho* in the Sierra but *cabayo* on the coast. Have fun learning to distinguish between the regional accents!

SLANG

As in any culture, slang terms develop that often replace standard language. Proper use of slang will help you break the ice more quickly with the locals. Slang or colloquialisms in any culture often distinguish the outsiders from the insiders of the culture and are considered informal in nature. However, many Ecuadorians will judge the social class they consider you to be in purely by your use of slang.

I remember the first time I used the slang word *pana* (good friend). The local I was speaking to was pleasantly surprised. It is important, however, to remember that slang takes time, study and experience to use properly. When I used the same word on a second occasion, the female Ecuadorian I was addressing was not impressed. She explained to me that she understood the term as being used with someone you wanted to smoke marijuana with. I quickly informed her that I had no intention of doing that, and learnt later that

this term had different meanings when used with different classes. Use of slang will often tell others what social rank you maintain.

Higher social class Ecuadorians believe slang is primarily used by the lower classes. When I used the word *pluto* to announce that I was drunk, a local friend haughtily replied that she didn't belong to the lower classes and not to use that term around her. (I have included some common middle and lower class slang words in the Glossary at the back of the book.)

However, there are numerous slang words which are used by every stratum of society. I was once in a cab several years ago when it ran over a speed bump very roughly. The driver exclaimed "*¡Odio el vigilante acostado!*" (Literally translated "I hate the traffic officer that is lying down!") I turned around thinking he had run over a traffic cop until I realised that, in Ecuador, a speed bump is referred to as a traffic officer lying down. (In the Sierra, the word for 'vigilante' is *chapa*.) Slang vocabulary should, in most cases, not be used during formal situations, job interviews or presentations.

'NICETIES'

In Ecuador, another aspect of Spanish is its use of 'niceties'. Ecuadorians are generally more courteous or formal in their language than the Americans. They try not to give commands but make requests to everyone from superiors to cabdrivers. This is especially true between employees and employers. For example, it is very rare for employees to call their boss by their first name.

Diplomacy is a common characteristic in much of the language used. A person might say "*No, usted no me ha comprendido.*" ("No, you don't understand me.") But the more appropriate and polite way to say this is "*Me he explicado mal—voy a expresarme mejor.*" ("I explained it poorly—I am going to express myself better.") Notice the attempt to avoid conflict. This is an important cultural custom in Ecuador.

Speak Elegantly

Ecuadorian writer Rómulo Vinueza explains that one should speak with 'elegance' and 'sincerity'. Another example of this is the various ways to express thanks. While saying *gracias* conveys thanks, the following phrases express the same emotion more genuinely and sincerely. In fact, after receiving a compliment it is considered rude by some to answer with a mere *gracias*!

Useful phrases include:
- "*¡Le quedo muy agradecido!*"—"I am very grateful!"
- "*¡No sé como agradercerle!*"—"I don't know how to thank you!"
- "*¡Muy agradecido!*"—"I am very grateful!"

NAMES

An Ecuadorian's first name is usually followed by his or her father's last name and the mother's maiden name. Juan García Lopez's father's last name is García and his mother's maiden name is Lopez. In the phonebook, you would look up Juan's name under García Lopez, Juan. In most cases, you would use the first last name, except at formal occasions, in writing or for legal purposes, i.e. Juan García Lopez would more often be referred to as Juan García.

The use of the last name with a married woman can also be confusing for an English speaker. If Julia Batista Guzman marries Juan García Lopez, she may be referred to in several ways. The one form she is never referred to is Señora Juan García, thus using her husband's last name. In a formal situation, *de* (which means 'of') is inflected after her husband's last name, i.e. Julia Batista de García. In many cases, she will still be referred to as Julia Batista or Julia Batista Guzman. When her husband introduces her he will say "May I introduce my wife, Julia Batista Lopez, to you". When referring to her, you may say "La Señora Julia Batista," still using her father's last name. Addressing her directly, you would say "Señora Batista (father's last name)" or "Señora García (husband's last name)".

Another confusion for foreigners is how to address a woman—Señorita (Miss) or Señora (Mrs)? There is no 'Ms' title in Ecuador. The simple rule I use is if the woman is relatively young, address her as Señorita. She will correct you if she is married and respond by saying "Señora". If she appears middle-aged or older it is relatively safe to address her as Señora.

TITLES

The most common professional titles in Ecuador are: Doctor/Doctora (male and female titles for Doctor), Ingeniero/Ingeniera (male and female titles for Engineer) and Licenciado/Licenciada (referring to a male or female who is a specialist or is qualified in a particular field, often a lawyer). The last name is usually used with the title, e.g. Licenciada Lopez or Ingeniero Guzman. It is just as common to address Ingeniero Guzman as Ingeniero, even in a room full of other Ingenieros!

Doctors are sometimes referred to as *medicos*. Even if the person does not actually hold such a title, titles are sometimes used in jest and as a form of endearment.

NICKNAMES

You will soon discover in Ecuador that most people have

a nickname of sorts among good friends or family. Nicknames or *apodos* are a very strong part of Ecuadorian culture. You will most probably be given one too.

I know someone who was a little chubby when she was young and was nicknamed Pocha (meaning short and pudgy). Nearing 50 years old, fit and slim, she's still called Pocha by her family and friends. She even introduces herself as Pocha.

Many of the nicknames in the Sierra use Quichua combined with Spanish. There are literally hundreds of nicknames, such as Huevito (little egg), Carepavo (turkey face) and Pelusa (referring to someone with fine hair). The Manta area nicknames are also used for people from different regions of Ecuador. Care should be used if you're going to use regional *apodos* as they are often perceived as derogatory. These should only be used if you're a close friend. Here are some examples: Guaitambos from Ambato, Morlacos from Cuenca, Morenos or Negros from Esmeraldas, Monos from Guayaquil, Puendos from Imbabura, Mashcas from Latacunga/Cotopaxi, Pata Amarilla from Manabí, Cara de Papa (meaning potato face), Longo and Pachuco from Quito.

Given names have a unique Ecuadorian twist to them in the Manta and the Manabi province. Mothers and fathers in this area often name a child after a product or event surrounding conception or birth. Such given names include Alka-Seltzer, gasoline and *aspirina*. You will also find along the coast many blacks with the given name of a former US president such as Washington or Jefferson.

FORMS OF ADDRESS

What is the correct way to address an individual? In English, there is only one word: 'you'. Spanish has two forms: *tú* or *usted*. *Tú* is considered the familiar form and *usted,* the formal.

Tú is primarily used with very close friends and family, although children may use *usted* with a parent. To be on the safe side, I always use *usted* if there is any ambiguity. This is the correct form with strangers or in business. If someone wishes you to refer to him or her with the *tú* form, they will let you know. *Tú* can also be used by someone wishing to put you down, indicating that the speaker is of a higher social standing.

INDIGENOUS LANGUAGES

It is believed that at the time of the Spanish conquest, some 30 indigenous languages were spoken in Ecuador. Today, only about 12 indigenous languages exist in the lowlands (of which nine are used in the Oriente: Siona; Secoya; Tetete; Cofán; Huaorani; the Jívaroan languages Shuaran and Achua; Quichua; and Zapora). Only three indigenous languages (Colorado, Cayapa, and Coaiquer) are still spoken in the western coastal lowlands, with a total of about 48,000 speakers. The only indigenous language left in the Sierra is the northern dialect of the Quichuan language family (known as high-land Quichua or *chinchay*), with about 3.5 million speakers.

The decline of many indigenous languages and the increasing bilingualism with Spanish is a product of the locals' increasing contact with whites and mestizos. The domination and exploitation of indigenous communities by whites and mestizos in the quest for 'progress' has posed a threat to the land, and to the people and cultures who originally inhabited it.

Quichua

The Quichua refer to themselves as *runa* (the people). The Quichuan languages were the languages of the former Inca Empire (Tawantinsuyu). There are at least 20 dialects of Quichua in Ecuador. Quichua in Peru is written Quechua.

Some Quechuan words have entered the English language: *cuca* (cocoa), *huanu* (*guano*), *huanaco, huanacu (guanaco)*, *pampa* (pampa), *puma* (puma), *quipu* (quipu) and *kinua, kinoa* (quinoa). The most difficult sound for English-speakers is the Quechuan *q*, which sounds like the German 'ch' in Bach, except it is pronounced even further back in the throat. Quichua can be heard in Andean music, which is getting easier to find in the United States, either in its purer form, used by groups such as Markahuasi, Ayllu Sulca and Ch'uwa Yacu, or its more Westernised forms, used by the group Inti-Illimani. The Peruvian singer Yma Sumac has the Quichuan name *ima sumaq*, which means 'how beautiful!'.

Quichua has been heavily influenced by Spanish. Some 30 per cent of the lexicon, even with monolingual speakers, comes from Spanish. Examples include *riru* (from Spanish *dedo* meaning 'finger'), *arwi* (from Spanish *adobe* meaning 'sun-dried brick' or 'seasoned'), *chufir* (from Spanish *chofer* meaning 'chauffeur') and *sirbisa* (from Spanish *cerveza* meaning 'ale' or 'beer'). Some Quichuan words have also passed into Latin American Spanish:

- *papa*   potato
- *choclo*   corncob
- *chompa*   jacket
- *cushma*   shirt
- *china*   maid or worker
- *cuy*   guinea pig
- *pachamanca*   earth oven
- *quena*   flute
- *cachaco*   cop
- *chacra*   farm

(There are over 100 Quichuan basic vocabulary words in the Glossary section at the back of this book.)

Quichua has become increasingly popular in US university programmes over the last five to ten years. It is a langauge now spoken by 11 million people in five countries straddling the Andes, from Colombia to Argentina.

One of the best programmes for Quichua is the Amazon and Andes Field School, open to university students and educators. Operated by Arizona State University, it runs a winter and summer programme which are offered on the banks of the Napo River, giving the student full immersion into the Quichua culture. Language programmes in Waorani and Shuar are also offered. For more information visit: http://www.asu.edu.

LEARNING SPANISH

Spanish schools are a very important source of income for Ecuador. Walking along Avenida Amazonas in Quito, you will find no shortage to choose from. But you will also find varying degrees of quality. The competition is so fierce that I have even seen language classes offered for as little as US$ 3 per hour. Most schools offer live-in arrangements with Ecuadorian families which will, no doubt, help you improve your Spanish.

School Tips

Here is a list of a few things you should look out for when choosing a school:

- How long has the school been in operation? (Newer schools may not necessarily be better.)
- What types of programmes do they offer?
- What is the teacher-student ratio?
- What is the educational level of the teacher?
- Will the school provide references?
- Will the school help you in the event of an emergency?

I believe that references are a very good indicator of what a good programme is. Another option for finding a programme is a broker or agent located in the United States representing the school. These are usually paid a commission and may represent several schools. Three such services based in the United States are Language Link (http://www.langlink.com), Spanish Abroad (http://www.Spanishabroad.com) and AmeriSpan (http://www.amerispan.com). These firms have been around for some time and have good reputations.

Additonal recommendations are:

- Academia De Español Quito
  Website: http://regio.com/ecuador/learnsp1.html
- Academia De Español 'Surpacifico'
  Website: http://www.surpacifico.k12.ec
- Academia Latínoamericana de Español
  Website: http://www.ecuador-Peru-bolivia.com
- Activa Spanish School
  Website: http://www.activa-spanish.com
- Andean Study Programs
  Website: http://www.andeanstudy.com
- Apuinty Spanish School
  Website: http://www.apuintyspanishschool.com
- Bipo and Toni's Academia de Español
  Website: http://www.bipo.net
- Centro de Español Vida Verde
  Website: http://www.vidaverde.com
- Escuela de Español Simón Bolívar or Simón Bolívar Spanish School
  Website: http://www.simon-bolivar.com
- Galápagos Spanish School
  Website: http://www.galapagos.edu.ec
- Instituto Superior de Español
  Website: http://www.instituto-superior.net
- Mitad Del Mundo
  Website: http://www.ecua.net.ec/mitadmundo
- Ordex Cultural Programs
  Website: http://www.ordex.org/pages/language_culture_programs.htm

- Otavalo Spanish Institute
  Website: http://www.otavalospanish.com
- Quito Spanish Institute
  Website: http://www.quitospanish.com

WORKING IN ECUADOR

CHAPTER 9

'We came back from (Ecuador) and
we were writing our recommendation.
We thought Ecuador was a very stable country.
There hadn't been a revolution in 40 years...
an Ecuadorian friend called to inform us
a revolution had just broken out.'
—Melvyn N Klein, founding partner of the
investment partnership GKH Partners, L P
(Quote taken from *Financial World*, 21 October 1996)

ECONOMY

Ecuador's economy is one of the smallest in Latin America and heavily dependent on external markets. This has made it vulnerable in terms of trade (the relation between export and import prices) shocks. This vulnerability, as well as inadequate export diversification and structural reform in the public and financial sectors, has resulted in a poor economic performance since the early 1980s.

The late 1990s found the economy shaken to its knees, resulting in its worst depression in 70 years. The economy has shrunk substantially with hyperinflation and the government has had to take the drastic step of replacing the country's currency, the sucre, with the US dollar. The middle class has virtually disappeared and those with the means have left the country in search of better opportunities.

Historically, much of Ecuador's economic past had revolved around agriculture. For many decades, Ecuador's largest export product was cocoa. Other agricultural products, primarily coffee and bananas, later increased in importance. Ecuador's economic landscape changed significantly when oil was found and exported. Almost overnight, Ecuador became flushed with oil earnings.

Oil is still Ecuador's largest export. This small nation is Latin America's fourth largest oil exporter and sixth biggest producer of oil. It produces an average of 500,000 barrels of crude oil daily. In recent years, at least 40 per cent of the country's budget has been derived from oil revenue. One third of the tax revenue is from petroleum.

The government tried to use the tremendous amount of new revenue coming from oil in the 1970s to finance the industrialisation of Ecuador. This resulted in a fiasco when interest rates were raised and oil prices fell. Import substitutions were used in an attempt to promote development by using high import taxes to discourage the cheaper, and thus more attractive, imports. This contributed to increased corruption and tax avoidance by such methods as double invoicing by many import companies. Guarantees of future oil revenue provided financing that established large state-owned industrial companies that were lethargic and bureaucratic. This plan didn't produce results.

Tough Times

I tried to start a sales agency in Ecuador during this period, in the early 1980s, and the experience was horrendous. The requirements for importation were enough to kill my company. Companies with deep pockets were the ones that survived. Between 1984 and 1988, the government's import substitution programme was wound down and some of the large state-owned companies were privatised.

Petroleum

Oil is a critical factor in Ecuador's economy. There is a long history of oil production in Ecuador, beginning in the first part of the 20th century along the coast of Ecuador. This was followed by major discoveries in the Amazon, beginning in 1917. It was in the late 1960s and the early 1970s that oil became a significant export product and gradually replaced Ecuador's dependency on agricultural exports. Production began at about 78,000 BPD (BPD = barrels per day) and has increased to present-day levels of around 500,000 BPD. About 4.6 billion barrels of proven oil reserves remain.

Oil exports produced a brief period of high growth for the country in the 1970s. But El Niño in 1998 led to widespread crop devastation. Then a sharp decline in world oil prices drove Ecuador's economy into a free-fall by 1999. This marked the beginning of the collapse of Ecuador's banking sector, and it defaulted on its external loans later that year. The currency depreciated by 70 per cent throughout 1999, forcing a desperate government to replace its local sucres with US dollars in 2000. This move stabilised the currency, but was followed by protests and riots, the deposits of some Ecuadorians having depreciated by as much as 400 per cent.

Petroecuador (previously CEPE) is the state oil company and has begun to open up some concessions, operating joint ventures with many foreign firms. All oil is the property of Ecuador. The main pipeline in Ecuador is the Trans-Ecuadorian (SOTE), which starts in Lago Agrio and transports about 380,000 BPD of oil some 300 miles to a port north of Esmeraldas. It was built in the early 1970s and has experienced numerous problems. More recently, these have been attributed to sabotage. International experts believe that some of the problems with the pipeline are due to lack of maintenance and earthquakes. In 2004, a major landslide stopped the flow of oil and Ecuador lost nearly 50 per cent of its revenues for the year. In 2001, a new pipeline was conceived called Oleducto de Crudos Pesados (OCP) and it runs almost parallel to SOTE. It began production in 2003 and almost doubled Ecuador's output. It was highly contested by a number of environmental and indigenous groups. This industry is susceptible to criticism due to the result of deforestation and pollution from the waste of oil products as well as to the effect on local cultures.

An environmental lawyer has blamed multinational oil companies for widespread skin, respiratory and other diseases; a rise in miscarriages; increased cancer rates for as many as 30,000 impoverished Indians and settlers; and widespread environmental damage. An Ecuadorian native has even launched a class-action lawsuit against Texaco (now Chevron) in the United States on behalf of

Wildlife and habitats have been devastated through pollution (including oil waste dumping) and accidents, such as oil spills. Oil exploration has contaminated water and land resources that the population itself depends on, ruining the indigenous lifestyles of hundreds of native communities.

Oriente residents. His allegation is that 'they poisoned the rivers, killed the fish and made the people sick'.

The effect that oil pollution has had on human society has led to anti-government movements and uprisings in many areas. As a result of the damaging effect oil production has had on the Indians in Ecuador for the past 20 years, the Indians have resisted government oil exploration efforts, demanding rights to their ancestral lands.

Bananas

Ecuador is king when it comes to bananas. It is the largest exporter of bananas in the world. Approximately one-third of Ecuador's bananas are exported to the United States, one third to Europe and the rest to other countries, including Russia, Argentina, Chile and Japan.

Ecuador's largest exporter is a national producer—Noboa, the world's fourth largest banana company. While the big three US-based companies of Dole, Fresh Del Monte and Chiquita control nearly all exports in South American countries, Ecuador's banana export industry is unique in its domination by national producers. Although Ecuadorian

Bananas for sale in the countryside between Guayaquil and Cuenca.

bananas have to cross the Panama Canal in order to reach the European market, Ecuador's banana industry is not unionised, which keeps labour costs low.

Most farms are medium-sized (about 120 acres in land area) and giant trading houses control the distribution. About 10 per cent of a population of approximately 13 million inhabitants is somehow connected to the banana industry. The mid-1990s saw a tremendous boom in sales, approaching a billion dollars a year. Everyone was planting bananas trying to make a quick dollar. A number of pesticides banned in foreign countries were permitted to be used in Ecuador.

Workers reported earning an average of US$ 56 per month, with few if any benefits. This compares to an average monthly wage of over US$ 500 in Panama, US$ 200 to US$ 300 in Colombia, US$ 200 in Costa Rica, US$ 150 to US$ 200 in Honduras and US$ 120 to US$ 150 on Guatemala's Atlantic Coast. In other banana-exporting countries, banana workers, even some non-union workers, typically receive social benefits such as housing, health care, potable water,

electricity and education for their children. In Costa Rica, even non-union banana workers get benefits left over from the time when unions were strong.

On many of these plantations, it is not uncommon to see warning signs telling workers that they must leave the fields when aerial spraying begins, and remain away for at least two hours after it stops. But at only one Ecuadorian plantation did workers report compliance with this norm, and only after the banana workers' union put up a fight. Where there is worker housing on the plantations, the houses are often located in the middle of the fields and are thus exposed to spraying. Workers know that exposure to these chemicals is unhealthy but complain that no one has ever informed them of the adverse effects of exposure. Packing workers report that they, especially women, are exposed to chemicals used to disinfect and clean the bananas prior to packing. They reported that they were not provided with any sort of safety equipment.

Banana workers have little power under the current structure and have expressed extreme distrust in the ability or the will of government authorities to protect their rights to free association and freedom of expression.

In the absence of social criteria governing world trade, consumers can play a strong role to support the rights of banana workers. Efforts are underway to organise unions in Ecuador's banana industry. Although this is a long-term project, it will need significant support from activists and consumers in countries like the United States that buy large quantities of Ecuadorian bananas.

Ecuadorian banana workers are not calling for a boycott; but consumers can express a preference for 'sweat-free' bananas to retailers. Likewise, we can pressure the Ecuadorian government to respect its citizens' labour rights.

Shrimp

Shrimp is Ecuador's third largest export after oil and bananas. Anyone visiting Ecuador will see and taste that shrimp is a staple and that some of the largest and best shrimps in the world are from Ecuador.

Mangrove Destruction

Besides the destruction of the mangrove forests, many shrimp producers have significant problems with pesticide runoff originally used to fumigate bananas. As of 1999, shrimp farmers have contributed to the destruction of more than 65 per cent of the Ecuador's mangrove habitat. This situation is set to worsen, due to a growing demand for shrimps from the United States, Japan and western Europe.

I first read about Ecuador's newfound wealth in shrimp farming in 1981. An American from the United States had been successful in other countries and began the shrimp farming process in Ecuador, making fortunes for some but taking a toll on Ecuador's beautiful mangrove forests. These forests have been decimated up and down the coast and significant intrusion has been made in the forests in northern Ecuador towards Esmeraldas. Ecuador is now the fourth largest producer of shrimp in the world and the largest in Latin America. There are at least 200,000 people with direct or indirect employment in the shrimp industry, and at least 105,000 hectares (259,460 acres) are dedicated to shrimp production.

The arrival of the lucrative commercial shrimp farms and the clearing of mangroves to construct aqua-culture ponds started in the 1980s. The net profits of the farms were so high that the idea caught on and spread rapidly along the coast. A one-hectare shrimp farm could earn a gross income of US$ 5,000 to US$ 15,000 per year. Once cut, however, the mangrove cannot fully recover for more than 100 years and many benefits to the ecosystem are lost. The waste water from the farms also pollute the surrounding area with antibiotics and chemicals used to prevent shrimp disease. There is growing conservation awareness among the local commercial farmers and foreign environmental organisations.

Flowers

Ecuador is home to literally thousands of species of plants that decorate the cities and countryside. In the last 20 years, a significant business has developed in the export of its beautiful roses, and sales of orchids and exotic plants are

on the rise, mostly to the United States, Russia and Europe. In 1997, flower exports represented about 70 per cent of non-traditional agricultural production.

Nestled in the deep valleys between the mountain ranges of the Andes, you will notice large flower plantations throughout the Sierra. Eighty per cent of the production of cut flowers come from the provinces of Cotopaxi, Pichincha (especially from Cayambe) and Imbabura. Ecuador is now producing over a billion roses a year and continues to produce good margins for the producers. Most of the Ecuadorian flower-growing companies are locally owned. It was in the late 1980s that many of the companies were started with an ever increasing world demand. In 1997 terms, each hectare required an investment of over US$ 250,000. Net prices for roses have been as high as US$ 0.25 in the last several years. In 2000, a check with a large grower in Cotopaxi revealed that its net sales price is often in the

US$ 0.10–US$ 0.11 range. Approxiamately 400,000 boxes of roses are shipped to the US in the two weeks prior to Valentine's Day.

There are substantial margins between the selling price from the grower and the retail price for the end client, primarily taking into consideration transportation, storage and marketing functions. Ecuador's competitive advantage has been that of labour. Flower growing is labour intensive, with between 10 to 12 labourers required per hectare (2.4 acres) of roses, for example. The marketing of flowers is done through specialist marketing companies, a number of which are foreign-owned. Contracts are not often the norm and business is often conducted on trust.

While Colombians and their influence in Ecuador are often depicted in a negative light by the press, this is one industry in which they have had a significant and profitable impact. Colombia, a major flower grower and exporter in its own right, has provided much of the technical know-how for developing the Ecuadorian flower industry. Flowers have officially been considered by the government to be a non-traditional export compared to such products as bananas or

Roses being readied for export near Cotopaxi.

petroleum. However, the impact on the economy has been substantial, especially in terms of offering employment opportunities in rural areas. Between 1990 and 1997, the number of flower producers jumped from 39 to 179 and from 286 to 1,549 hectares (706–3,827 acres). In 2005, there were over 300 flower companies. Production has also begun in the lower Sierra. Flower production along the coast presents opportunities, especially for orchids and other tropical varieties.

During the same period mentioned above, employment increased an average of 8 per cent per annum. Women make up 70 per cent of the labour pool for the flower industry and they are primarily involved in the areas of cultivation and harvesting. It is believed by most management that women are more adept at the growing of flowers, it being compared to child-rearing. Men are primarily involved in the maintenance, irrigation and fumigation processes. Younger workers are often preferred, with an average age of between 22 to 25 years old. These jobs are highly desirable in rural areas and in 1997-terms, paid about US$ 190 per month. Many new employees have been hired because of references from current levels using the *palanca* system, which is discussed in Chapter Four, Fitting into Society.

One of the major concerns of labourers is getting ill or injured due to pesticides and chemicals (currently 100 different pesticides are used). The Flower Label Programme, an organisation comprised of flower importers and buyers from Germany, provides certification (The Green Seal), which promotes environmental consciousness and the good health of employees. In 1997, there were only a small number of firms certified in Ecuador but many were awaiting approval. Maintenance and harvesting are risk areas and cuts are common. The main physical complaints from workers are colic, blurred vision and headaches. In November 2000, I visited a large plantation in Cotopaxi which clearly had responsible management. Workers seemed to be very well protected, and wore masks to full suits for fumigation. It was truly a first-class operation. This industry has a bright future in store for it.

Exports

I once spoke to a friend who said, "If Ecuador could get its act together there could be thousands of millionaires." She was alluding to the economic potential of Ecuador's fruits, flowers, artisan crafts and so on. While her statement may be somewhat true, Ecuador has some significant roadblocks to overcome before this Utopia can be reached. Some of these roadblocks include: the oligarchy present in much of Ecuador which wants to keep things as they are; low production numbers; a dependence on centralism by the government; the fragile nature of financial institutions; the lack of reinvestment or investment of capital (capital flight risk); and significant deforestation and environmental stress.

UNEMPLOYMENT

One thing about visiting or working in Ecuador is the amount of activity. It always looks bustling and as though there is a lot of commerce going on. But the truth of the matter is that most people are working hard just to survive. More than 50 per cent of the population live below the poverty line, leading lives of quiet desperation. The rural areas, for the most part, are more impoverished than the urban sector. In my interviews with numerous small businesspersons in October 2005, they indicated that everybody looks busy but no one is making money—just treading water.

Competitive Business

I visited a Pilates studio owner in October 2005. When she first opened she was the only studio in Guayaquil and was quite popular and making good money. Soon, other studios began to open and offer lower prices and her business began to decrease. She surmised that Ecuadorians are much more price driven than other cultures.

Because of large migration patterns to cities such as Guayaquil and Quito, unemployment rates are usually higher. Men suffer a higher level of unemployment in the cities than women and the reverse is true in rural areas. During the 1990s, the official unemployment rate was 9 per cent. This has risen to 11 per cent in 2005. But the real rates are generally much higher.

The economic situation of both unemployment and underemployment has contributed greatly to what is called the 'informal economy', to which thousands belong. This is evident throughout the country. Several years ago, you could walk along any major street in Guayaquil and Quito and see hundreds of people camped out on pavements with blankets spread out or cardboard boxes displaying their wares. These wares for sale ranged from batteries to watches and everything in between. What was really amazing is that these so-called *ambulantes* were often parked right in front of a large shop selling the same type of items and no one seemed concerned about the so-called 'illegal operators'. On almost every corner, you could also find small portable stands where the vendor sold different types of sweets and small items. However, both Quito and Guayaquil have basically eliminated the street vendor by moving him to shopping centres designed for small vendors. In Quito, there are 12 such centres. Vendors on the street can be arrested and

Even foreign currency can be hawked on the streets.

fined in Quito and Guayaquil. While it looks better without the vendors lining the pavements, it certainly has been a cultural transition. The street vendors have always been an integral part of the culture.

For the most part, lower-class Ecuadorians live a sub-standard existence. I wanted to experience the vendors-life back in the 1990s and took to Ecuador some watches that I had bought at a liquidation sale. I took a blanket and walked down to 9 de Octubre in Guayaquil, parked my blanket and laid out the watches. I attracted a huge crowd who seemed more interested to see a foreigner on the street than the watches. I spent several hours there and imagined how difficult it must be to do this every day with no protection from the heat or bathrooms available. The lowest strata of society and members of all races who were just amazed that I was there at all, surrounded me. Luckily, traffic police, who often chase street vendors away unless they are paid a small bribe, did not approach me. I did manage to sell all the watches and moved on, grateful not to have to earn my living in such a manner.

This type of operation still exists in many of the smaller towns in Ecuador. The streets throng with these vendors, especially during the Christmas holidays. There are also thousands of *ambulantes* that sell juice or popcorn in the streets via pushcarts in the suburbs and smaller cities.

One of my most poignant memories of Ecuador is that of the popcorn-makers, who, with a small cart, roast up the delicacy on a small flame. There are also a number of vendors who cook food at home and visit shops and bars to hawk their food. Goods sold via vendors have often been obtained by legitimate means but a large number may have been stolen. There are also a number of people who have a full-time job and yet look for other sources of income. I have met many people who sell goods such as jewellery from their homes, operate beauty shops, sell imported clothing or who open up small shops selling small items such as soft drinks, toilet paper and necessities. There is not a block in Ecuador where you can't find such a set-up. Just look for signs that read: *Se Vende Colas*.

Jobs are highly prized in Ecuador compared to the United States where most people feel it is relatively easy to find some type of employment. Individuals keep jobs for longer periods of time and when jobs are advertised, the competition can be very fierce.

Fight for Survival

I once had a friend who put an advertisement in the paper for a delivery person. The ad stated that interviews would start at 9:00 am. On that particular day, he heard a large commotion outside his office at about 8:00 am. He discovered that a small riot had broken out with people fighting for a place in the queue.

Many accounting or CPA firms, especially for large companies, act as an intermediary when hiring employees. The CPA firm will usually place anonymous advertisements requesting that a resume be sent to a post box. A survey of such adverts might lead one to believe that there is age discrimination in Ecuador in terms of employment. Many advertisements will state that the applicant must be under a certain age (usually under 40 years old). Also, most requests for resumes require a photograph of the applicant.

MANAGING EMPLOYEES

Consensus management is not the norm in Ecuador. Management decisions often come from high up in an organisation (*as previously mentioned in the palanca scenario above*). While labour unions do have clout in Ecuador and it is hard to fire someone, most employees seem to fear their supervisors.

Ecuadorians as employees will often tell supervisors or managers what they want to hear, trying to avoid conflict. Ecuadorians are generally viewed as hard workers who show up on time, but more out of fear than punctuality. A foreign manager from Denmark, interviewed for this book, feels that Ecuadorian employees need lots of direction and guidance, even after having done a specific job for a length of time.

Managers will not generally socialise with subordinates, and if you're a male with a female secretary it will be assumed by many employees that she is also your mistress. Foreign women managers must set a, serious tone, especially with male subordinates. You're already fighting a tough stereotype; Ecuadorian men think that most foreign women (especially from the United States) are available for sexual liaisons. It is important to understand as a manager that joking or laughing at one's self should be minimised as you will not, then, be respected. It is important to remember that yelling or criticising employees in front of others will cause great embarrassment for the employee. Remaining calm and under control will yield better results with employees.

NEGOTIATING

Here are some general guidelines that are important to successful negotiations while in Ecuador:

- You really should speak Spanish at an acceptable level. If you don't, you will need an interpreter or representative who speaks both languages. When using an interpreter, you should meet with him beforehand and discuss his preferences while conducting a negotiation. Make sure you are speaking more slowly than normal and do not use slang. You may have to go over highly technical terms together before your negotiations. You should also keep comments brief by pausing to allow the interpreter to convey the message. Speak to the recipient of your message and not to the interpreter.

- You will be judged by your appearance. Be sure that your shoes shine and your fingernails are clean and manicured. You should dress appropriately, depending on the business you are visiting. Suits are the norm in Quito. You cannot go wrong with grey or navy blue. White shirts and ties make a good impression. If you have a limited wardrobe, I suggest mixing several grey and tan trousers with a navy blue sports jacket. White and light blue shirts should work well. It does not look good to show up in Quito dressed as if you're going to a beach resort. Guayaquil is a little less formal. However, businessmen, especially from financial institutions, do wear suits. Lighter material is preferred to help beat the heat. Women should also dress conservatively in business attire suitable for conducting business in places such as San Francisco or New York.

- Pleasantries and small talk are often good ways to start conversations. Avoid talking about Ecuador's problems with Peru or Colombia. I like to focus on positive things about the region that I am in. While in Quito, for example, you might talk about the beautiful architecture. In Guayaquil, you can comment on the beautiful Malecón project along the Guayas River. Remember, regionalism is a very serious issue. I suggest that, during negotiations, you try to ascertain as quickly as possible where the other parties are from. That would help you make conversation.

- Politeness is a sign of breeding to most Ecuadorians and it is almost impossible to be too polite. However, remember that their politeness is no indication which way they are leaning in a negotiation.

- Negotiations take time and it may take you several trips to build up a relationship with a potential customer or partner. Once, I used a representative that had been in Ecuador for over 30 years and was well trusted. Even then, the customers for our product started off by purchasing small amounts. Assure Ecuadorians that their market is important to your firm and don't group Ecuador with all the other Latin American countries.

- Remain patient throughout all negotiations. Ecuadorians will try to exploit any show of temper. Assure them that you're interested in both parties succeeding and that you are after long-term results.

- Talk to non-competitive companies doing business in Ecuador for advice on dealing with Ecuadorians.

- Don't underestimate the influence that secretaries and support staff can have. They can make things very difficult for you, for example, by taking any opportunity to delay you. Being courteous and cheerful will reap rich dividends.

- Remember, being direct or frank doesn't normally produce good results. Keep things open-ended. Don't show all your cards at once. Keep alternative plans that may be acceptable to both parties.

- Most Ecuadorians will never say 'no' and will evade the final decision. They may also be trying to gain more in the negotiations by this method. Friderich Hassaurek commented in his book *Four Years Among the Ecuadorians* (a reprint of the 1867 book *Four Years Among the Spanish-Americans*) that Ecuadorians are very difficult to deal with in business. Often when agreements had been made, they would change things right at the end and demand more or change prices. I once contacted a Spanish school in Quito who was not really known on the Internet but had a website. I suggested that they place an advertisement. The lady proprietor stated how hard business was and that, if a small discount could be offered, she would place an advertisement. I told her that I would have to think about it. I told her that I would be back in a week to ask her again. The next week I approached her and agreed to the discount and she replied that she would love to do it in the future, not actually saying 'no'. I was very polite and suggested that I would e-mail her in the future to see if she were ready. Ecuadorians love to haggle politely and never want to pay full price.

FAST FACTS ABOUT ECUADOR

CHAPTER 10

'In this country you might as well throw your watch away.
Nobody, not even the police, are on time.'
—Herr Vogeli, *The Donkey Inside*

Official Name
Republic of Ecuador

Capital
Quito

Flag
The Ecuadorian flag comprises three horizontal bands. The first band is yellow and is double the width of the blue and red bands. The colour yellow symbolises the abundance and fertility of Ecuador's crops and land. The second band is blue and represents the sea and the sky. The last band is red and signifies the blood shed by soldiers in the battles for independence.

The Ecuadorian coat of arms is positioned at the centre of the flag. The condor is seen as a symbol of protection but at the same time, it is ready to attack any enemy. At the centre of the coat of arms is Ecuador's highest mountain, Chimborazo, and the steamboat Guayas.

National Anthem
Salve, Oh Patria! (We Salute You Our Homeland!)

Official Languages
Spanish
Amerindian languages (especially Quechua)

Time
Greenwich Mean Time minus 5 hours (GMT −0500)

Telephone Country Code
+593

Land
Ecuador is located between Colombia and Peru in the western region of South America and borders the Pacific Ocean at the Equator.

Area
Total: 283,560 sq km (109,483.1 sq miles)
Land: 276,840sq km (106,888.5 sq miles)
Water: 6,720 sq km (6720.6 sq miles)

Highest Point
Chimborazo Volcano 6,267 m (20,567 ft)

Climate
Ecuador experiences different climates in the different regions. The rainy season in the Pacific coast area is between December and May while the dry one is from June to November. The temperature here ranges from 23°C to 26°C (73.4°F to 78.8°F). The Galápagos has a temperate climate with temperatures ranging from 22°C to 32°C (71.6°F to 89.6°F). The weather in the Amazon is rainy and humid between January and September and dry between October and December. The temperature here ranges from 23°C to 36°C (73.4°F to 96.8°F). The Highlands experience a rainy and cold climate from November to April and a dry one from May to October. The temperature here ranges from 13°C to 18°C (55.4°F to 57.2°F).

Natural Resources
Petroleum, fish, timber, hydropower

Population
13,363,593

Currency
US Dollar (US$)

Ethnic Groups
Mestizo (mixed Amerindian and white): 65 per cent
Amerindian: 25 per cent
Spanish and others: 7 per cent
Black: 3 per cent
(2005 estimates)

Religion
Roman Catholic: 95 per cent
Others: 5 per cent
(2005 estimates)

Government Structure
Republic with an elected president and a unicameral National
Congress

Adminstrative Divisions
22 provinces: Azuay, Bolivar, Canar, Carchi, Chimborazo,
Cotopaxi, El Oro, Esmeraldas, Galapogos, Guayas, Imbura,
Loja, Los Rios, Morona-Santiago, Napo, Orellana, Pastaza,
Pichincha, Sucumbios, Tungurahua, Zamora-Chinchipe

Gross Domestic Product (GDP)
US$ 49.51 billion (2004 estimate)

Agricultural Products
Bananas, coffee, cocoa, rice, potatoes, manioc (tapioca),
plantains, sugarcane; cattle, sheep, pigs, beef, pork, dairy;
balsa wood; fish, shrimp

Industries
Petroleum, food processing, textiles, wood products,
chemicals

Exports
Petroleum, bananas, cut flowers, shrimp

Imports
Vehicles, medicinal products, telecommunications equipment, electricity

Airports
The main international airport is Simón Bolívar International Airport in Santiago de Guayaquil.

FAMOUS PEOPLE
- Jefferson Pérez from Cuenca stepped onto the world stage in the 1996 Olympics. He became the first Ecuadorian to win a gold medal when he won the 20km speed-walking marathon. He is an icon now in Ecuadorian society and while still competing, he has used his fame to encourage Ecuadorians to better themselves and set goals through many of his youth conferences. For more information visit http://www.jeffersonperez.com.
- **Iván Vallejo,** a world famous mountaineer became the first Ecuadorian to climb Mount Everest without the use of oxygen in 1999. His dream of climbing mountains began as a youth when he was amazed by the Tungurahua volcano. He was trained as a chemical engineer and is a past mathematics professor. However, he continues his climbing expeditions of Ecuadorian mountains and sites around the world. For more information visit http://www.ivanvallejo.com.
- **Luis Noboa Naranjo** (d.1994), from very humble beginnings in Ambato, amassed the largest personal fortune in Ecuador. After his father's death, he moved with his family to Guayaquil where he sold magazines and rags. His destiny changed when he met the son of one of Ecuador's richest men (Juan Marcos) and went to work for his father's bank. In 1955, he made his first US$ 1 million through exporting banana and coffee. At the time of his death (aged 78), his holdings were in excess of US$ 800 million.
- **Elsie Monge** was born into a comfortable existence in 1933. Highly educated in anthropology, she made a significant decision early in her life not to marry into

a prestigious family and became a nun with Maryknoll Catholic Mission. After working for many years for human rights in Guatemala and Panama, she returned to Ecuador where she heads the Ecumenical Commission of Human Rights. For more information visit:

http://www.cedhu.org/html/index.php

ACRONYMS

ID	Izquierda Democrática (Democratic Left), Ecuador
FECD	Fondo Ecuatoriano-Canadiense de Desarollo, Ecuador
ADEFOR	Asociación para el Desarrollo Forestal, Ecuador
OCE	Customs Corporation of Ecuador
PSP	Partido Sociedad Patriótica (Spanish: Patriotic Society Party), Ecuador
CES	Centro Especial de Seguimiento (Special Centre of Pursuit), Ecuador
PRONADER	National Sustainable Rural Development Program
PROTECA	Programa de Desarrollo Tecnologico Agropecuario (World Bank Ecuador)
FORTIPAPA	Fortalecimiento de la Investigación y Producción de Semilla de Papa en el Ecuador
INIAP	Instituto Nacional Autónomo de Investigaciones Agropecuarias
MICIP	El Ministerio de Comercio Exterior, Industrialización, Pesca y Competitividad

PLACES OF INTEREST
Coast

Ecuador offers fantastic whale watching between June and September. Many of the tours for this experience originate from Puerto Lopez in the Manabi province and include tours to Isla de la Plata which, in many ways, is similar to the Galápagos but without the huge number of tourists, and is much less expensive to visit.

Bird watching is a hugely popular pastime in Ecuador. Isla Corazon near Bahia Carquez has a protected mangrove area where bird life abounds. There are a number of tour companies specialising in the area. For more information visit http://www.riomuchacho.com/html/bird.html.

Sierra

The Sierra region is paradise for those interested in river rafting and kayaking. In 2005, the World Rafting Championships were held in Ecuador. Three hours from Quito, near Santo Domingo, lies the popular Toachi river-run.

Intag Cloud Forest

Intag Cloud Forest is a privately owned lodge which provides outstanding vistas of the mountains and wonderful bird-watching. Situated near Apuela. Prices are US$ 45 per day. For reservations (necessary):

Fax: (06) 923-392

Email: intagcz@uio.satnet.net

CULTURE QUIZ

SITUATION 1

You are standing in a queue at an airline counter in Guayaquil. You notice that fellow passengers are going to the counter past you, apparently just to ask a quick question. You also notice an elderly person cut straight to the front of the queue and is served before the other passengers. Then you notice an agent signal to someone in the queue and take him around the counter. The agent furnishes him with a ticket and then escorts him through the terminal and onto the plane before general boarding occurs. You become upset at the general lack of regard for queues. Do you?

A Start raising your voice and telling others to get back in the queue?

B When you get to the clerk, demand to see the manager in a loud voice and become quite irate? You begin thinking like a gringo might: 'The squeaky wheel will get the grease.' Yelling, you exclaim 'I will never fly this airline again because you allow customers to cut the queue ahead of others!'

⊙ Smile and keep moving with the queue but curse quietly to yourself? You keep reminding yourself how lucky you are to be in this unique and beautiful country.

Comments

Ⓐ would be considered very rude by Ecuadorians, despite your desire for order. Ecuadorians have a much higher tolerance for queue-cutting than most North Americans or Europeans. You would be considered most rude if you started yelling at an older person, as they are usually allowed to be served before others. However, in some cases, if you politely point out to the person who cuts into the queue that he/she has done so, the meeker people in the queue might appreciate your attempt, even if that doesn't produce any results.

Ⓑ is very similar to **Ⓐ**. The clerk and manager will not argue with you. However, they will start to think of ways to make your life miserable. Challenging the manager will not change the situation. Getting angry will create the opposite effect. The person who received the preferential treatment was probably a friend of the agent or had connections in the airline.

⊙ is the correct choice. Smiling and going with the flow is the best solution. Arriving at the airport as early as possible might reduce your stress.

SITUATION 2

You meet an Ecuadorian friend for lunch at a restaurant. When the bill arrives you suggest that each of you pay for your meal. He wants to pay the bill but you insist that you pay your half. Do you:

Ⓐ Continue to press the issue and insist you pay your portion of the bill?

Ⓑ Decide to pay for the bill as he has been very kind in the past and you know his funds are limited?

⊙ Allow him to pay the bill? You comment that you will allow him to do so this time but you will treat him for lunch the next time.

Comments

Ⓐ would be considered very rude. Splitting bills or asking for separate bills at a public meal is not practised by Ecuadorians. Being a host is considered an honour and you should accept the hospitality graciously. The general rule in Ecuadorian society is that the inviting party is obligated to pay for any entertainment as well. Also, please don't negotiate in advance for separate bills.

Ⓑ is acceptable unless your Ecuadorian friend asked you out for lunch. **⊙** is also acceptable.

SITUATION 3

While at the home of an Ecuadorian, he asks you about your children and how tall your son is. Not knowing his height measurements, you use your hand as a ruler for his height. Do you:

Ⓐ Demonstrate the height of your son with your palm facing down?

Ⓑ Demonstrate the height of your son by turning your hand in a 90-degree angle with the bottom of the hand being the ruler?

Comments

Ⓐ is an extremely rude gesture to make in Ecuador. Measuring things with the palm down is only used for animals, not for people.

Ⓑ is the correct answer and used to show the height of someone.

SITUATION 4

An Ecuadorian friend has just visited your home in Quito. When he leaves, should your appropriate gesture be:

A Shake his hand as he is leaving and see him off until he is in his car and well on his way, making sure you leave the front door open?

B Wave him goodbye at the front door and shut the door after he has left.

Comments

A is the appropriate response. Ecuadorians shake hands a great deal, both when meeting and parting with each other. Letting the friend leave the house and closing the door behind him would be considered rude. The door should be left open until you are sure he is well on his way.

SITUATION 5

While at a party, you are drinking glasses of beer or whisky. You realise that you have consumed your limit. Do you:

A Finish the glass and tell your host you have had enough to drink?

B Accept one more glass but continue to sip it and don't finish all of it?

Comments

A would not be appropriate. By finishing the beverage you are telling your host you would like some more. This is especially so among the lower classes. **B** is the appropriate response as you will be allowed to nurse your drink and will probably not be offered any more.

SITUATION 6

You have a business appointment for four o'clock in the afternoon. Should you:

A Arrive exactly at four o'clock and expect to wait for your meeting?

B Arrive 15 minutes early and expect to wait for your meeting?

C Arrive 10 minutes late and expect to wait for your meeting?

Comments

All answers are correct in this scenario. It is not considered rude to arrive a few minutes late for a business meeting, on time, or early. However, it is always best to be punctual and please be prepared to wait. (However, this is not the rule for a private party, arriving half an hour to 40 minutes late is fine.)

SITUATION 7

You are the new country manager in Ecuador for a foreign major export company. One of your duties is to assign a manufacturing representative for Ecuador. You have found two qualified people, one from Quito and the other from Guayaquil. However, your firm's practice in the past has been to assign only one representative. Do you:

A Choose the agent from Quito because he has a little more technical experience than the agent in Guayaquil for your particular product?

B Choose the agent from Guayaquil who is of Lebanese descent and has an excellent reputation in sales?

C Divide the territory up for the agents giving the Sierra region to the agent from Quito and the Costa market to the agent from Guayaquil?

Comments

Choosing **A** may cause your firm to have representation problems, especially on the coast. The Serrano will always be viewed as an outsider by many of the Guayaquil clients and not trusted.

B causes the same problem in reverse, although some businesspeople may disagree with me and decide to take the risk, given his expertise. The Costeño will, however, have problems operating in the Sierra.

C is the best choice for market penetration, as numerous companies have found. This will also minimise travel expenses, resulting in a higher profit margin.

SITUATION 8

You are attending a friend's party and you join a group at the party outside the residence. One of the partygoers opens up a bottle of beer, fills his glass up and consumes the alcohol. He then fills up the glass and hands it to you so you too can enjoy a glass of beer. Being concerned about hygiene, do you:

A Say "No thank you" and pass the glass on to the next person?

B Say "Don't you know you can pass germs and illness by drinking out of the same glass with a number of other people"?

C Say "I'm sorry I have diabetes and I am not allowed to consume alcohol"?

D Say "I'm sorry, I have a bad cold and don't want to infect anyone"?

E Say "Thank you" and drink up while you say a silent prayer that you won't catch anything?

Comments

The first two responses would definitely offend the people you are with. **C** has worked for me in the past and didn't seem to offend others. **D** and **E** may be the best responses to being invited for a drink. This cultural practice is deeply imbedded in much of Ecuador's culture and is seen as a sharing and bonding experience. You really need to make the call yourself on this social activity and realise how your actions may offend your new Ecuadorian friends.

DO'S AND DON'TS

DO'S

- Speak as loudly as you like (in many situations). Conversations here are often louder than those that North Americans are accustomed to. Ecuadorians may also interrupt each other by using their hands. Loudness is not an indicator of confrontation or disagreement.
- Arrive at a party half an hour to 40 minutes after the stated time. However, be on time for business meetings even though your Ecuadorian counterpart may be late.
- Present your host/hostess with a box of chocolates or flowers if you are invited to an Ecuadorian home. However, don't pay too much attention to the lady of the house.
- Defer to older people in conversation or when entering or exiting a building. Age is openly respected in Ecuador.
- Feel free to display open affection for children in public. Be prepared to witness much more permissiveness to children by parents and family in public.
- Laugh at jokes about Pastuzos. Pastuzos hail from Pasto (Colombia) and this name is given to people from Tulcán, a town near the Ecuadorian–Colombian border who are considered naive. Many Ecuadorians use Pastuzo as the subject of jokes, much as Polacks are in the United States.

  An example of such a joke is: "How does a Pastuzo tie the shoelace on his right foot?" Answer: He puts his left foot on a chair and bends down to tie the shoelace on his right foot on the floor.
- Keep your hands above the table when you eat. Ecuadorians often rest their forearms on the table while they eat.
- Remember that women from Manabí are viewed by most Ecuadorian men as very attractive.
- Remember that women from the United States are often seen by Ecuadorian men as being sexually permissive.
- Feel free to breast-feed in public.
- Accept that begging is common in Ecuador. People just learn to ignore it or give a small amount.

- Remember that people from Europe or the United States are viewed by most Ecuadorians as being wealthy.
- Be aware that many Ecuadorians group people from Asia into one race, calling them 'chinos'.
- Haggle or bargain in open markets—this is an accepted practice. If you are the first customer of the day, you no doubt will be in a good position to bargain as the first sale of the day indicates good luck to the merchant. If you don't attempt to get a lower price, you will be seen as being naïve.
- Open doors or get a female's chair for her.
- Upon entering a room with a number of people, address each individual with a handshake.
- Get used to addressing people by their professions or titles as this is seen as a sign of respect. Men you are friendly with can be addressed as Don, followed by that person's first name. (In my first few months in Ecuador, I actually believed people thought my name was Don.)
- Understand that elephants are seen as a sign of good luck in Ecuador. Many houses have a number of elephant ornaments. There is a phrase that says each home should have one elephant ornament that was given, one bought and one stolen. Many Ecuadorians will have the elephant ornaments facing a window or door for good luck.
- Allow women and older people to board the lift first.
- Know that Tuesday the 13th is viewed as a day of bad omen.
- Give a light kiss on the cheek when greeting a female whose acquaintance you have made. Many women also kiss each other on the cheek.
- Remember that conduct in the workplace is generally more formal in Ecuador than in the United States.

DON'TS

- Don't yawn in public. It is considered rude.
- Don't point at people.
- Don't arrive at a party at the designated hour.
- Don't discuss the border disputes with Peru or Colombia. In 2006, Colombia is a particularly touchy subject for Ecuadorians.
- Don't 'Go Dutch.' If you invite a friend/s out you are expected to pay. This is especially true if you're a male and you have invited a female out.
- Don't give money openly to a female in public. This may have negative connotations.
- Don't finish all the food on your plate when eating as a guest in someone else's home. If you clear the plate, the hostess may feel that the food wasn't sufficient.
- Don't spit in public.
- Don't clap your hands or hiss for service in a restaurant.
- Don't feel inhibited about seeing others urinate in public. It is a common practice.
- Don't be too direct or frank. The white lie is a practised art in Ecuador. Ecuadorians will often tell you what you want to hear. This is especially true between a subordinate and a superior or between someone from a lower and higher social class.
- Don't ask someone not to smoke in public places as smoking is widely accepted here.
- Don't curse in public.
- Don't extravagantly flaunt your wealth. This is looked down upon.
- Don't walk barefooted in public.
- Don't bare all on public beaches.
- Don't use your mobile phone in banks. Do not forget that, although mobile phones are used in many public places, they are seen as a sign of wealth.
- Don't laugh very loudly.
- Don't expect Ecuadorians to stand in a straight or orderly queue. You will usually notice more of a circling or rounding of the group trying to get to the cash register or service counter.

- Don't forget that people of the middle and upper social classes view manual labour as below their station in life.
- Don't be offended if you are called a hippy. Hikers and campers are often called hippies here, especially if they have long hair.
- Don't forget that formalities and good manners are important to Ecuadorians, much more so than in the United States. Manners also are a sign of education to an Ecuadorian.
- Don't forget to shake the hand of the person you are greeting or parting from. Handshakes here are generally less firm but longer than in other Western countries.

GLOSSARY

It is recommended that you read Chapter Eight: Language, prior to using the colloquialisms presented here.

A la johnny	Going to the United States
A precio de huevo	Cheap price (literally price of an egg)
Abreboca	Appetiser
Abrir cancha	Move out of the way
Achumarse	To get drunk (Costa)
Acolitar	To help, stand by someone
Afrecho	Crybaby (Cuenca)
Agringado	Refers to a local trying to act like someone from the United States
Aguaje	High tide
Aguatero	Water seller
Aguinaldo	Christmas gifts from employers
Alhaja	Nice party
Allulla	A corn flour bread which is typical of Latacunga
Aló	Hello (when answering the phone)
Ancheta	Good price
Ardilla	Poorly behaved child (literally means squirrel)
Arenilla	Small mosquito in the jungle
Atatay	Horrible! (Sierra)
Ayayay	Hurt, sore (Sierra)
Bacan	It's OK

Bachacha	Jail
Balde	Back of a pickup truck
Bambu	Cigarette from the United States
Biela	Beer
Boche	Fight
Botadero	City dump
Buena facha	Good dresser (Cuenca)
Buseta	Small bus that travels between the provinces
Cabeza de huevo	Bald man (literally means egghead)
Cacharrero	Seller of contraband along the borders with Peru and Colombia
Cachero or Maricón	Homosexual
Cachos	Jokes
Caído del petate	Fool
Caimán	Lazy person
Cajonera	Street salesperson (these operate off the pavements, especially in Quito)
Caleta	House
Calzonazo	Lazy man
Calzonudo	Fool (Costa)
Camarón	Inexperienced person (literally 'shrimp')
Cana	Jail
Capillo	Loose coins (usually thrown by the bridegroom to children when leaving the church after a wedding ceremony)
Cari	Macho (Cuenca)

Cháchara	Jokes
Chacra	Small garden plot outside the home
Chancho en bandeja	Fat (literally 'pig in a tray')
Chanchullo	Bribe, usually between an individual and a public official
Chancleta	Baby (literally 'sandal')
Chapa	Disrespectful term for a police officer
Chapudo	Cheeks/red face
Chevere	Good
Chimbo	Bounced cheque. Also refers to witchcraft. (Esmeraldas)
China	Maid
Chinear	To assault
Chiro	Broke
Chirona	Jail
Chiva	Old bus with no doors or windows used in places with hot weather
Chocha	To be fond of someone or something new
Chompa	Jacket
Choro	Thief
Choza	Hut (Sierra)
Chuamarse	To get drunk (Sierra)
Chuchos	Breasts
Chupón	Baby's dummy (pacifier)
Chuta	Exclamation of surprise
Conchudo	A person with no scruples
Cromo	Referring to a person's face
Cucaracha	Old car (literally 'bug')

Cuentero	A person who tells stories or lies.
Cucayo	Lunch
Dar para la cola	Bribe (literally refers to providing someone a payment to purchase a Coca-Cola)
Dele no mas	Go ahead
Domingo chiquita	Drunk or Monday morning hangover (literally refers to someone who continues drinking on Monday.)
Entrar de gancho	Two people admitted on one ticket
Estar con la leona	Hungry
Estar con la luna	Crazy (literally 'with the moon')
Estar frito	Bad situation (literally 'fried')
Estar limpio	Broke (literally 'to be clean')
Fachosa	Badly dressed (Costa)
Farra	Party
Foco	Embarrassed
Gallada	Gang (literally refers to group of young people out having fun and raising a ruckus)
Gato	Blue or green eyed person
Hacer cola	Queueing
Hacer dedo	Hitchhiking
Huasipungo	House (Sierra)
Jamar	Eat
Jeva	Girlfriend

La familia pavoni	Trying to get something for nothing, broke (literally 'turkey family')
La llapa	Baker's dozen (Sierra)
Ladrar	Drunk (Literally 'to bark' in Spanish)
Liga	To befriend
Mama cuchara	Dead end street
Mantel largel	Banquet in the house
Mario	Husband (Costa)
Matute	Contraband
Melindrosa	Picky eater
Michelin	Fat
Morder	To understand
Motoso	Curly hair
Mucha	Kiss (Sierra)
ñaño	Brother or good friend
No sea mailto	Expression used when a favour is needed
Norro	A disrespectful term for someone from the Sierra or Quito
Nuevón	New employee
Papear	Eat
Palo grueso	Influential person with a lot of power
Pana	Friend
Pega	Work
Pelado (a)	Boyfriend, girlfriend
Pelar el ojo	Alert, awake
Petate	Bed or straw mat used in the Costa
Picado	A person that wants revenge

Pichón	Loan (Cuenca)
Pinganillo	Elegant
Pipón	Lazy person (literally a person who receives his pay every 15 days but doesn't do any work)
Pite	A little bit
Plana calles	Lazy person who 'levels the streets with his feet'
Pleno	It's OK
Pluto	Drunk
Prenda el foco	Think (literally 'let me turn the lightbulb on')
Ruquear	Sleep
Sambo	Person with curly hair
Sapo	Person who is corrupt or takes advantage of a situation to the detriment to others
Ser del otro equipo	Homosexual
Simón	Yes
Sobrado	Arrogant, proud
Soplar	To make love (literal Spanish meaning 'to blow in the wind')
Sumercé	Your mercy (usually used in the Sierra between a person of indigenous origin and a white person or one of a higher social status)
Shunsho	Fool (Quichua)
Tiempo Alemán	To be on time (referring to German time which is seen as being exact)
Traguear	Drinking *aguardiente*

Trinche	Fork (Cuenca)
Turro	Broken, ugly, or of bad quality
X	Wife or husband (say 'La X' or 'El X')
Zorro	Homosexual or female prostitute

MEDICAL TERMS IN SPANISH

Alergia	Allergy
Amigdalitis	Tonsillitis
Ardentina	Fever
Arthritis	Arthritis
Asma	Asthma
Ataque al corazón	Heart attack
Bronquitis	Bronchitis
Diarrea	Diarrhoea
Difteria	Diphtheria
Dolor de cabeza	Headache
Dolor de garganta	Sore throat
Dolor de oido	Ear ache
Conjuntivitis	Conjunctivitis
Erupción cutánea/salpullido	Rash
Fiebre	Fever
Fiebre amarilla	Yellow fever
Fiebre escarlatina	Scarlet fever
Fiebre tifoidea	Typhoid
Gripe	Cold/flu
Hepatitis	Hepatitis
Manchas rojas en la piel	Spots
Meningitis	Meningitis
Mordedura or picadura	Bite
Neumonia/pulmonia	Pneumonia

Paludismo	Malaria
Paperas/parotiditis	Mumps
Polio	Polio
Rabia	Rabies
Reumatismo	Rheumatism
Rubeola	German measles
Sarampión	Measles
Tétanos	Tetanus
Tos	Cough
Tosferina	Whooping cough
Varicela	Chicken pox
Viruela	Smallpox

QUICHUA
Examples of Basic Vocabulary

Words are given in Spanish along with Quichua equivalent and the meaning in English.

Spanish	Quichua	English
abajo	*urai*	below, down, beneath
abierto	*pascashca*	open
abogado	*camachic*	lawyer
abrigado	*cunuella*	wrapped up, protected
abrir	*pascana*	to open
apestar	*ashnana*	to stink
bailar	*ashnana*	to dance
bien	*alli*	fine, good, OK
boca	*shim*	mouth
bosque	*sacha*	forest
bravo	*millai*	brave, angry
brazo	*ricra*	arm
cabello	*accha*	hair

Spanish	Quichua	English
caliente	*cunuc*	hot
calle	*ñan*	street
cama	*cahuitu*	bed
caminar	*purina*	to walk
campo	*panpa*	countryside
cara	*ñahui*	face
carne	*aicha*	meat
casa	*huasi*	house
color	*tullpu*	colour
comenzar	*callarina*	to start
comer	*callarina*	to eat
comprar	*rantina*	purchase
decir	*nina*	to say
dedo	*ruca*	finger
despacio	*allimanta*	slowly
dia	*puncha*	day
dulce	*mishqui*	sweet, candy
enviar	*cachana*	to send
escoba	*pichana*	broom
esposa	*huarmi*	wife
esposo	*cusa*	husband
estar	*tiyana, cana*	to be
familia	*aillu*	family
feliz	*cushilla*	happy
fiesta	*raimi*	party
frío	*chiri*	cold
fuerte	*sinchi*	strong
ganado	*huacra*	livestock
gordo	*huira*	fat
grande	*jatun*	big
hablar	*rimana*	to speak

Spanish	Quichua	English
hormiga	*añancu*	ant
huevo	*lulun*	egg
impuesto	*jucha*	tax
jardín	*sisapanpa, muya*	garden
labio	*shimicara*	lip
lavar(ropa)	*tacshana*	to wash clothes
leche	*ñeña*	milk
lejos	*caru*	far
limpio	*chuya*	clean
lugar	*cusca*	place
luna	*quilla*	moon
luz	*achic*	light
maestro	*yachachic*	teacher
maiz	*sara*	corn
maleta	*quipi*	suitcase
mano	*maqui*	hand
medicina	*janpi*	medicine
mesa	*churai*	table
miedo	*manchai*	fear
mitad	*chaupi*	half
mono	*cushillu*	monkey
mujer	*huarmi*	woman
oír	*uyana*	to hear
ojo	*ñahui*	eye
olivdar	*cuncana*	to forget
país	*mamallacta*	country
palo	*caspi*	stick
pan	*tanta*	bread
patio	*pancha*	yard, courtyard
perro	*alleu*	dog
pobre	*huaccha*	poor

Spanish	Quichua	English
precio	*chani*	price
problema	*llaqui*	problem
profesor	*yachachic*	professor
pronto	*utca*	soon
puente	*chaca*	bridge
queso	*maquinchu, masharu*	cheese
ratón	*ucucha*	rat
respirar	*samana*	to breathe
reír	*asina*	to laugh
rojo	*puca*	red
ropa	*churana*	clothes
sal	*cachi*	salt
sangre	*yahuar*	blood
selva	*sacha*	jungle
ser	*cana*	to be
sierra	*punasuyu*	mountain range
todo	*tuci*	all, everything
tonto	*muspa, upa*	fool
triste	*llaquilla*	sad
tú	*can*	you (familiar)
usted	*quiquin*	you (formal)
valor	*chani*	value
vender	*catuna*	to sell
verdad	*ilu*	truth
vivir	*causana*	to live
zapato	*ushuta*	shoe

RESOURCE GUIDE

EMERGENCY PHONE NUMBERS
Quito

Alcoholics Anonymous	(02) 252-6527
Ambulance/Red Cross	131
Blood Bank	(02) 258-2480
Civil Defence	(02) 243-9433/
	(02) 2469-009
Criminal Investigations	(02) 255-0918
Emergency	911
Fire Department	102
Police Radio Patrol	101
Police Regiment	(02) 245-9811
Detention Centre	(02) 295-0250
Airport	(02) 294-4900
Public Water	(02) 250-1375
Time	109

Guayaquil

Airport	(04) 228-2100
Alcoholics Anonymous	(04) 230-0871
Ambulance/Red Cross	(04) 256-0674
Blood Bank	(04) 2560-675
Civil Defence	(04) 232-1111
Criminal Investigation	(04) 287-0439
Fire Department	102
Police Radio Patrol	101
Transit/Vehicular Commission	103
Tourist Information	(04) 232-1160

TELEPHONES

If you have family calling you from Ecuador they can compare the rates of numerous carriers at the following website:
http://www.abelltolls.com/compare/international/ longdistancerates/ecuador.htm.
There are two major players in the mobile phone market in Ecuador:

- Porta
  Website: http://www.porta.net
- Movistar
  Website: http://www.movistar.com.ec

(For more information on telephone numbers in Ecuador, please refer to Chapter Five, Settling In.*)*

AIRLINES
- Exito Travel; tel: 1-800-655-4053
  Website: http://www.exito-travel.com
- Intratours; tel: 1-800-334-8069
  Website: http://www.intratours.com
- Latin Cheap Tickets; tel: 1-888-590-3152
- Mill Avenue Travel
  International tel: 1-800-815-6455
  US Tel: (01) 602-966-6300
  Website: http://www.millavenuetravel.com
  I have used this agency for a number of years.
- Safar International; tel: 1-800-544-2369
  Email: safarinc@ameritech.net
  Website: http://www.safarint.com
- TAME; toll free within Ecuador: 1-800-555-999
  Website: http://www.tame.com.ec

TOURIST OFFICES
Ecuador Government Tourist Office
- Reina Victoria 514 y Ramon Roca, Quito
  Tel: (02) 252-7002
- Avenida Venezuela y Chile (smaller office)
  Tel: (02) 251-4044

Ecuador Government Tourist Corporation
- Airport Executive Tower II, Suite 400, 7270 NW 12th Street, Miami, FL 33126
  Tel: (01-305) 477-0041
- Website: http://www.ecuadorexplorer.com
  This is a comprehensive website for anyone travelling or moving to Ecuador. While highly commercial in nature, it does list good information.

CAB SERVICES

In Quito, there is a radio taxicab company that you can call to your location—Taxi Amigos (Tel: (02) 222-2222). It often uses cars that are not marked as cabs for security purposes, as thieves do think that foreigners who take cabs may have large amounts of cash. You can always ask for the identification of the driver. I have found that making good connections at your hotel can often yield good reliable transportation. If you indicate to the help desk that you are looking for a cab available for long term trips, such as to Guayaquil, you will often be referred to someone who is reliable. Other cab companies in Quito are:

- Autoexpress; tel: (02) 227-1742
- Taxiexpress; tel: (02) 221-1111

BANKING

- Banco Bolivariano
  Website: http://www.bolivariano.com
- Banco de Guayaquil
  Website: http://www.bankguay.com
- ABN Amro Bank
  Website: http://www.abnamro.com
- Banco de Austro
  Website: http://www.baustro.fin.ec
- Banco Pacifico
  Website: http://www.bp.fin.ec

ACCOUNTANTS
Price Waterhouse Coopers

- Carchi 702 2nd Floor, Guayaquil
  Tel: (04) 228-1555
- Diego de Almagro N 32-48 y Whymper, Edificio IBM 1st Floor, Quito
  Tel: (02) 226-3530

TAXES

The tax system is quite complicated and has changed significantly in the last several years with the government's attempt to increase revenues. The taxable rate for most foreigners who reside in Ecuador is usually about 25 per cent. The government website for tax issues (in Spanish only) is:

http://www.sri.gov.ec

BANK ACCOUNT

Opening up an account in Ecuador is quite straightforward. A savings account will usually require a minimum of a few hundred dollars. You will also have to produce an identification card. Current (checking) accounts require, in some cases, at least several hundred dollars with a previous banking reference and two commercial references. Writing invalid cheques is serious business in Ecuador and can land you in jail. In 2000, at a certain bank, customers withdrawing money from its cash machines had the amount debited twice. Also, there have been several cases where money withdrawals were attempted but the machine didn't dispense the funds. Always keep your receipts when withdrawing money.

CREDIT CARDS

The most commonly accepted cards are Diners Club, Mastercard, Visa and American Express.

American Express
Quito
- Through Ecuadorian Tours
  Avenida Río Amazonas
  Tel: (02) 256-0488

Guayaquil
- Through Ecuadorian Tours
  Avebuda 9 de Octubre 1900
  Tel: (02) 228-7111

Diners Club
- Edificio Diners
  Avenidas de la Republica 710 y Eloy Alfaro, Quito
  Tel: (02) 222-1372
  Website: http://www.dinersclub.com.ec

This is an excellent website with lots of information about upcoming events and special discounts. If you're moving to Ecuador for the long term, I would recommend that you obtain this card as it is considered prestigous and is widely accepted in Ecuador.

DOCTORS
Quito
- Dr John Rosenberg (Internal Medicine)
  Foch 476 y Almagro
  Tel: (02) 252-1104
  Email: jrd@pi.pro.ec
- Alvaro F Davlos P M D
  La Colina 202 y San Ignacio
  Tel: (02) 250-0267, (02) 250-0268
  Email: adavalos@pi.pro.ec

Guayaquil
- Dr Roberto Calderon
  Clinic Alcivar Centro Medico, #2, 2nd Floor
  Tel: (04) 234-3575, (04) 244-7354
- Dr Rafael Caputi
  Clinica Kennedy Seccion Beta #21
  Tel: (04) 229-3526
- Telmo Fernandez
  L Urdaneta 1401 y Garcia Moreno
  Tel: (04) 229-4515
- Dr Gilberto R Peñafiel, M D
  Tel: (04) 228-5886
- Ma Fernanda Ayala de Hidalgo (Dentist)
  Orrantiz MZA 2 y #503
  Tel: (04) 268-0105

HOSPITALS
Quito
- Hospital Metropolitano
  Avenida Mariana de Jesús y Nicolas Arteta y Calisto
  Tel: (02) 226-1520, (02) 226-9030
  Website: http://www.hospitalmetropolitano.org

- Hospital Vozandes
  254 Villa Lengua
  Tel: (02) 226-2142

Guayaquil
- Clinica Alcivar
  Coronel y Azuy Esquinas (Sur)
  Tel (04) 244-4287, (04) 258-0030
- Clinica Kennedy
  Av San Jorge entre 9a y 10a
  Tel: (04) 228-6963, (04) 228-9666
  Ambulance: (04) 228-8888
- Clinica Kennedy
  Alvorada Guill Pareja R y Benj Carrion
  Tel: (04) 224-7900

HEALTH SERVICES
Ambulances
Quito
- ADAMI
  Tel: (02) 226-5020
- UTIM
  Tel: (02) 256-2613, (02) 256-2614

Air Ambulances/Evacuation
- Aeromedevac Inc (US based)
  Tel: 1-800-462-0911 (from the US)
  Tel: 1-800-832-5087 (from Mexico)
  Website: http://www.aeromedevac.com
- Ambulancias Aereas del Ecuador
  Tel: (02) 244-9191 (Quito)
  Tel: 1-800-523-8930 (International SOS, US based)
- Life Flight
  Tel: 1-800-231-4357; Non-emergency tel: 713-704-4014;
  Emergency tel: 713-704 HELP (4357)
  Email: webmaster@lifeflight.com
  Website: http://www.lifeflight.com
- National Jets; tel: 1-800-327-3710
  Website: http://www.nationalairambulance.com

International Health Insurance
- Carefree Travel Insurance
  Tel: 1-800-645-2424
- International SOS
  Website: http://www.internationalsos.com
- Wallach & Co
  Tel: 1-800-237-6615, (540) 687-3166
  Email: info@wallach.com
  Website: http://www.wallach.com

Other Contacts
- International Association for Medical Assistance to Travelers (IAMAT)
  Tel: (716) 754-4883 (Lewiston, New York)
  Website: http://www.iamat.org
  Free membership with listings of doctors who speak English. There is a set fee for the first visit. This is a very good organisation funded by donations. Some donations include excellent climate and tropical disease charts covering the world.
- Website: http://www.travmed.com
  It is a very good source of general and specific information on travelling around the world and travelling to Ecuador.

POST OFFICES
Quito
Main Post Office
- Eloy Alfaro 354 and 9 de Octubre
  Open: Mon–Fri, 7.30 am–7:00 pm; Sat, 8:00 am–2:00 pm

Branch Post Offices:
- Reina Victoria and Colón (Edificio Torres de Almagro).
  Open: Mon–Fri, 7.30 am–5.45 pm; Sat, 8:00 am–11.45 am
- Espejo y Guayaquil (between Guayaquil and Venezuela)
  Open: Mon–Fri, 7:30 am–7:00 pm; Sat, 8:00 am–2:00 pm
- Japón and Naciones Unidas
  Open: Mon–Fri, 7:30 am–7:00 pm; Sat, 8:00 am–2:00 pm
- Airport Mariscal Sucre (National Departures)
  Open: Mon–Fri, 7:30 am–7:00 pm; Sat, 8:00 am–1:00 pm

Guayaquil

The main post office is located at Pedro Carbo y Clemente Ballén. Another option for receiving your mail while you are overseas is by using a private company. Personal Mail International out of New Jersey offers such a service.

Tel: 1-800-548-3622, (973) 543-6001

Website: http://www.pmipmi.com

EMBASSY LIST

Most of the foreign embassies and consulate offices are in Quito. I have provided a list of foreign embassies and consulates in Quito and Guayaquil. Their addresses and telephone numbers are below but please take note that these are subject to change. To verify this information, here are some related websites:

- http://www.goabroad.com/embassy

Embassies in Quito

- **Argentina:** Amazonas Ave. 477, 8th Floor
  Tel: (02) 562-2921
- **Austria:** Of Comercial, Av Gaspar de Villarroel E9-53
  Tel: (02) 246-9468
- **Belgium:** Av Rep de El Salvador 1082 y Av Naciones Unidas, Edf Mansión Blanca
  Tel: (02) 246-4387
- **Bolivia:** Av Eloy Alfaro 2432 y Fernando Ayarza
  Tel: (02) 244-6652
- **Brazil:** Av Amazonas 1429 y Colón, Edf. España
  Tel: (02) 256-3086
- **Canada:** 6 de Diciembre Avenida 2816 y Paul Rivet, Josueth Gonzales Building, 4th Floor
  Tel: (02) 2232-114, (02) 2506-162
- **Chile:** Juan Pablo Sanz 3617 y Av. Amazonas, Ed. Xerox, Floor 3 y 4
  Tel: (02) 246-6780
- **China:** Atahualpa 349 y Av Amazonas
  Tel: (02) 243-3337
- **Colombia:** Av Colón 1133 y Amazonas, Ed Arista, Floor 7
  Tel: (02) 222-2486

- **Costa Rica:** Rumipamba 692 y República, Floor 2
  Tel: (02) 225-4945, (02) 225-6016
- **Dominican Republic:** Av de los Shyris 1240 y Portugal,
  Edf. Albatros Of. 201
  Tel: (02) 243-4232
- **Egypt:** Baquedano 222 y Reina Victoria
  Tel: (02) 222-5240
- **France:** General Plaza 107 y Avenida Patrtia
  Tel: (02) 256-0789
- **Germany:** Avenida Naciones Unids y Avenida Repúbublica
  El Salvador
  Tel: (02) 297-0822
- **Great Britain:** Avenida Naciones Unidas y República El
  Salvador 14th Floor-City Plaz
  Tel: (02) 297-0800
- **Holland:** Avenida 12 de Octubre 1942 y Cordero–World
  Trade Center, Tower 1, 1st Floor
  Tel: (02) 252-5461
- **Israel:** Avenida 12 de Octubre y General Salazar
  Tel: (02) 256-2152
- **Italy:** La Isla y 111 y Humberto Albornoz
  Tel: (02) 2561-077
- **Japan:** Avenida Patria 130 y Juan Leon Mera
  Tel: (02) 256-1899
- **Mexico:** Avenida 6 de Deciembre N 36–165
  Tel: (02) 225-8788
- **Peru:** Avenida República de El Salvador 495 y Irlanda
  Tel: (02) 246-8410, (02) 246-8411
- **Russia:** Reina Victoria 462 y Roca
  Tel: (02) 252-6375
- **Spain:** La Pinta 455 y Av Amazonas
  Tel: (02) 225-64373
- **Switzerland:** Avenida Amazonas Xerox Building
  Tel: (02) 243-4949
- **United States:** Avenida 12 de Octubre y Patria
  Tel: (02) 254-9083
  Website: http://www.usembassy.org.ec
- **Venezuela:** Av Amazonas 5546
  Tel: (02) 224-6526

BUSINESS CONTACTS

- Ecuadorian–American Chamber of Commerce (Quito)
  Edificio Multicentra 4 floor, La Nina y Avda. 6 de
  Diciembre, Quito
  Tel: (02) 250-7450
  Website: http://www.ecamcham.com
- Ecuadorian–American Chamber of Commerce (Guayaquil)
  Edificio Centrum 6th floor, Office 5, Francisco de Orellna
  Avenue, Kennedy Norte, Guayaquil
- Ecuadorian American Chamber of Commerce of Los Angeles
  701 N. Alvarado Street, Los Angeles, CA 90026, USA
  Tel: (1-323) 939-6568
  Email: franklinfigueroa@hotmail.com
- Ecuadorian-American Chamber of Commerce
  4100 Westheimer, Suite 200, Houston, TX 77027-4427, USA
  Tel: (1-713) 877-8534
  Email: james@eacc.org
  Website: http://www.eacc.org
- Export and Investment Promotion Corporation
  (CORPEI)
  Cdla. Kennedy Norte, Avda. Francisco de Orellana y Miguel
  H. Alcívar, Edificio Centro Empresarial Las Cámaras, Torre
  de Oficinas, 2nd Floor, Guayaquil
  Tel: (04) 681-550
- CORPEI
  Avenida 12 de Octubre y Cordero, World Trade Center
  Torre B office 1406
  Website: http://www.corpei.org
- Federación Ecutoriana de la Pequeña y Mediana Industría
  (CAPEIPI)
  Avenida Amazones y Atahualpa, Centro de Exposiciones
  Quito 2nd Floor, Quito
  Tel: (02) 244-3388
  Website: http://www.capeipi.com

LAWYERS

- Aguiar Law Group
  Tel: (02) 256-4721
  Website: http://www.aguiarlaw.com

- Bermeo & Bermeo
  World Trade Center, Building Tower II, 12th Floor, 12
  Octubre y Cordero, Quito
  Tel: (02) 225-4587
- Bustamante Cia. Ltd
  Tel: (02) 256-2680
  Website: http:/www.bustamante.com.ec

REAL ESTATE BROKERS
Quito

- Frave Real Estate
  Corunia Av. 10 de Agosto 7080 y Amazonas, Quito
  Tel: (02) 246-6217
  Website: http://www.ecuainternet.com
- Quito Real Estate Service
  Calle Leonids Plza 353 y Roca

If you're moving appliances or going to purchase appliances for your move to Ecuador, there is a very good company in New York called Appliances Overseas where you can purchase items plus have them shipped overseas:

- Appliances Overseas
  276 Fifth Avenue & 30th Street, Suite 407 New York, NY
  10001-4509
  Tel: (212) 545-8001
  Email: help@appliancesoverseas.com
  Website: http://www.appliancesoverseas.com

SCHOOLS
Quito

- Academia Cotopaxi
  Website: http://www.cotopaxi.k12.ec
  Probably the best private school in Quito.
- Alliance Academy
  Website: http://www.alliance.k12.ec
  Used primarily by Christian missionaries.

Guayaquil

- Inter-American Academy
  Website: http://www.interamerican.edu.ec

STUDY ABROAD PROGRAMMES

- Boston University
  Website: http://www.bu.edu/abroad
  College credit language and liberal arts programme in Quito. Also offers a tropical ecology programme with intensive fieldwork on the coast of Ecuador.
- Elderhostel
  Website: http://www.elderhostel.org
  Offers numerous tours exploring Ecuador's history and culture. They also offer a Spanish language programme.
- Marist College
  Website: http://www.marist.edu/international
  Offers a programme with Pontifica Catholic University of Ecuador in Quito. Semester and full year programmes for variety of subjects including Ecuadorian studies.
- University of Minnesota
  Website: http://www.umabroad.umn.edu
  Semester and year-long programme offered in numerous subjects including agriculture and Andean studies.

RELIGIOUS AND SOCIAL WORK
Quito
Baptist
- First Baptist Church (English), El Telérapho 281 y Juan de Alcántara

Catholic
- El Girón Church, Avenida 12 de Octubre y Veintimilla
- El Batán Church, Av Gaspar de Villareal y 6 de Deciembre

Christian
- English Fellowship Church, Villalengua 884
- Presbyterian Church of Ecuador, Río Coca 1025

Mormon
- Iglesia de Jesuscristo de los Santos de los Ultimos Días Av Colón 706- y Almagro

Synagogue:
- Israelite Society Synagogue, 18 de Septiembre 954

VOLUNTEER OPPORTUNITIES
- CEIBA (Foundation for Tropical Conservation)
  Website: http://www.ceiba.org/index.htm
- Earthwatch Institute
  Website: http://www.earthwatch.org
- Partners of the Americas
  Website: http://www.partners.net
- Global Volunteers; tel: 1-800-487-1074
  Website: http://www.globalvolunteers.com.
- HCBJ World Radio
  Website: http://www.hcjb.org
  A number of Christian opportunities in technical fields and medicine.
- Reformed Church in America
  Website: http://www.rca.org
  This organisation needs Doctors, Nurses, Construction and Agricultural Workers.
- United Nations Volunteers
  Website: http://www.unv.org

VOLCANO INFORMATION
Volcano information may be obtained at
        http://www.ssd.noaa.gov/VAAC/guag.html

WRITING NUMBERS
Dates are normally written as day-month-year (3-1-2002). Full stops indicate thousand and millions, and commas are used for decimals, e.g. 1.101.800,10.

FURTHER READING

Reading as much as possible about Ecuador will enhance your understanding of this unique country. During the last several years, there has been substantial new material published in English about Ecuador.

BOOKS
Business
Doing Business Guide: Ecuador. Price Waterhouse Coopers, 1995.
- Much of the information here is dated but it is informative about the intricacies of operating a business in Ecuador.

Culture
Del Tiempo De La Yapa. Jenny Estrada. Guayaquil: El Universo, 1996 (2nd Edition)

Ecuador, Portrait Of A People. Albert B Franklin. Garden City, New York, NY: Doubleday Doran & Company Inc., 1943.
- Travel account that explores the culture of the Ecuadorians. While it is dated, the information is invaluable for understanding Ecuador.

Comidas Del Ecuador: Recetas Tradicionales Para Gente de Hoy. Michelle O Fried. Quito: Impreseñal Cía Ltda, 1993.

Culture and Customs of Ecuador. Michael Handelsman. Westport, CT: Greenwood Publishing Group, 2000.
- Professor Handelsman writes in detail about many aspects of Ecuadorian society. A concise and well-written work, it contains seldom-covered subjects in English about Ecuadorian culture. It provides excellent insights into a broad spectrum of Ecuadorian society that includes its media, music and performing arts.

The Panama Hat Trail: A Journey from South America. Tom Miller. New York, NY: Vintage/Random House, 1998.

- One of the best books on the unique Panama hat industry in Ecuador. Tom Miller really knows how to tell a story. If you have an interest in Ecuador, this is a very hard book to put down.

Ecuador and the Galápagos Islands. Victor Wolfgang Von Hagen. Norman, OK: University of Oklahoma Press, 1959.
- Excellent description of Ecuador's culture and geography.

Millennial Ecuador—Critical Essays on Cultural Transformations & Social Dynamics. Ed. Norman Jr Whitten. Iowa City, IA: University of Iowa Press, 2003.
- This is an excellent compilation of essays about Ecuador by leading experts. It is in-depth in its presentation of material about social and cultural aspects of Ecuador.

Fiction
Don Goyo. Demetrio Aguilera Malta. Dlifton, New Jersey: Humana Press, 1980.
- Originally published in 1933 with a translation by John and Carolyn Brushwood. A mythical tale of the mestizos on the coast and their fight to keep the mangrove swamps from being torn down by the hated white class of Ecuador.

Huasipungo. Jorge Icaza. London UK: Dennis Dobson, 1962. Buenos Aires: Editorial Losada, 2005.
- First published in 1934 with the 1962 edition translated by Mervyn Savill. This novel deals with the racism that the Indians suffered in a small mountain village.

General
Enciclopedia del Ecuador. La Editorial Océano de Barcelona, Barcelona: 2000.
- Excellent reference work in Spanish covering all subjects about Ecuador.

Four Years Among the Ecuadorians. Friedrich Hassaurek. New York, NY: Hurd & Houghton, 1867. Carbondale: IL: Southern Illinois University Press, 1967.

- A frank account of Mr Hassurek's travels in Ecuador in the 1860s and his observations of Ecuadorian life.

Political Power in Ecuador. Osvaldo Hurtado. (Translated by Nick D Mills, Jr). Albuquerque, NM: University of New Mexico Press, 1977.
- Osvaldo presents an excellent political history of Ecuador.

Savages. Joe Kane. New York, NY: Vintage Departures, 1996.
- An excellent account of the Huaorani Indians and their struggle with oil companies and the government of Ecuador.

The Inca Smiled: The Growing Pains of an Aid Worker in Ecuador. Richard Poole. England: Oneworld Publications, 1997.
- Excellent accounts from a Peace Corps volunteer in Ecuador and his experience of the culture of Ecuador. This story is highly personal and examines in detail the problems of understanding another culture, its food and its language.

The Farm on the River of Emeralds. Mortitz Thomsen. New York, NY: Vintage/Random House, 1979.
- A crusty old codger writes about his attempts at farming in the province of Esmeraldas.

Food, Gender, and Poverty in the Ecuadorian Andes. Mary J Weismantel. Philadelphia, PA: University of Pennsylvania Press, 1989. Illinois: Waveland Press, 1998 (Reprint).
- This book is an in-depth study of the role food plays in the lives of the residents of Zumbagua, a small mountain village in the Andes.

Travels Amongst The Great Andes Of The Equator. Edward Whymper. Layton, UT: Gibbs M Smith Inc, 1987.
- Originally published in 1892, this is an account of Whymper's studies of the altitude and natural science.

History

The Redemptive Work: Railway and Nation in Ecuador, 1895-1930. A Kim Clark. Wilmington, DE: SR Books, 1998.

- Another fascinating, newer work in English regarding the construction of the railroad in Ecuador.

Indians, Oil, and Politics, a Recent History of Ecuador. Allen Gerlach. Wilmington, DE: SR Books, 2003.

- Without hesitation, this is one of the best recent works about culture and politics in Ecuador. You will no doubt have a better understanding of the country by reading this volume.

Tumult at Dusk: Being an Account of Ecuador. Walker Lowry. San Francisco, CA: The Grabhorn Press, 1963.

- This is a very unique book that covers both the culture and history of Ecuador. I highly recommend it. However, there are only 100 printed copies. There is one available at the UCLA special collections unit.

The Kingdom of Quito in the Seventeenth Century: Bureaucratic Politics in the Spanish Empire. John Leddy Phelan. Madison, WI: University of Wisconsin, 1968.

- An excellent account of Ecuador in the 17th century with good material about graft and life in general.

Poetry

Between the Silence of Voices: An Anthology of Contemporary Ecuadorian Women Poets. Ed. Alicia Cabiedes-Fink and Ted Maier. Ecuador: Associación Ecuatoriana de Ejecutivas de Empresas Turísticas, Cayambe, 1997.

- An excellent edition.

Travel

Let's Go Ecuador Including the Galápagos Islands. Ed. August Dietrich. New York, NY: Saint Martin's Press, 2005.

- Overall, this is a very good guide for the visitor or resident in Ecuador. Strongest point of this book is the budget recommendations.

Ecuador and Galapagos Handbook: The Travel Guide. Robert Kunstaetter and Daisy Kunstaetter. Bath, UK: Footprint travel Guides, 2005.

- In my view, probably the best travel book about Ecuador. Very in-depth coverage with accurate information.

INTERNET SITES
Business
- http://www.barternews.com/ecuadorian_bartering.htm
  Information on bartering and negotiating in Ecuador's markets.
- http://www.economist.com/countries/Ecuador/
  Excellent information about business in Ecuador. Some material is not free.
- http://www.ecuadorexplorer.com/html/ecommerce_investment_.html (ecommerce in Ecuador)
- http://www.goinglobal.com/hot_topics/ecuador_business_mamarb.asp
  Guidelines for conducting business in Ecuador.
- http://www.miagencia.net
  Ecuador advertising and marketing portal in Spanish.

Cities
Quito
- http://www.quito.gov.ec
- http://www.inquito.com
  Good overall site

Guayaquil
- http://www.guayaco.com
- http://www.inguayaquil.com
- http://www.guayaquil.gov.ec
  Government site

Otavalo
- http://www.otavalo.com/main.html

Culture
- http://arts.ucsc.edu/faculty/Schechter
  Dr Schechter is an expert on Ecuadorian music.

- http://www.ecuador.com
- http://www.ecuadornostalgia.com
  Very good site about Ecuadorian culture.
- http://www.ecuadorprofundo.com
  Excellent resource in Spanish on Ecuador culture.
- http://ecuatorianistas.org
  Organisation of professionals that specialise in Ecuadorian studies.
- http://www.globalvolunteers.org/1main/ecuador/ecuadorculture.htm
  Excellent general resource about most aspects of Ecuadorian culture.
- http://www.vivecuador.com/html2/eng/culture.htm

General
- http://www.cdc.gov/travel/diseases.htm
  Centre for Infectious Diseases
- http://www.chevrontoxico.com
  Excellent site about the oil contamination disaster in Ecuador.
- http://www.derechos.org/nizkor/ecuador
  Human Rights Group
- http://www.elmilagrodemindo.com
  Orphanage
- http://www.explored.com.ec
  Huge collection of articles published about Ecuador—searchable database under Archivo Digital
- http://www.globalvolunteers.org/ecdrmain.htm
  Volunteer Work in Ecuador
- http://www.paho.org/english/sha/prflecu.htm
  Pan-American Health Organisation with excellent information about society and health in Ecuador.

Geography & Weather
- http://www.cimas.edu.ec
  Environmental Groups
- http://www.gct.org
  Galápagos Conservation Trust
- http://www.jatunsacha.org
  Conservation Project

- http://www.weatherhub.com/global/ec.htm
  Links to weather reports on a number of cities in Ecuador.
- http://www.weather.com

Government & Politics
- http://www.bce.fin.ec
  Central Bank of Ecuador
- http://www.odci.gov/cia
  Listing of government ministers.
- http://www.britembquito.org.ec
  British Embassy
- http://www.conaie.nativeweb.org
  Site dealing with indigenous issues.
- http://www.ecuador.org
  Ecuador Embassy in the US
- http://www.embassyworld.com/embassy/ecuador.htm
  Lists many of the Ecuadorian embassies worldwide
- http://www.estade.org
  Study of government organisations in Ecuador
- http://www.mmrree.gov.ec
  Minister of Foreign Relations

Internet Directories
- http://www.bacan.com
- http://www.ecua.net.ec
- http://www.ecuaworld.com

Magazines
- *Cosas* (National magazine)
  Website: http://www.cosas.com.ec
- *El Financiero* (Finance)
  Website: http://www.elfinanciero.com
- *Gestión*
  Website: http://www.gestion.dinediciones.com
- *Revista Estadio* (Sports)
  Website: http://www.revistaestadio.com
- *Vistazo* (Magazine covering the country)
  Website: http://www.vistazo.com

Newspapers

- *Cronica* (Loja).
  Website: http://www.cronica.com.ec
- *El Comerico* (Quito).
  Website: http://www.elcomercio.com
- *El Hoy* (Quito).
  Website: http://www.hoy.com.ec
- *La Hora* (Quito)
  Website: http://www.lahora.com
- *Diario Expreso* (Guayquil)
  Website: http://www.diario-expreso.com
- *Diario El Extra* (Guayaquil)
  Website: http://www.diario-extra.com
- *Diario La Hora* (Quito)
  Website: http://www.lahora.com.ec
- *El Universo* (Guayaquil)
  Website: http://www.eluniverso.com
- *El Telégrafo* (Guayaquil)
  Website: http://www.telegrafo.com.ec
- *El Mercurio* (Cuenca)
  Website: http://www.elmercurio.com.ec
- *El Diario* (Portoviejo)
  Website: http://www.eldiario.com.ec
- *La Prensa*
  Website: http://www.laprensa.com
- *Orenses* (Machala)
  Website: http://www.orenses.com

Tourism

- http://www.darwinfoundation.org
  Galápagos Information
- http://www.discovergalapagos.com/default.html
  Galápagos Tours
- http://www.ecuaventura.com
- http://www.ecuadorexplorer.com
- http://www.ecuaworld.com
- http://www.thebestofecuador.com
- http://www.voyage.gc.ca
  Excellent safety updates on Ecuador and the world.
  Sponsored by the Canadian government

ABOUT THE AUTHOR

Nicholas Crowder began his Ecuadorian experiences more than 25 years ago after studying at the American Graduate School of International Management. Selling automotive and industrial parts throughout Ecuador in the early 1980s and marrying an Ecuadorian, provided him an insight into the culture not seen by most outsiders. He was enthralled with the beauty and diversity of the country and this has led to a long-term observation and study of Ecuador.

His love both for Ecuador and Latin America was the genesis for his ever expanding website of over 10,000 links about Latin America (http://www.latinamericalinks.com). He is also the editor of Spanish Word of the Day (http://www.spanishwordoftheday.com). In 2006, his new site about culture and travel around the world was launched at http://www.dragomanchronicles.com. However, his fascination and love for Ecuador continues in his desire to share the beauty and nuances of this highly interesting and fascinating country, which he calls the 'jewel of the Andes'.

INDEX

Titles in the CULTURE**SHOCK**! series:

Argentina	Hawaii	Pakistan
Australia	Hong Kong	Paris
Austria	Hungary	Philippines
Bahrain	India	Portugal
Barcelona	Indonesia	San Francisco
Beijing	Iran	Saudi Arabia
Belgium	Ireland	Scotland
Bolivia	Israel	Sri Lanka
Borneo	Italy	Shanghai
Brazil	Jakarta	Singapore
Britain	Japan	South Africa
Cambodia	Korea	Spain
Canada	Laos	Sweden
Chicago	London	Switzerland
Chile	Malaysia	Syria
China	Mauritius	Taiwan
Costa Rica	Mexico	Thailand
Cuba	Morocco	Tokyo
Czech Republic	Moscow	Turkey
Denmark	Munich	Ukraine
Ecuador	Myanmar	United Arab
Egypt	Nepal	Emirates
Finland	Netherlands	USA
France	New York	Vancouver
Germany	New Zealand	Venezuela
Greece	Norway	Vietnam

For more information about any of these titles, please contact any of our Marshall Cavendish offices around the world (listed on page ii) or visit our website at:

www.marshallcavendish.com/genref